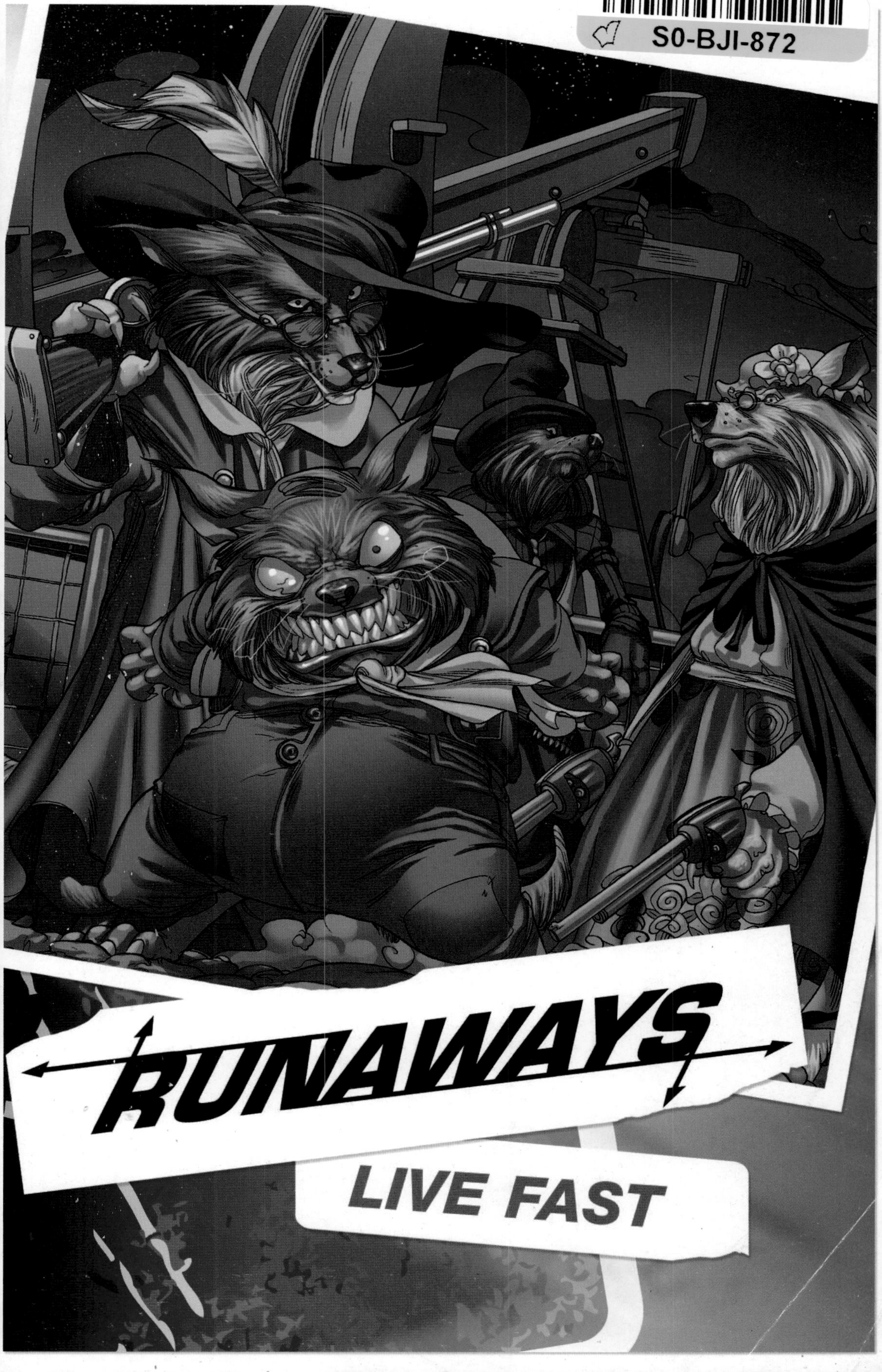

RUNAWAYS

LIVE FAST

RUNAWAYS

LIVE FAST

WRITER: **BRIAN K. VAUGHAN**
PENCILERS: **ADRIAN ALPHONA**
AND **MIKE NORTON** (ISSUES #19-21)
INKER: **CRAIG YEUNG**
COLORIST: **CHRISTINA STRAIN**
LETTERER: VC'S RANDY GENTILE
COVER ART: **MARCOS MARTIN**
ASSISTANT EDITORS: **DANIEL KETCHUM, SEAN RYAN**
AND **NATHAN COSBY**
EDITOR: **NICK LOWE**
SPECIAL THANKS TO C.B. CEBULSKI
& MACKENZIE CADENHEAD

RUNAWAYS CREATED BY **BRIAN K. VAUGHAN**
& **ADRIAN ALPHONA**

COLLECTION EDITOR: **JENNIFER GRÜNWALD**
ASSISTANT EDITOR: **ALEX STARBUCK**
ASSOCIATE EDITOR: **JOHN DENNING**
EDITOR, SPECIAL PROJECTS: **MARK D. BEAZLEY**
SENIOR EDITOR, SPECIAL PROJECTS: **JEFF YOUNGQUIST**
SENIOR VICE PRESIDENT OF SALES: **DAVID GABRIEL**

EDITOR IN CHIEF: **JOE QUESADA**
PUBLISHER: **DAN BUCKLEY**
EXECUTIVE PRODUCER: **ALAN FINE**

RUNAWAYS: LIVE FAST. Contains material originally published in magazine form as RUNAWAYS #19-24. First printing 2010. Hardcover ISBN# 978-0-7851-4154-9. Softcover ISBN# 978-0-7851-4155-6. Published by MARVEL WORLDWIDE, INC., a subsidiary of MARVEL ENTERTAINMENT, LLC. OFFICE OF PUBLICATION: 417 5th Avenue, New York, NY 10016. Copyright © 2006, 2007 and 2010 Marvel Characters, Inc. All rights reserved. Hardcover: $19.99 per copy in the U.S. (GST #R127032852). Softcover: $16.99 per copy in the U.S. (GST #R127032852). Canadian Agreement #40668537. All characters featured in this issue and the distinctive names and likenesses thereof, and all related indicia are trademarks of Marvel Characters, Inc. No similarity between any of the names, characters, persons, and/or institutions in this magazine with those of any living or dead person or institution is intended, and any such similarity which may exist is purely coincidental. **Printed in the U.S.A.** ALAN FINE, EVP - Office of the President, Marvel Worldwide, Inc. and EVP & CMO Marvel Characters B.V.; DAN BUCKLEY, Chief Executive Officer and Publisher - Print, Animation & Digital Media; JIM SOKOLOWSKI, Chief Operating Officer; DAVID GABRIEL, SVP of Publishing Sales & Circulation; DAVID BOGART, SVP of Business Affairs & Talent Management; MICHAEL PASCIULLO, VP Merchandising & Communications; JIM O'KEEFE, VP of Operations & Logistics; DAN CARR, Executive Director of Publishing Technology; JUSTIN F. GABRIE, Director of Publishing & Editorial Operations; SUSAN CRESPI, Editorial Operations Manager; ALEX MORALES, Publishing Operations Manager; STAN LEE, Chairman Emeritus. For information regarding advertising in Marvel Comics or on Marvel.com, please contact Ron Stern, VP of Business Development, at rstern@marvel.com. For Marvel subscription inquiries, please call 800-217-9158. Manufactured between 3/29/10 and 4/28/10 (hardcover), and 3/29/10 and 8/25/10 (softcover), by R.R. DONNELLEY, INC., SALEM, VA, USA.

10 9 8 7 6 5 4 3 2 1

PREVIOUSLY

AT SOME POINT IN THEIR LIVES, ALL KIDS THINK THAT THEY HAVE THE MOST EVIL PARENTS IN THE WORLD, BUT NICO MINORU AND HER FRIENDS REALLY DID.

DISCOVERING THEY WERE THE CHILDREN OF A GROUP OF SUPER VILLAINS KNOWN AS THE PRIDE, THE LOS ANGELES TEENAGERS STOLE WEAPONS AND RESOURCES FROM THESE CRIMINALS BEFORE RUNNING AWAY FROM HOME AND EVENTUALLY DEFEATING THEIR PARENTS. BUT THAT WAS JUST THE BEGINNING. TOGETHER, THE TEENAGE RUNAWAYS NOW HOPE TO ATONE FOR THEIR PARENTS' CRIMES BY TAKING ON THE NEW THREATS TRYING TO FILL THE PRIDE'S VOID.

AFTER A FEROCIOUS BATTLE WITH AN ALL-NEW PRIDE LED BY A TEMPORALLY DISPLACED GEOFFREY WILDER (FATHER OF THE LATE ALEX WILDER, THE RUNAWAYS' TRAITOROUS LEADER), GERT YORKES DIED IN THE ARMS OF HER BOYFRIEND. WITH HER FINAL BREATH, GERT "WILLED" CONTROL OF HER TELEPATHIC DINOSAUR TO CHASE STEIN, JUST BEFORE THE DEVASTATED YOUNG MAN STOLE A DECODER RING AND WILDER'S COPY OF THE ABSTRACT, A MYSTICAL TOME CONTAINING POWERFUL SECRETS.

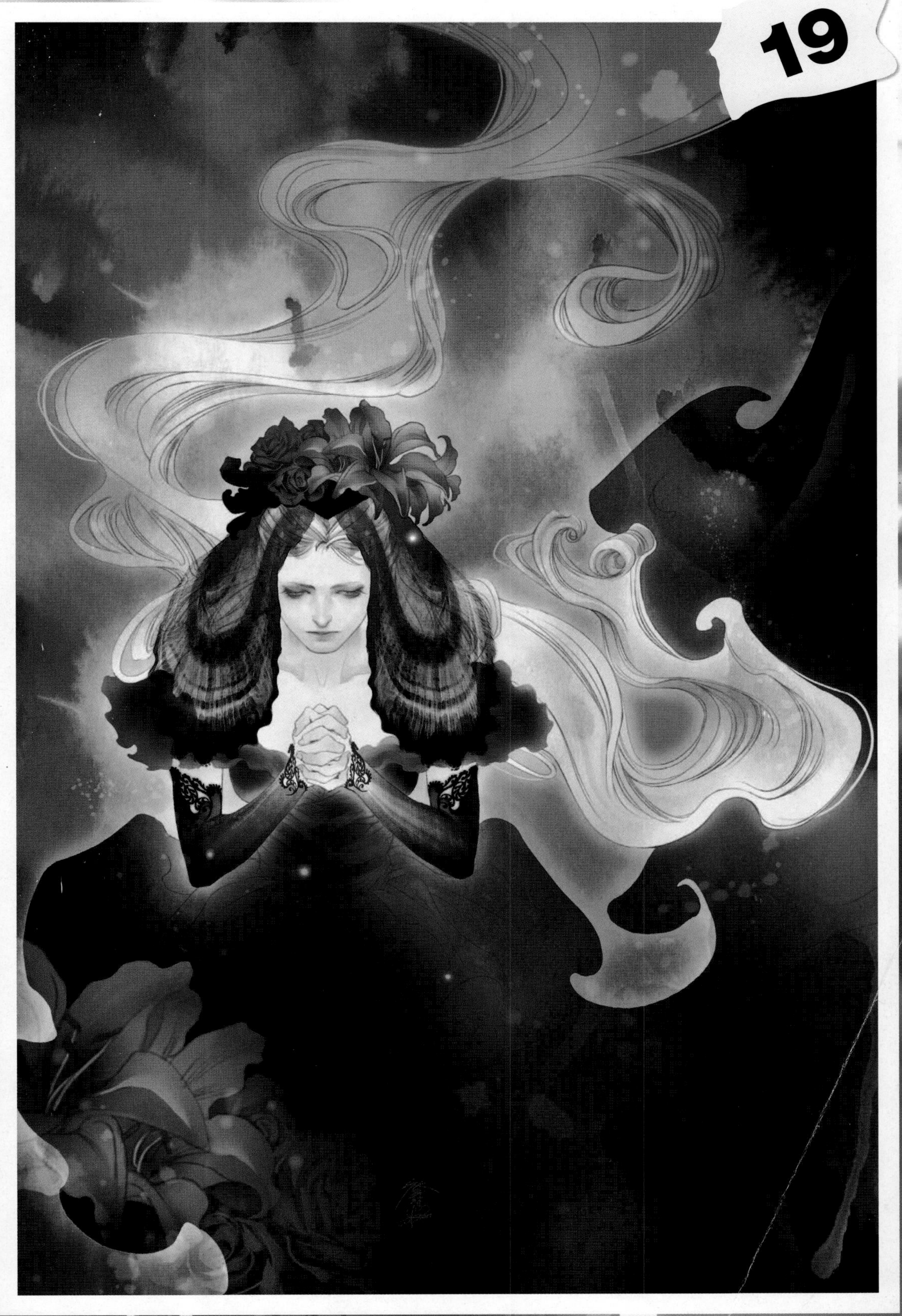
19

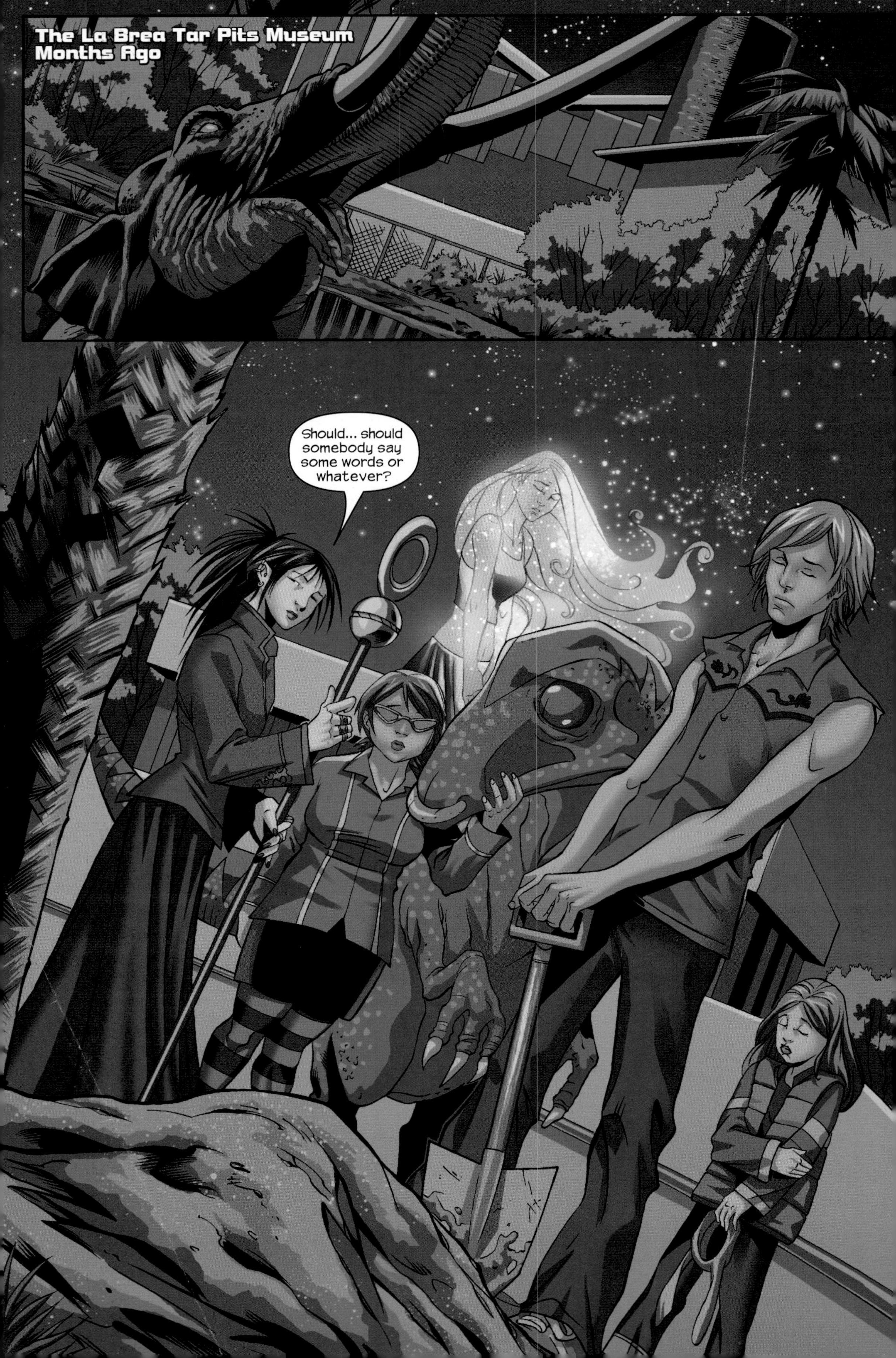
The La Brea Tar Pits Museum
Months Ago
Should... should somebody say some words or whatever?

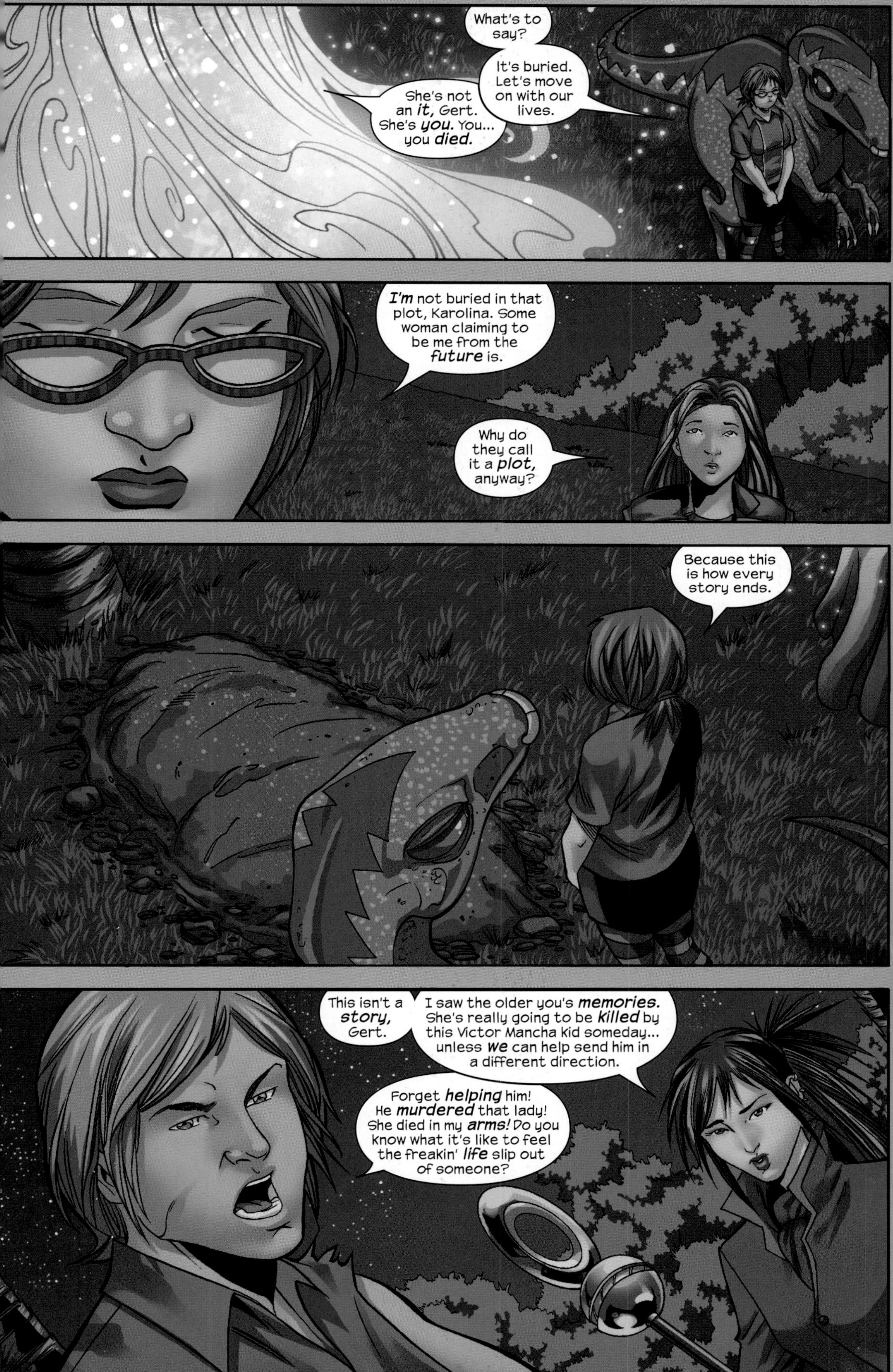
What's to say?
It's buried. Let's move on with our lives.
She's not an *it,* Gert. She's *you.* You... you *died.*
I'm not buried in that plot, Karolina. Some woman claiming to be me from the *future* is.
Why do they call it a *plot,* anyway?
Because this is how every story ends.
This isn't a *story,* Gert.
I saw the older you's *memories.* She's really going to be *killed* by this Victor Mancha kid someday... unless *we* can help send him in a different direction.
Forget *helping* him! He *murdered* that lady! She died in my *arms!* Do you know what it's like to feel the freakin' *life* slip out of someone?

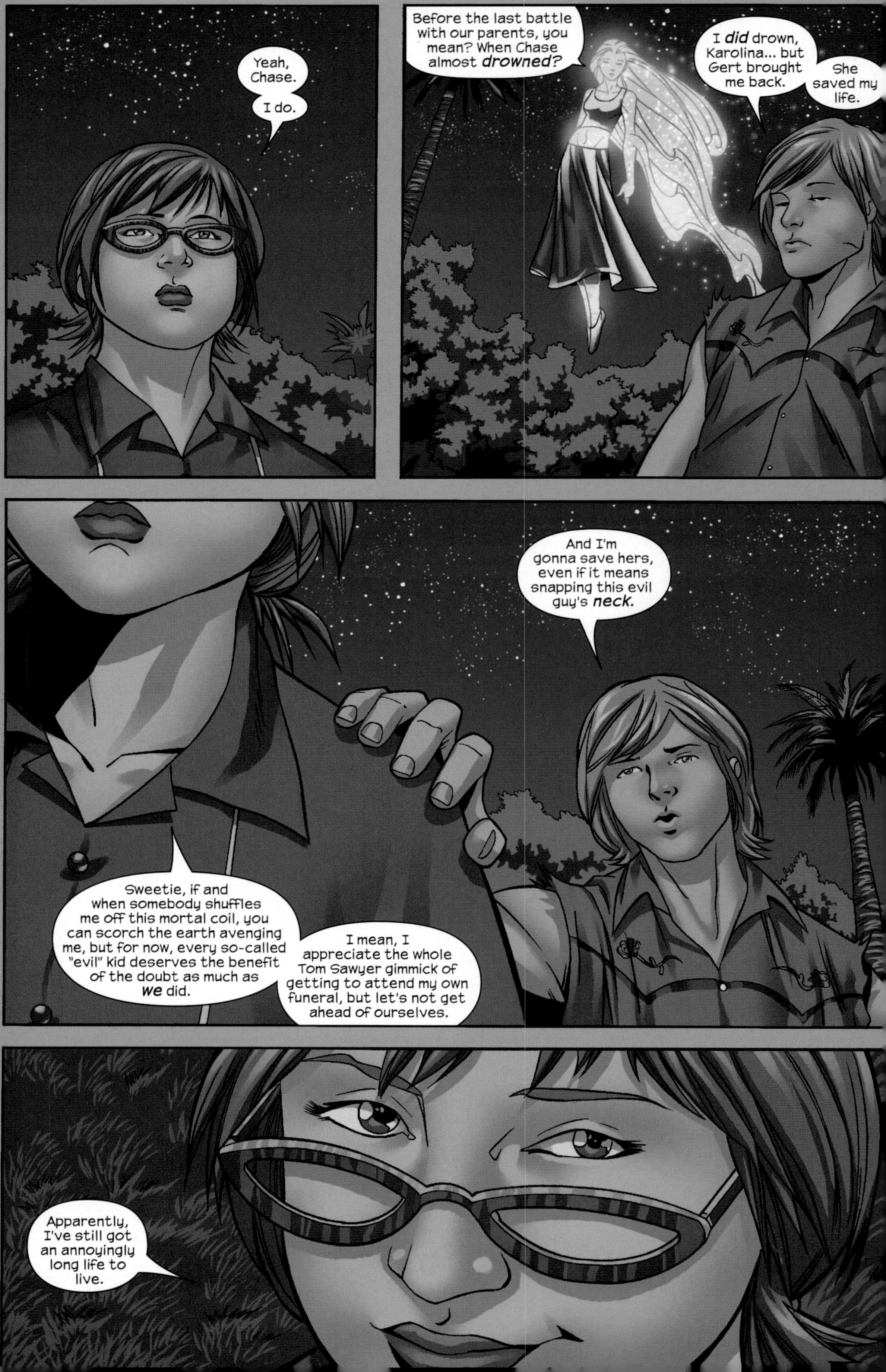

Yeah, Chase.
I do.
Before the last battle with our parents, you mean? When Chase almost *drowned*?
I *did* drown, Karolina... but Gert brought me back.
She saved my life.
And I'm gonna save hers, even if it means snapping this evil guy's *neck.*
Sweetie, if and when somebody shuffles me off this mortal coil, you can scorch the earth avenging me, but for now, every so-called "evil" kid deserves the benefit of the doubt as much as *we* did.
I mean, I appreciate the whole Tom Sawyer gimmick of getting to attend my own funeral, but let's not get ahead of ourselves.
Apparently, I've still got an annoyingly long life to live.

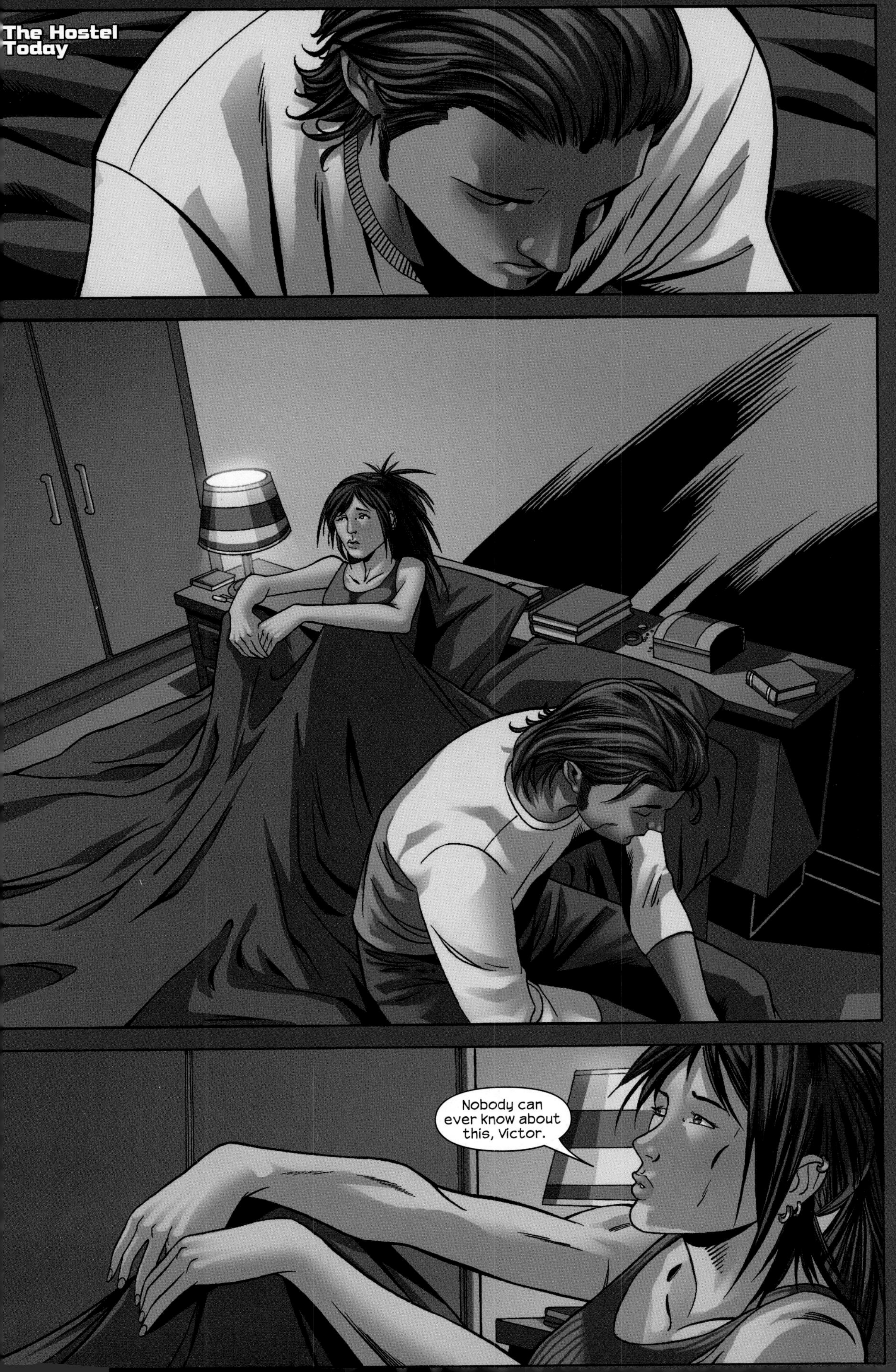
The Hostel
Today
Nobody can ever know about this, Victor.

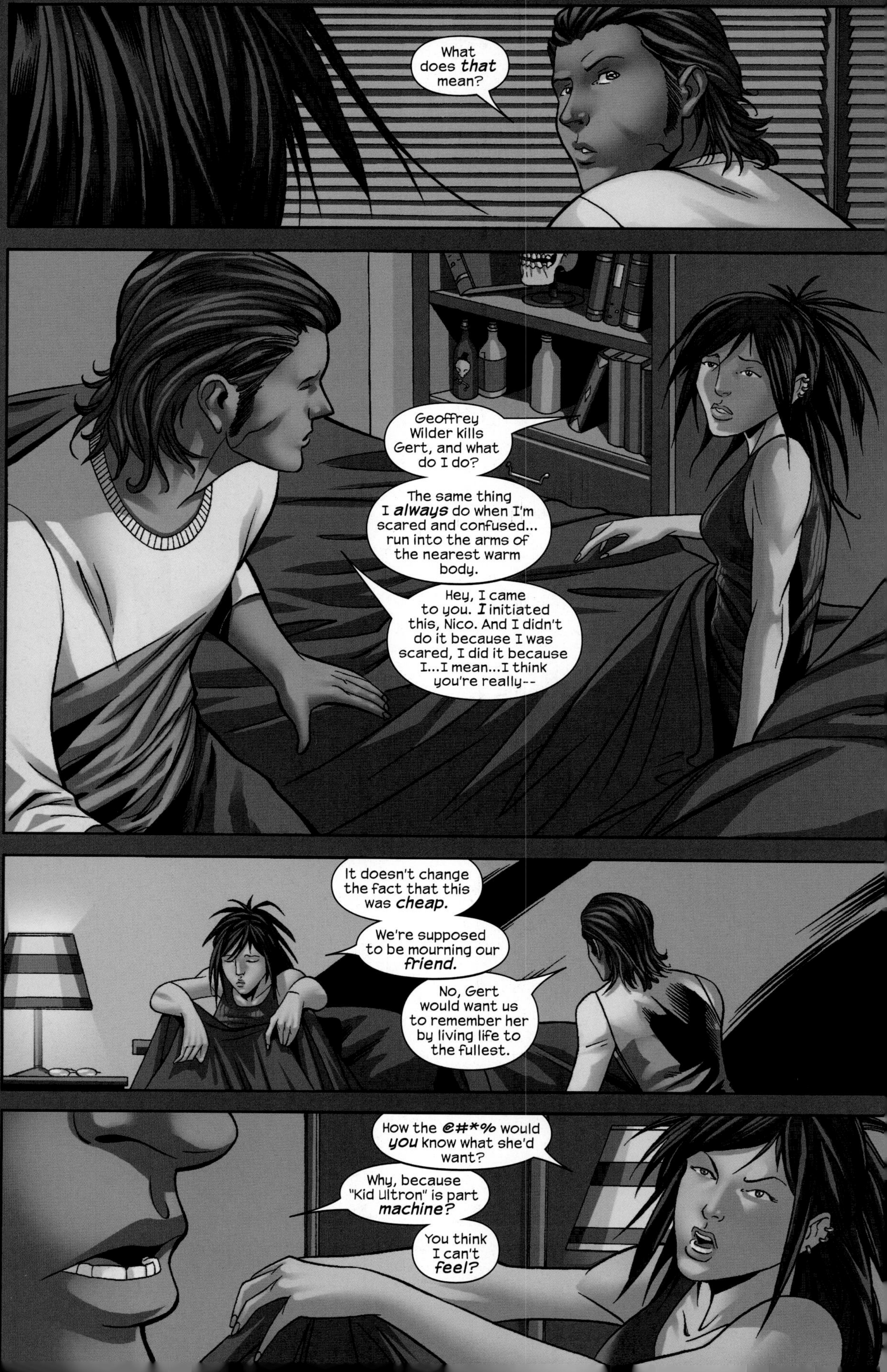
What does *that* mean?
Geoffrey Wilder kills Gert, and what do I do?
The same thing I *always* do when I'm scared and confused... run into the arms of the nearest warm body.
Hey, I came to you. *I* initiated this, Nico. And I didn't do it because I was scared, I did it because I...I mean...I think you're really--
It doesn't change the fact that this was *cheap.*
We're supposed to be mourning our *friend.*
No, Gert would want us to remember her by living life to the fullest.
How the @#*% would *you* know what she'd want?
Why, because "Kid Ultron" is part *machine?*
You think I can't *feel?*

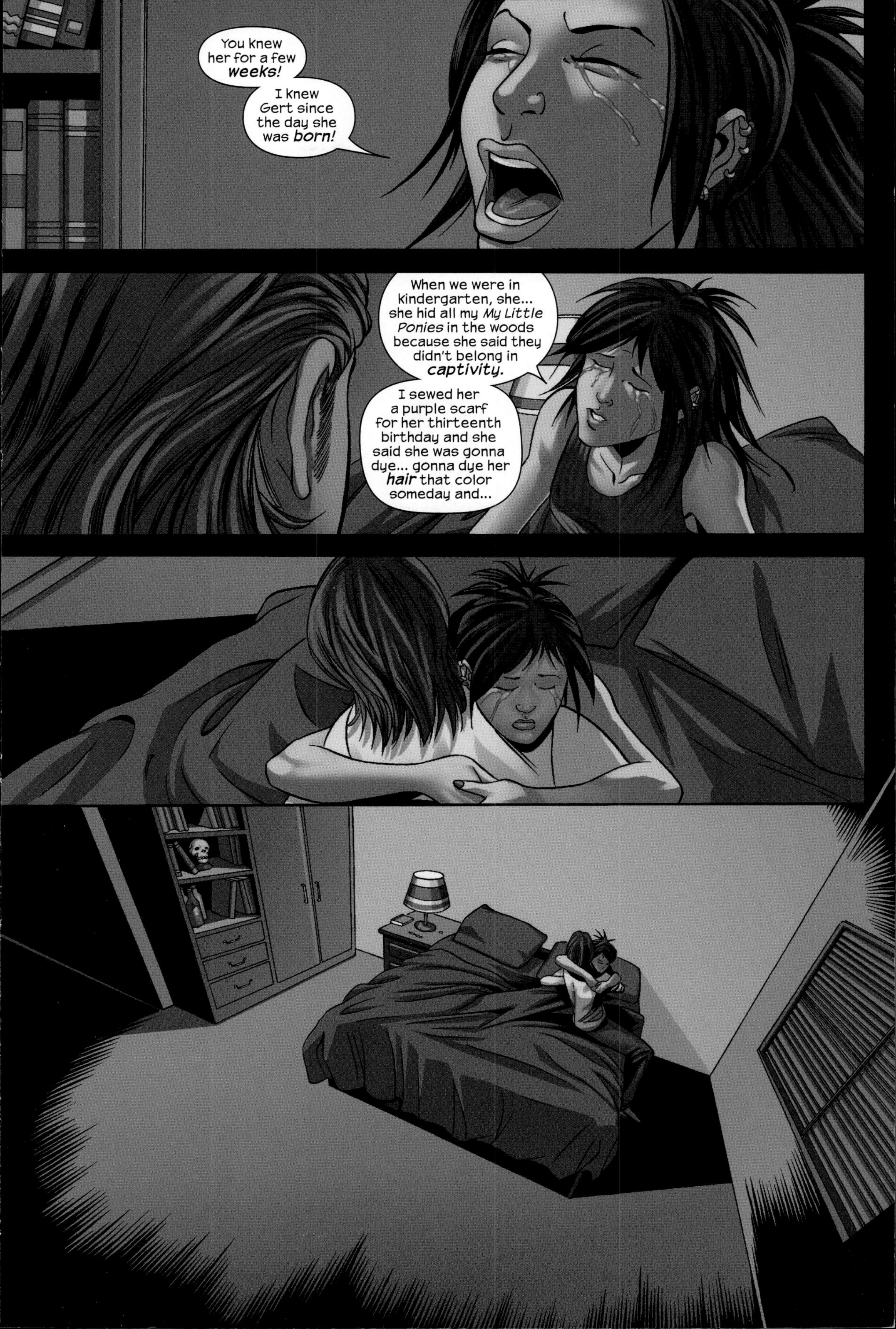
You knew her for a few *weeks!*
I knew Gert since the day she was *born!*
When we were in kindergarten, she... she hid all my *My Little Ponies* in the woods because she said they didn't belong in *captivity.*
I sewed her a purple scarf for her thirteenth birthday and she said she was gonna dye... gonna dye her *hair* that color someday and...

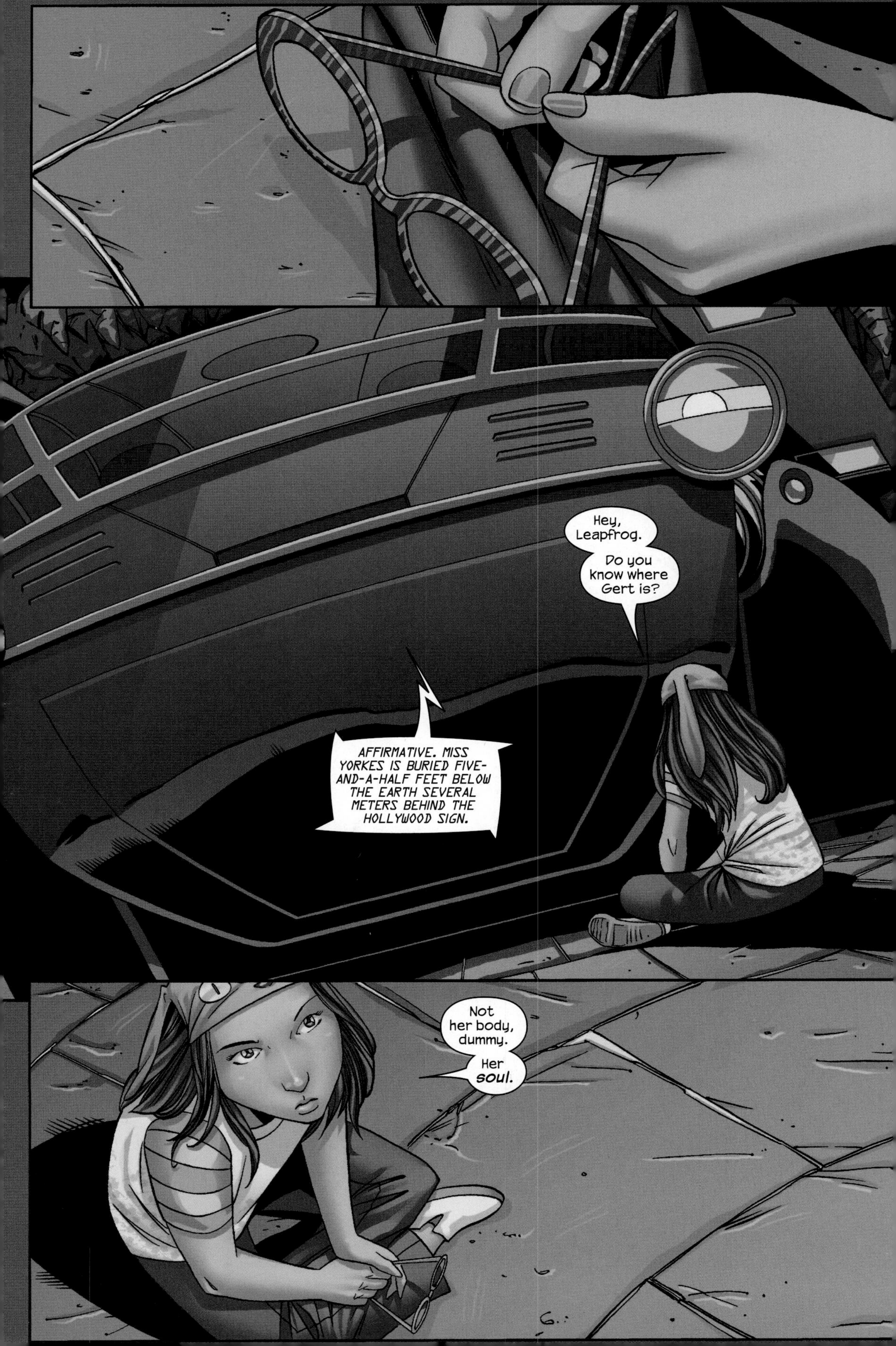
Hey, Leapfrog.
Do you know where Gert is?
AFFIRMATIVE. MISS YORKES IS BURIED FIVE-AND-A-HALF FEET BELOW THE EARTH SEVERAL METERS BEHIND THE HOLLYWOOD SIGN.
Not her body, dummy.
Her *soul*.

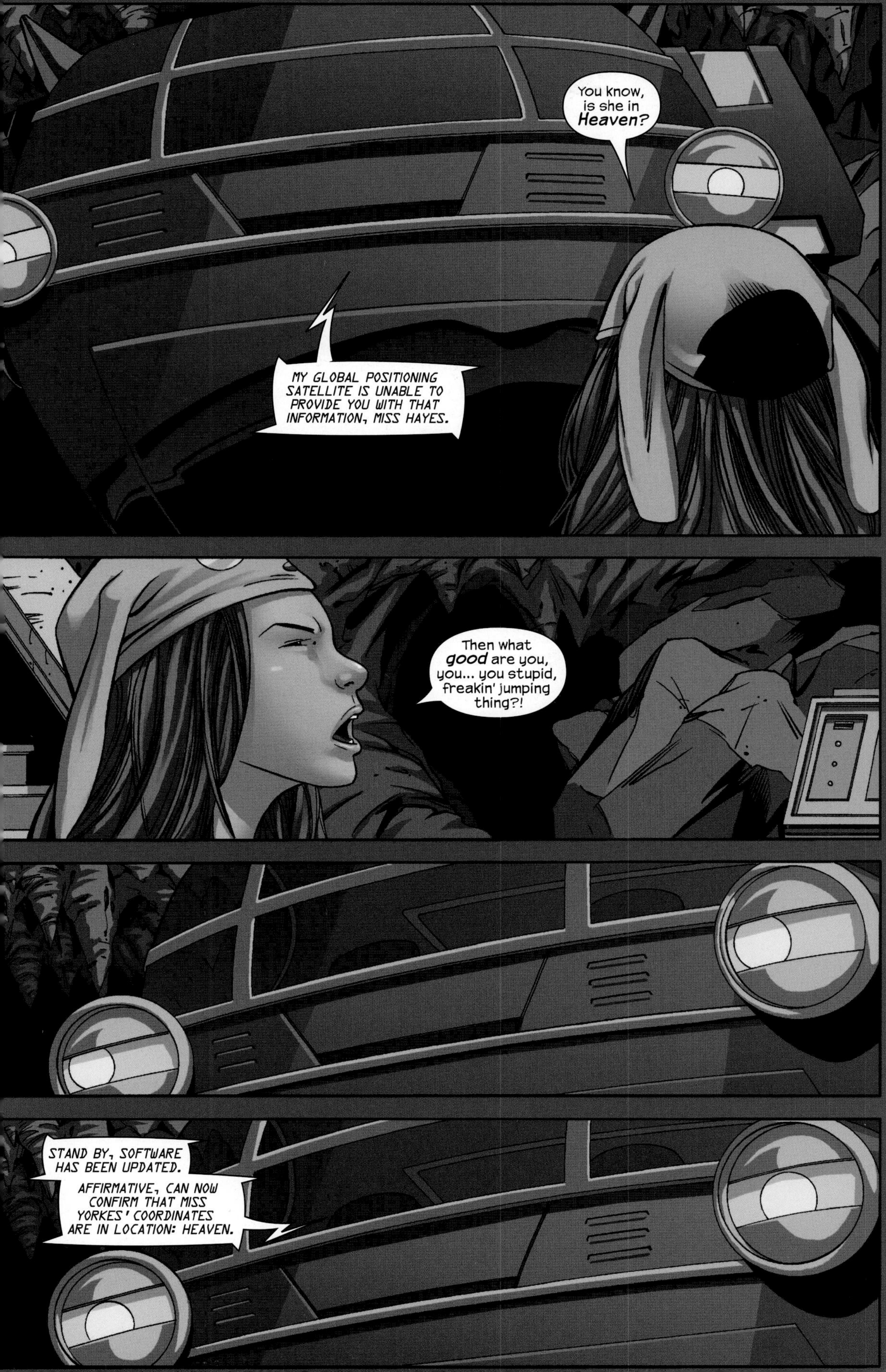
You know, is she in Heaven?
MY GLOBAL POSITIONING SATELLITE IS UNABLE TO PROVIDE YOU WITH THAT INFORMATION, MISS HAYES.
Then what good are you, you... you stupid, freakin' jumping thing?!
STAND BY, SOFTWARE HAS BEEN UPDATED.
AFFIRMATIVE, CAN NOW CONFIRM THAT MISS YORKES' COORDINATES ARE IN LOCATION: HEAVEN.

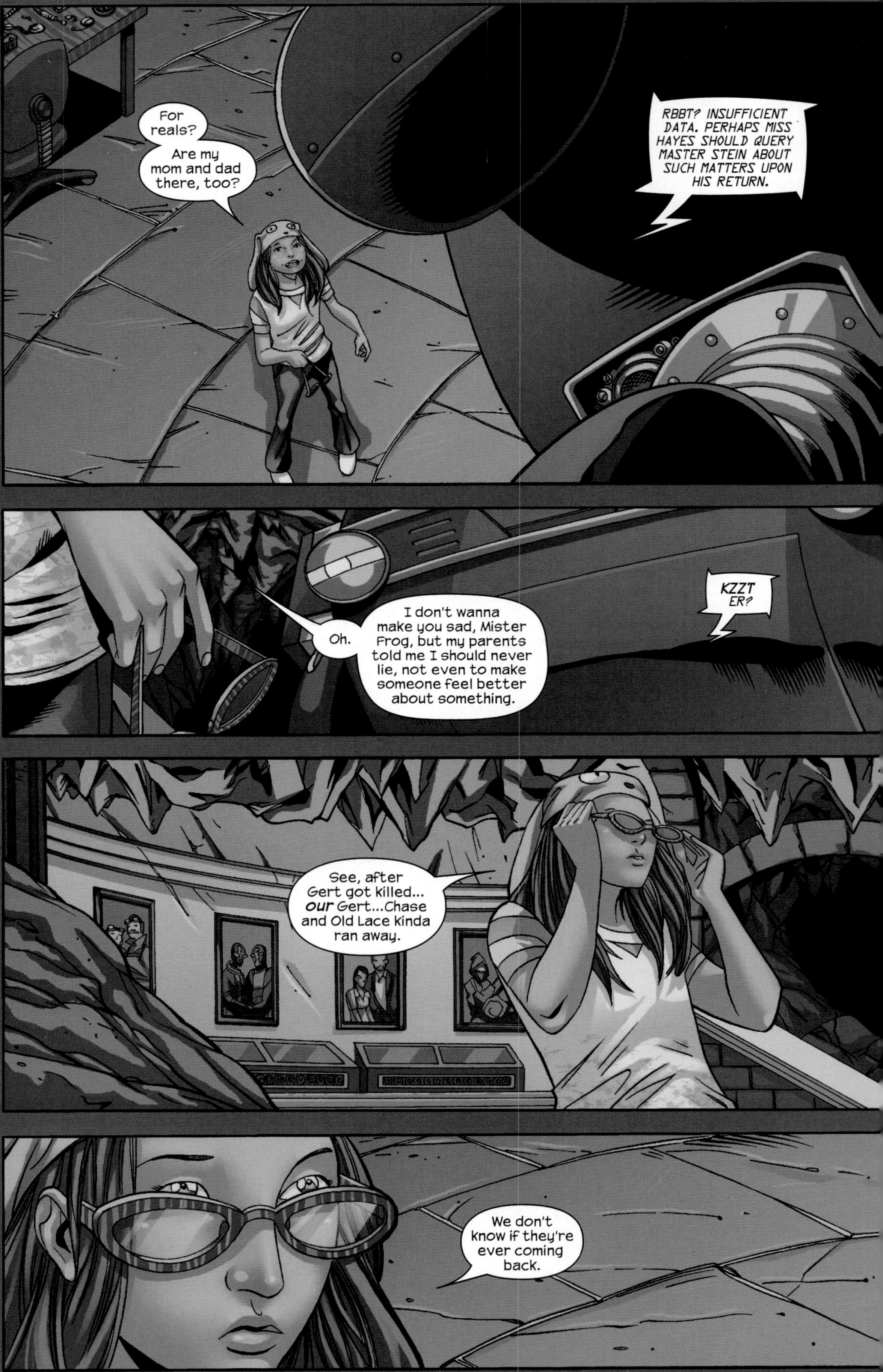
For reals?
Are my mom and dad there, too?
RBBT? INSUFFICIENT DATA. PERHAPS MISS HAYES SHOULD QUERY MASTER STEIN ABOUT SUCH MATTERS UPON HIS RETURN.
Oh.
I don't wanna make you sad, Mister Frog, but my parents told me I should never lie, not even to make someone feel better about something.
KZZT ER?
See, after Gert got killed... *our* Gert...Chase and Old Lace kinda ran away.
We don't know if they're ever coming back.

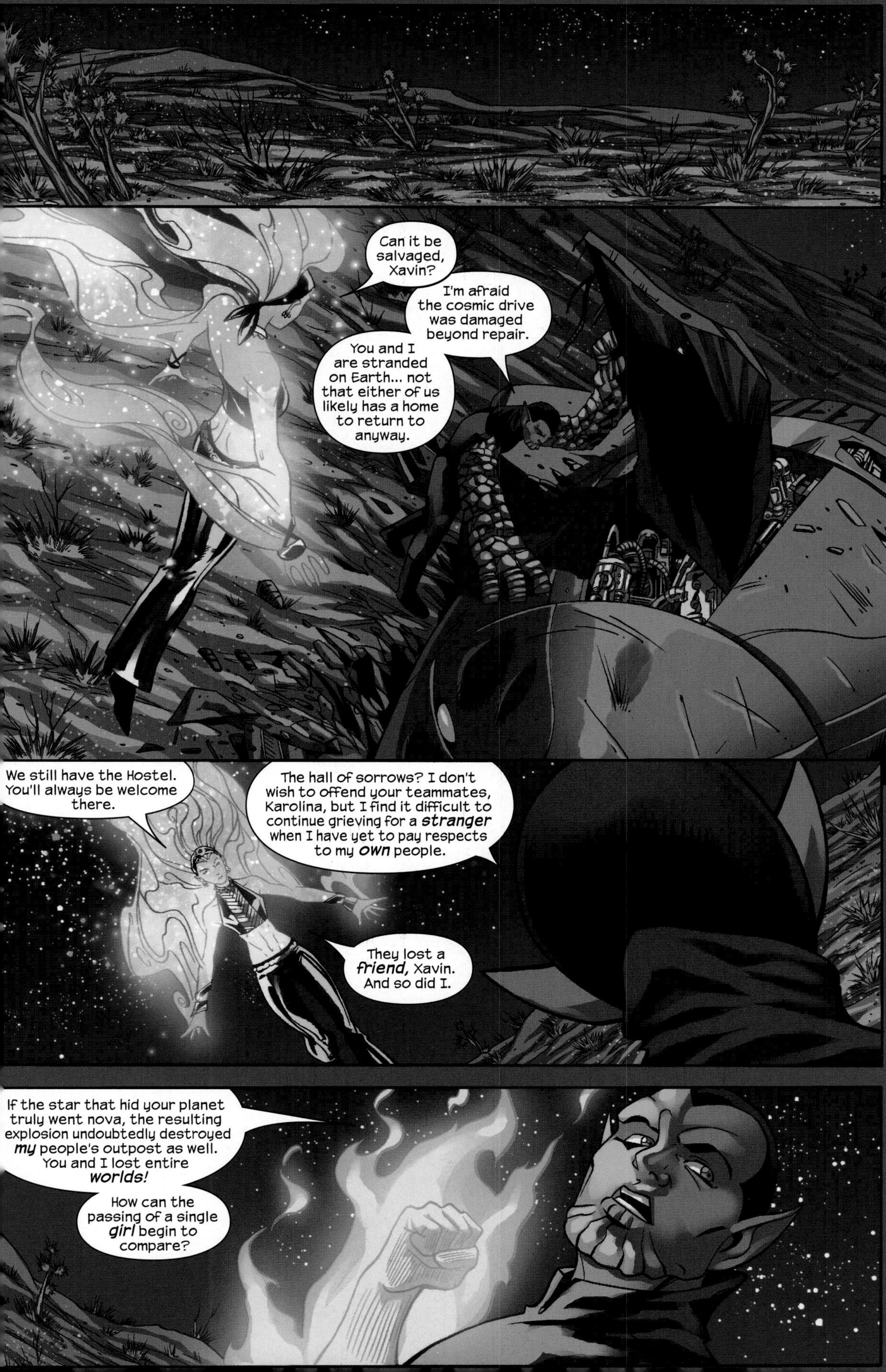

Can it be salvaged, Xavin?
I'm afraid the cosmic drive was damaged beyond repair.
You and I are stranded on Earth... not that either of us likely has a home to return to anyway.
We still have the Hostel. You'll always be welcome there.
The hall of sorrows? I don't wish to offend your teammates, Karolina, but I find it difficult to continue grieving for a stranger when I have yet to pay respects to my own people.
They lost a friend, Xavin. And so did I.
If the star that hid your planet truly went nova, the resulting explosion undoubtedly destroyed my people's outpost as well. You and I lost entire worlds!
How can the passing of a single girl begin to compare?

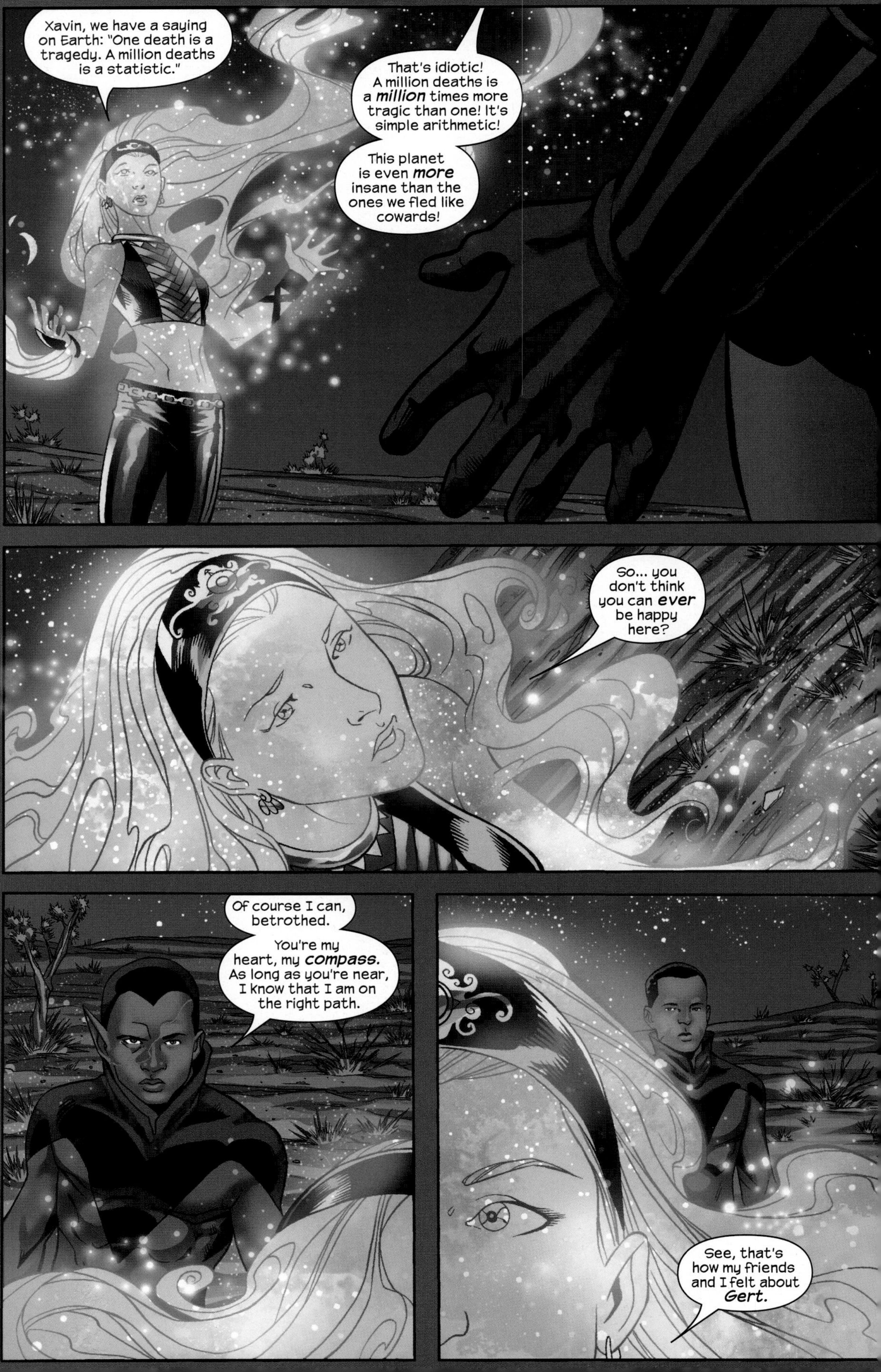
Xavin, we have a saying on Earth: "One death is a tragedy. A million deaths is a statistic."
That's idiotic! A million deaths is a *million* times more tragic than one! It's simple arithmetic!
This planet is even *more* insane than the ones we fled like cowards!
So... you don't think you can *ever* be happy here?
Of course I can, betrothed.
You're my heart, my *compass.* As long as you're near, I know that I am on the right path.
See, that's how my friends and I felt about *Gert.*

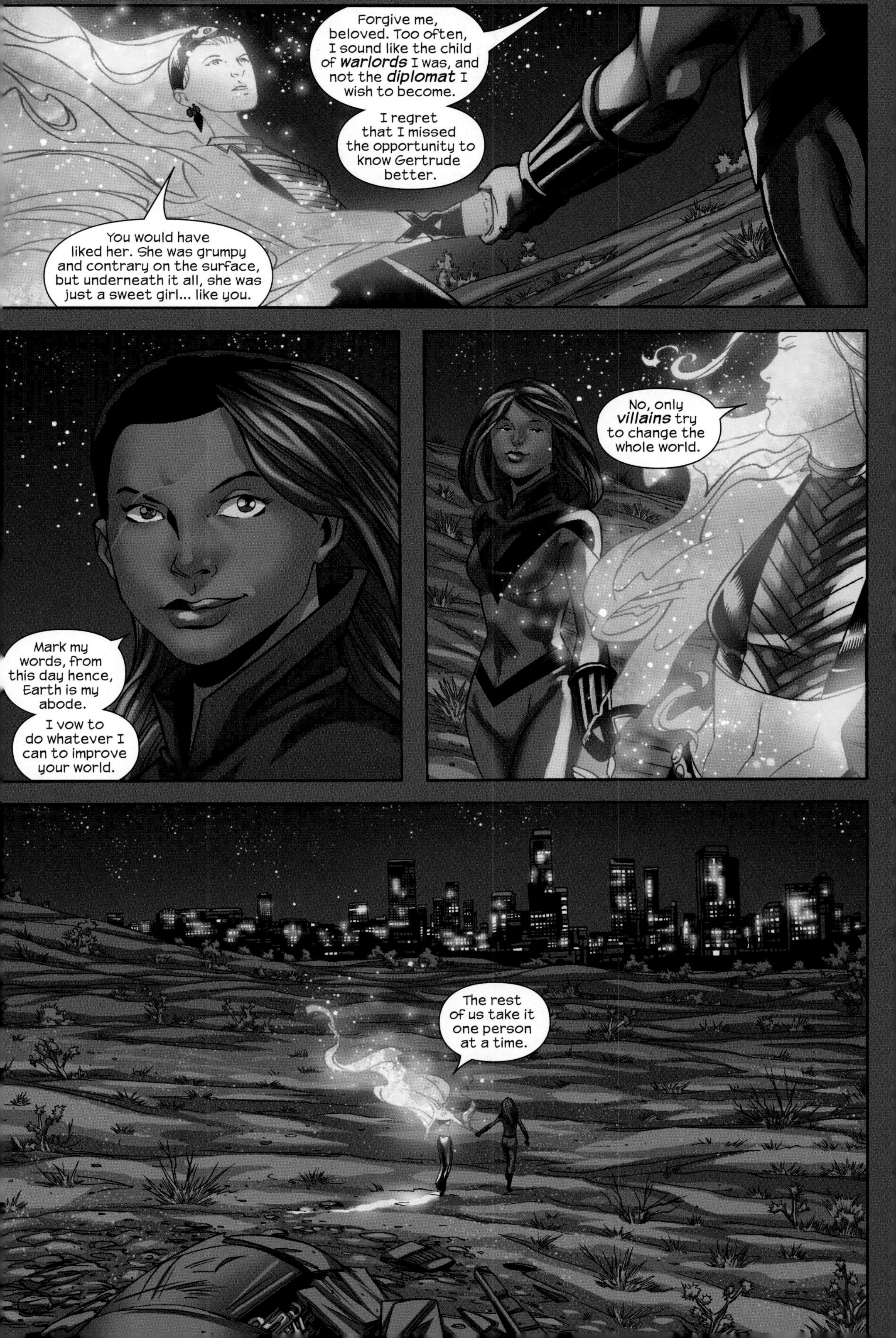
Forgive me, beloved. Too often, I sound like the child of warlords I was, and not the diplomat I wish to become.
I regret that I missed the opportunity to know Gertrude better.
You would have liked her. She was grumpy and contrary on the surface, but underneath it all, she was just a sweet girl... like you.
Mark my words, from this day hence, Earth is my abode.
I vow to do whatever I can to improve your world.
No, only villains try to change the whole world.
The rest of us take it one person at a time.

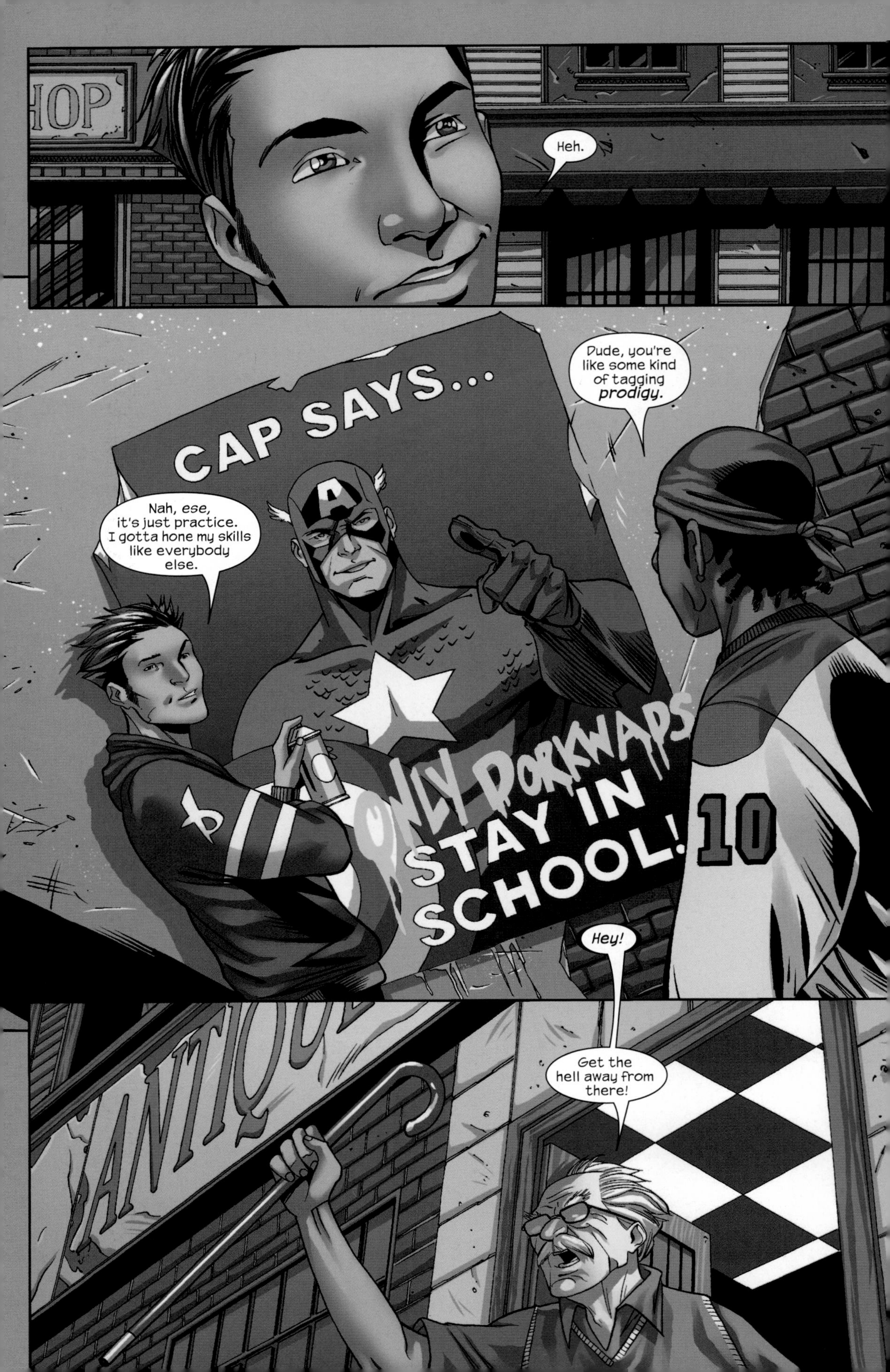

HOP
Heh.
CAP SAYS...
Dude, you're like some kind of tagging *prodigy*.
Nah, *ese*, it's just practice. I gotta hone my skills like everybody else.
ONLY DORKWAPS
STAY IN SCHOOL!
10
Hey!
ANTIQUE
Get the hell away from there!

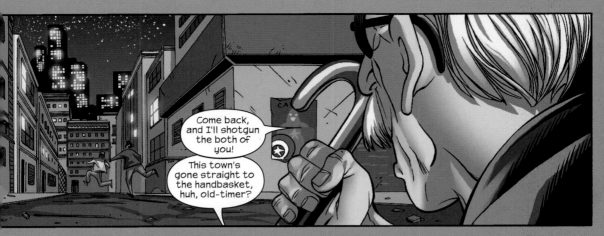

Come back, and I'll shotgun the both of you!

This town's gone straight to the handbasket, huh, old-timer?

No respect, no responsibility.

Angeles used to be the crown jewel of Cali, but these kids have turned it into worthless *crap*.

I know, that's why I left the force.

But not before I took this.

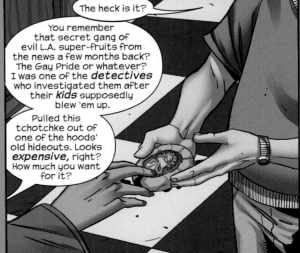

The heck is it?

You remember that secret gang of evil L.A. super-fruits from the news a few months back? The Gay Pride or whatever? I was one of the *detectives* who investigated them after their *kids* supposedly blew 'em up.

Pulled this tchotchke out of one of the hoods' old hideouts. Looks *expensive*, right? How much you want for it?

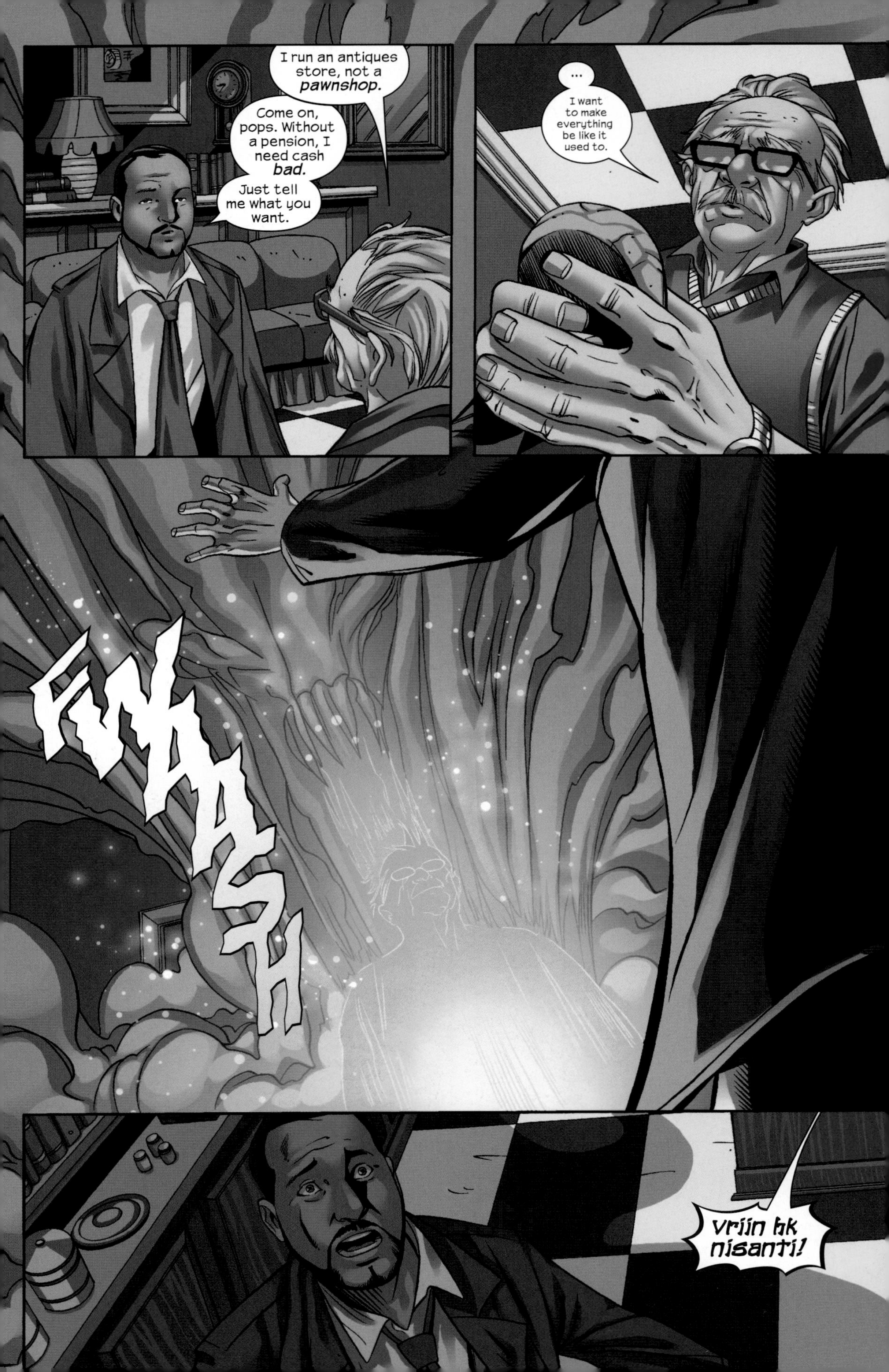
I run an antiques store, not a pawnshop.
Come on, pops. Without a pension, I need cash bad.
Just tell me what you want.
...
I want to make everything be like it used to.
FWASH
Vriin hk nisanti!

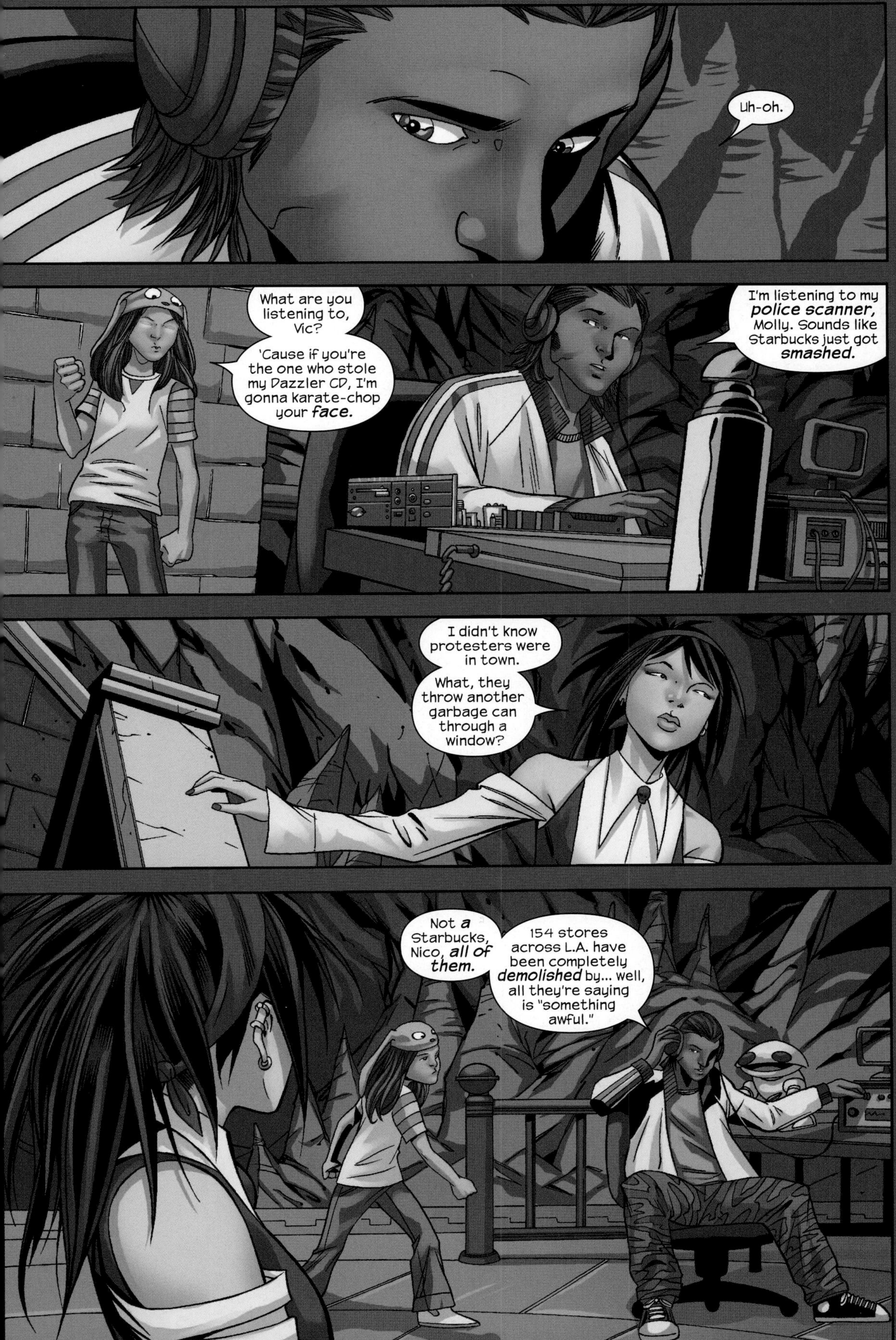
Uh-oh.
What are you listening to, Vic?
'Cause if you're the one who stole my Dazzler CD, I'm gonna karate-chop your *face.*
I'm listening to my ***police scanner,*** Molly. Sounds like Starbucks just got ***smashed.***
I didn't know protesters were in town.
What, they throw another garbage can through a window?
Not ***a*** Starbucks, Nico, ***all of them.***
154 stores across L.A. have been completely ***demolished*** by... well, all they're saying is "something awful."

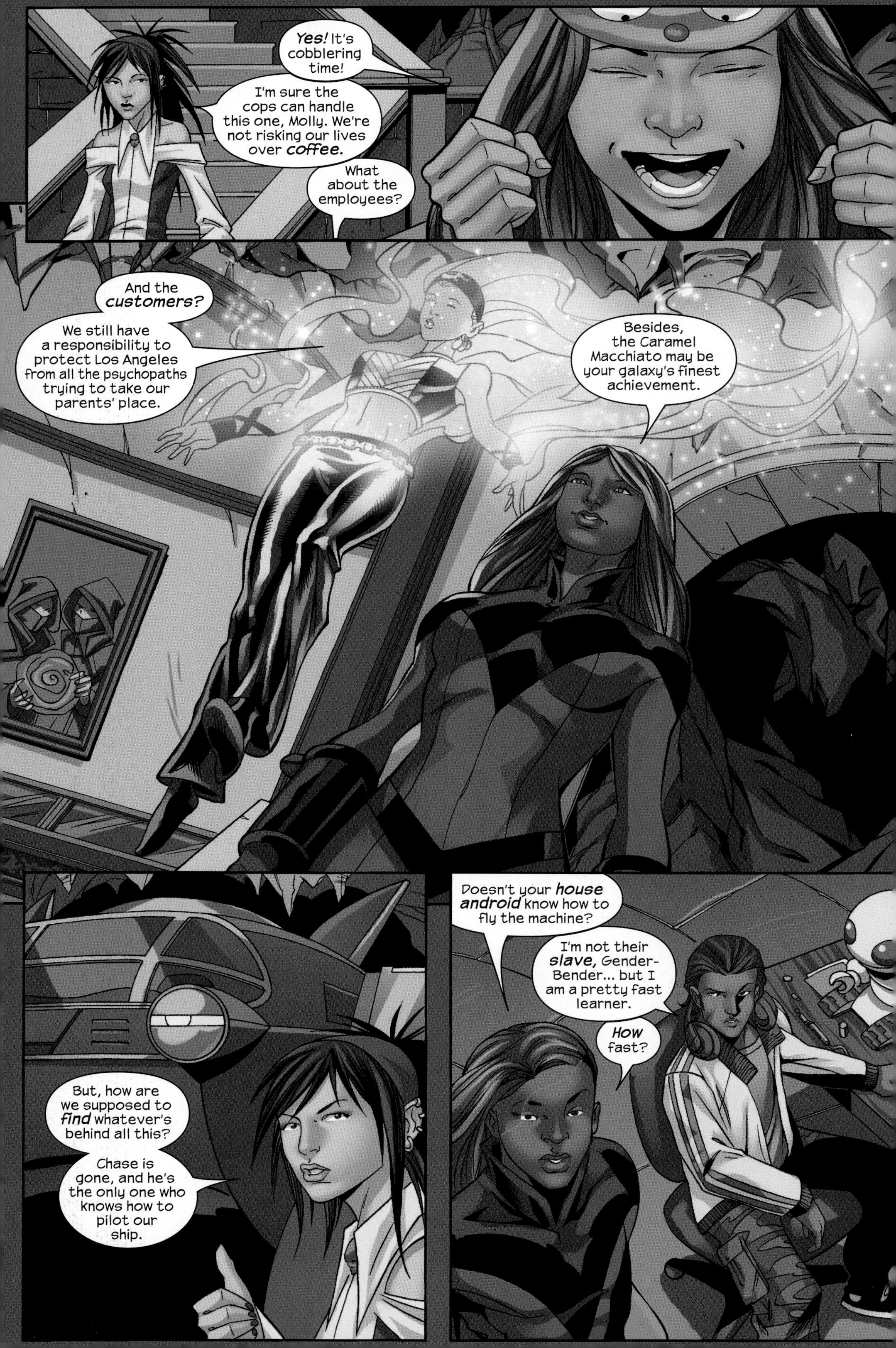
Yes! It's cobblering time!
I'm sure the cops can handle this one, Molly. We're not risking our lives over coffee.
What about the employees?
And the customers?
We still have a responsibility to protect Los Angeles from all the psychopaths trying to take our parents' place.
Besides, the Caramel Macchiato may be your galaxy's finest achievement.
But, how are we supposed to find whatever's behind all this?
Chase is gone, and he's the only one who knows how to pilot our ship.
Doesn't your house android know how to fly the machine?
I'm not their slave, Gender-Bender... but I am a pretty fast learner.
How fast?

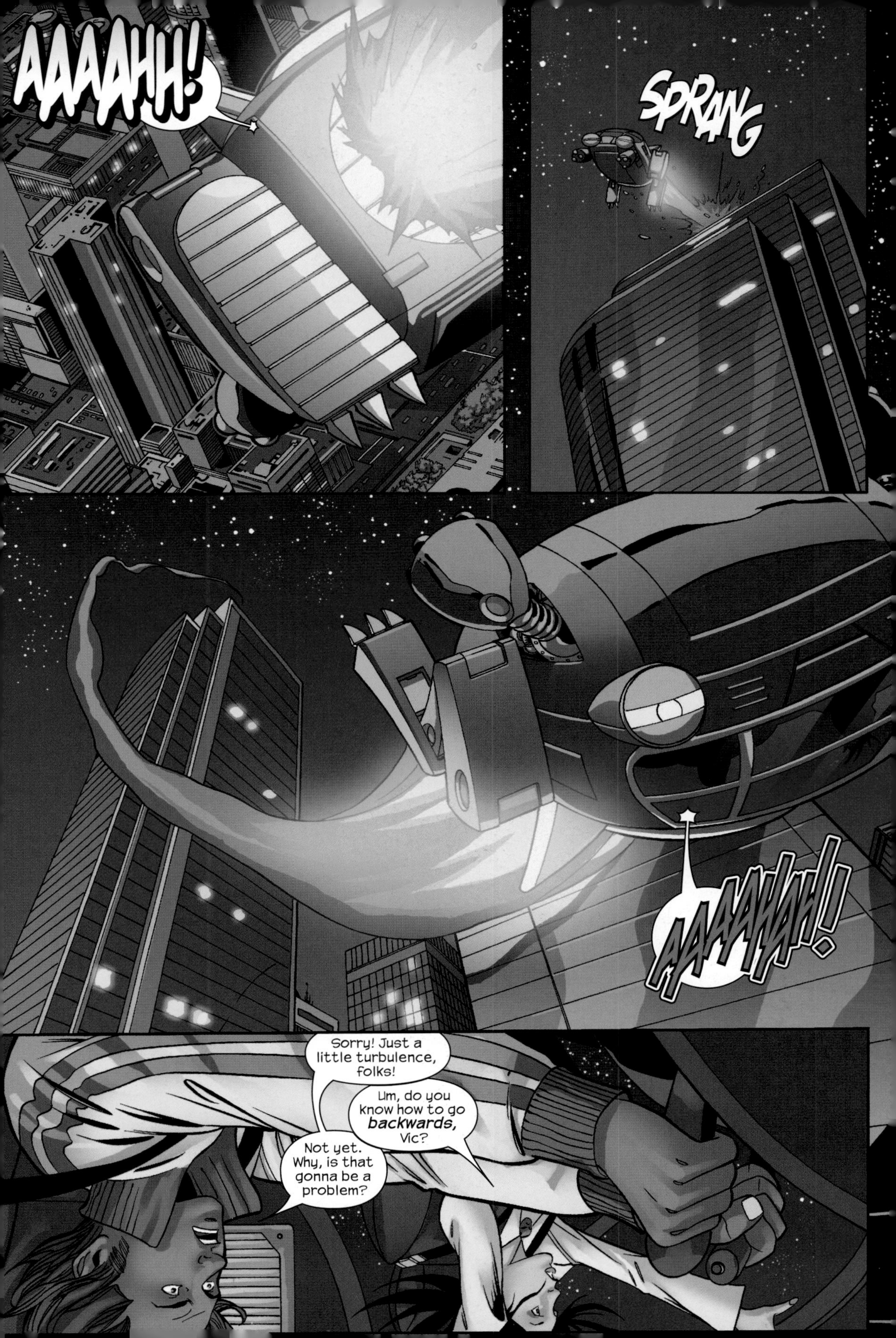
AAAAHH!
SPRANG
AAAAAHH!
Sorry! Just a little turbulence, folks!
Um, do you know how to go *backwards,* Vic?
Not yet. Why, is that gonna be a problem?

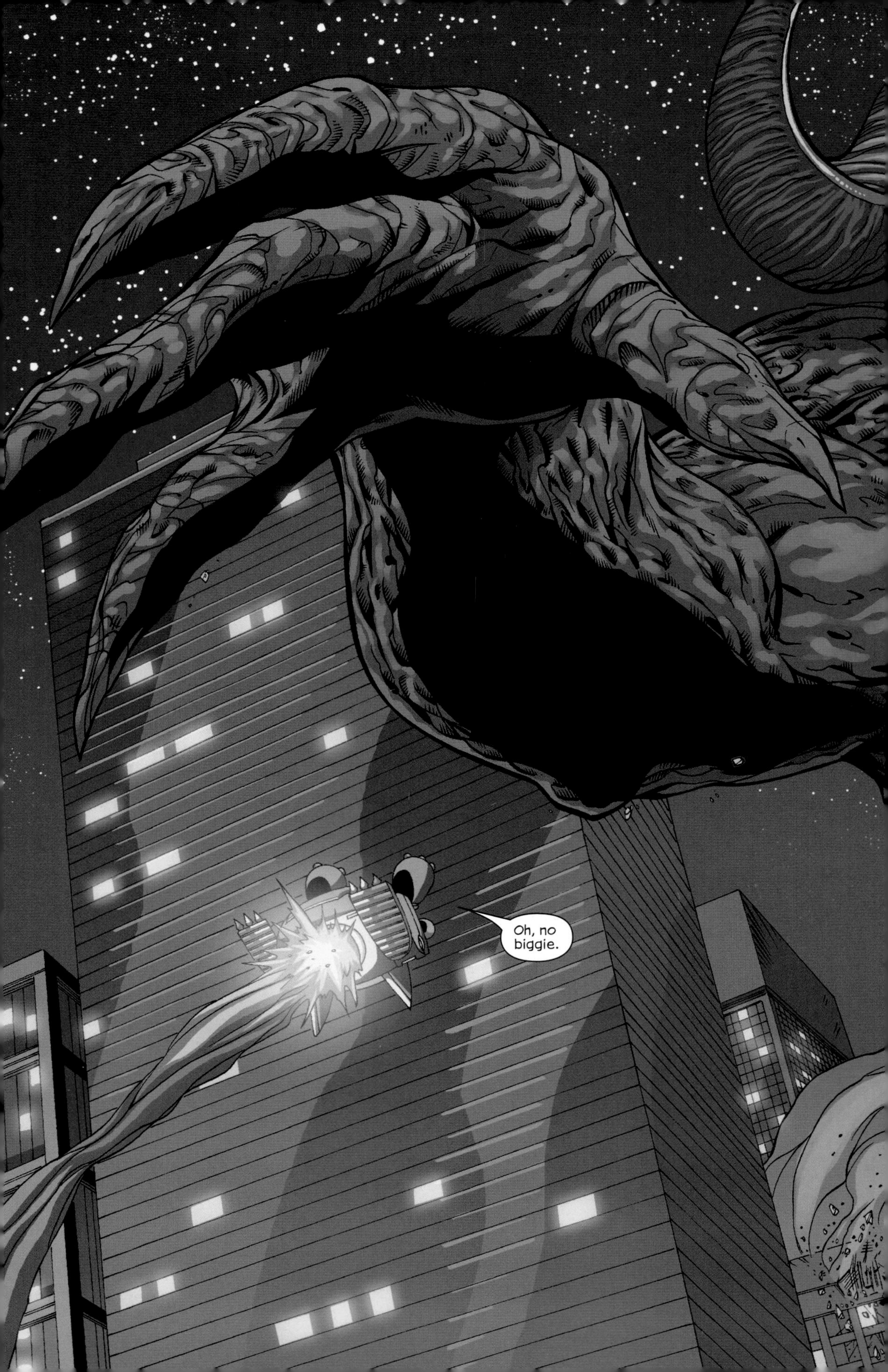
Oh, no biggie.

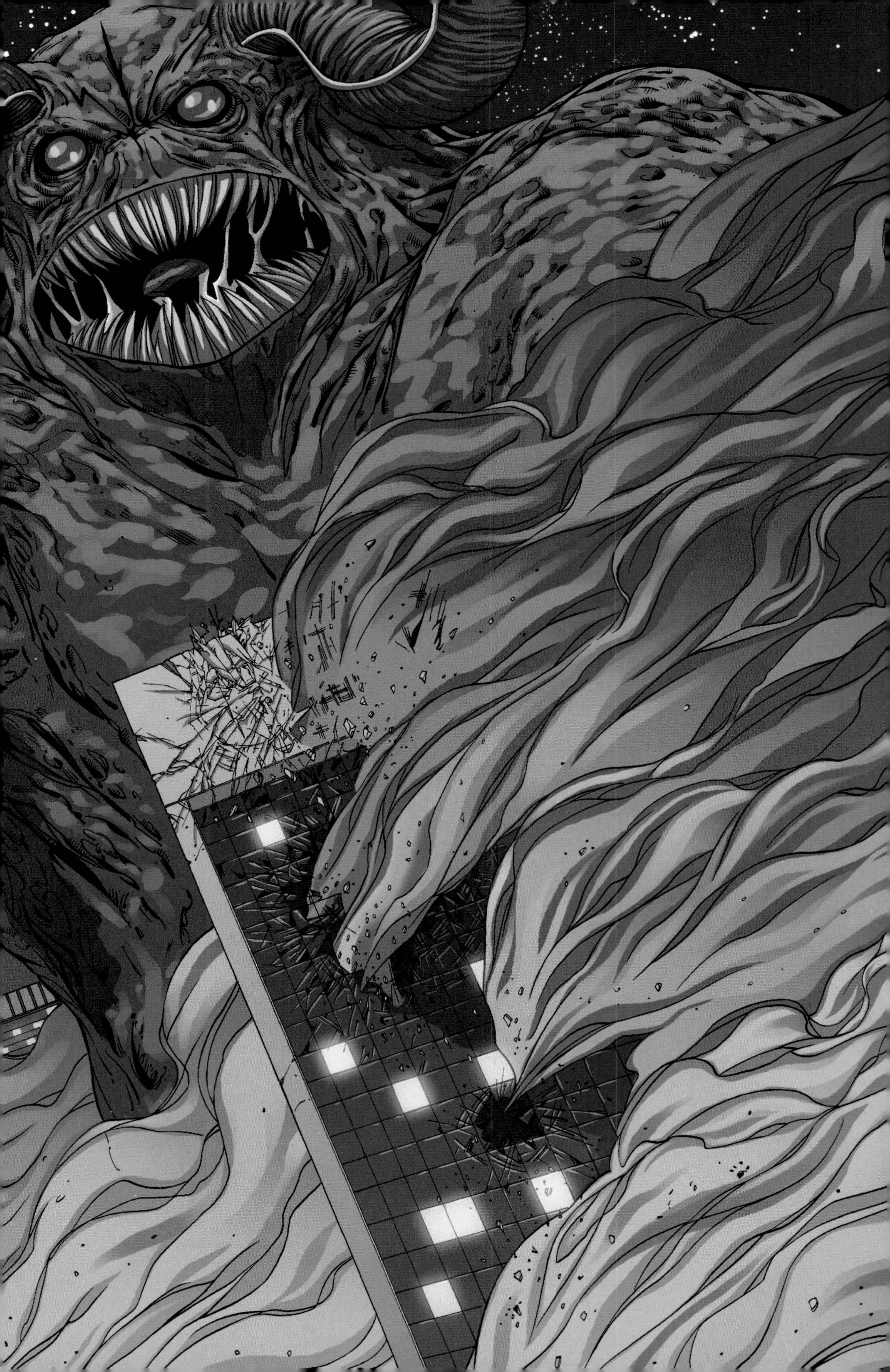

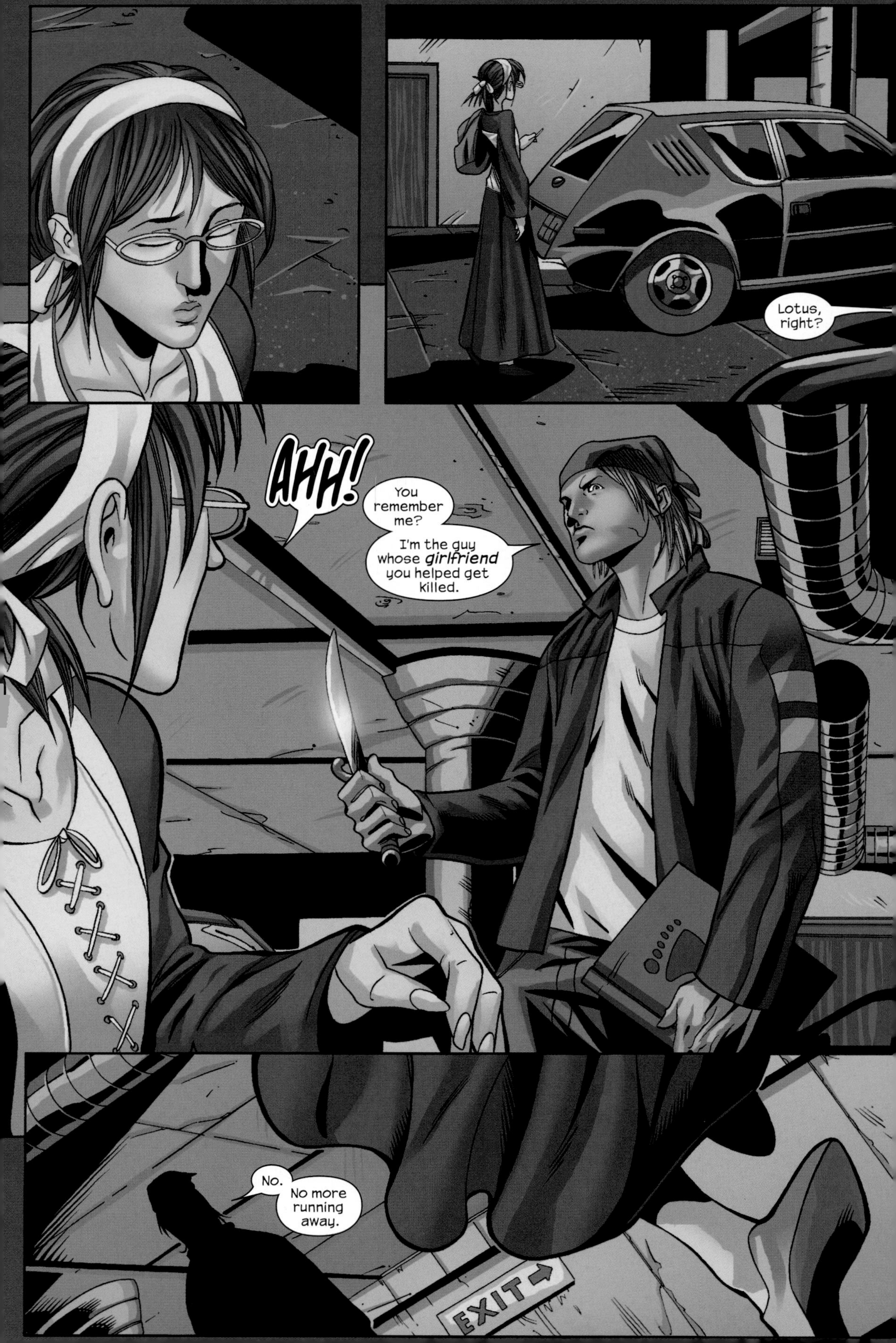

Lotus, right?
AHH!
You remember me?
I'm the guy whose *girlfriend* you helped get killed.
No.
No more running away.
EXIT
EXIT

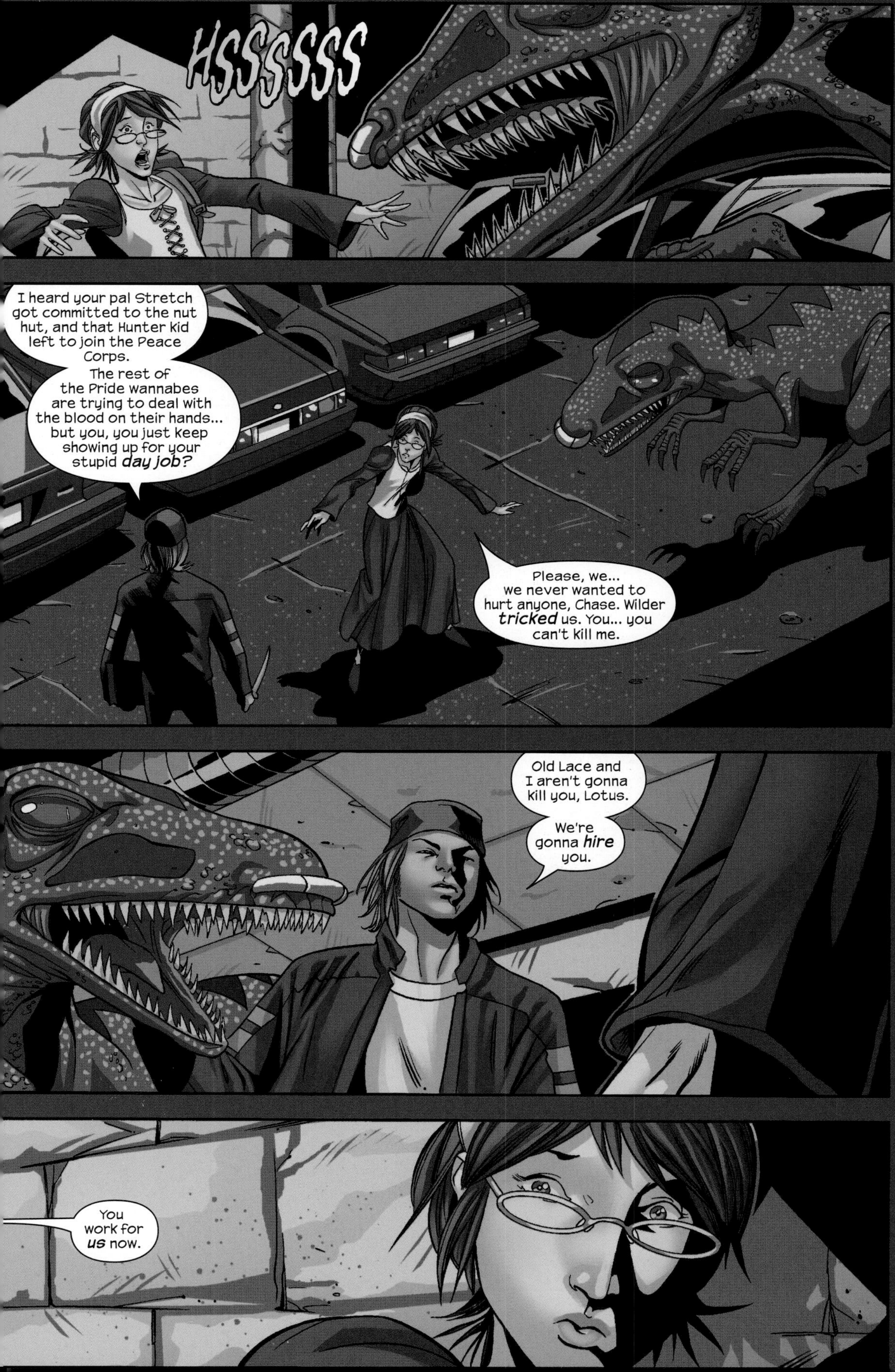
HSSSSSS
I heard your pal Stretch got committed to the nut hut, and that Hunter kid left to join the Peace Corps.
The rest of the Pride wannabes are trying to deal with the blood on their hands... but you, you just keep showing up for your stupid day job?
Please, we... we never wanted to hurt anyone, Chase. Wilder tricked us. You... you can't kill me.
Old Lace and I aren't gonna kill you, Lotus.
We're gonna hire you.
You work for us now.

20

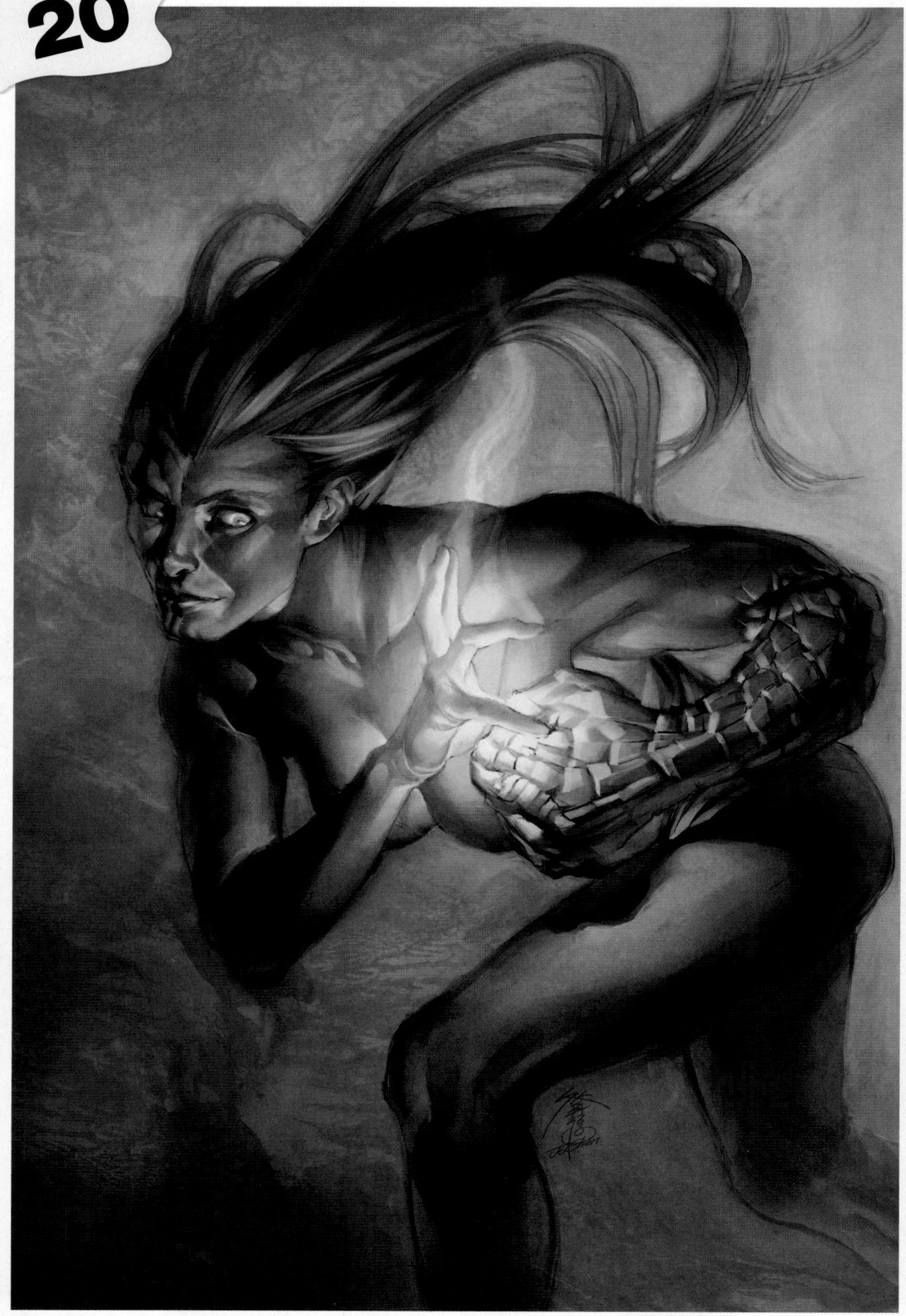

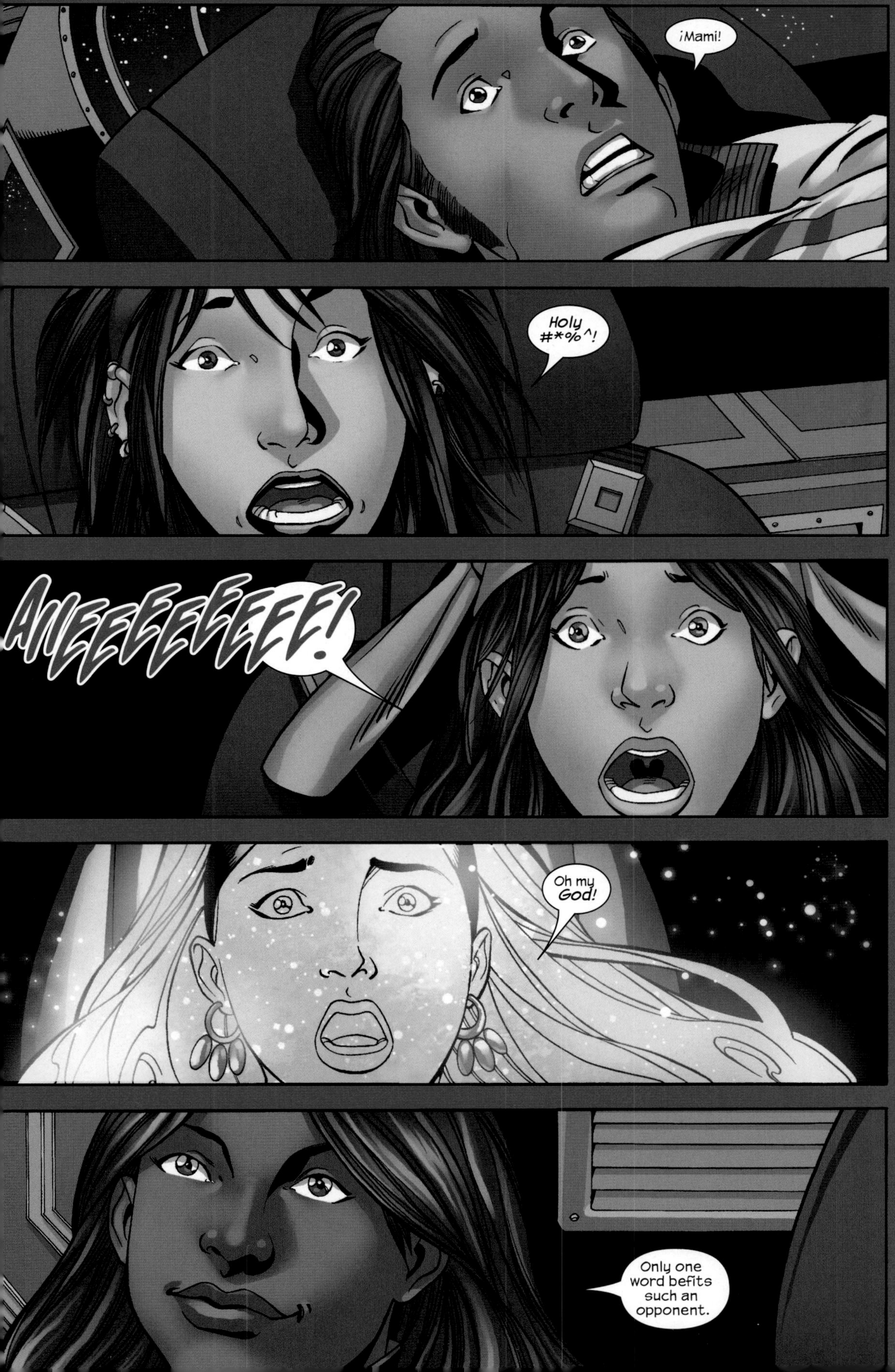

¡Mami!
Holy #*%^!
AIIEEEEEEEEE!
Oh my God!
Only one word befits such an opponent.

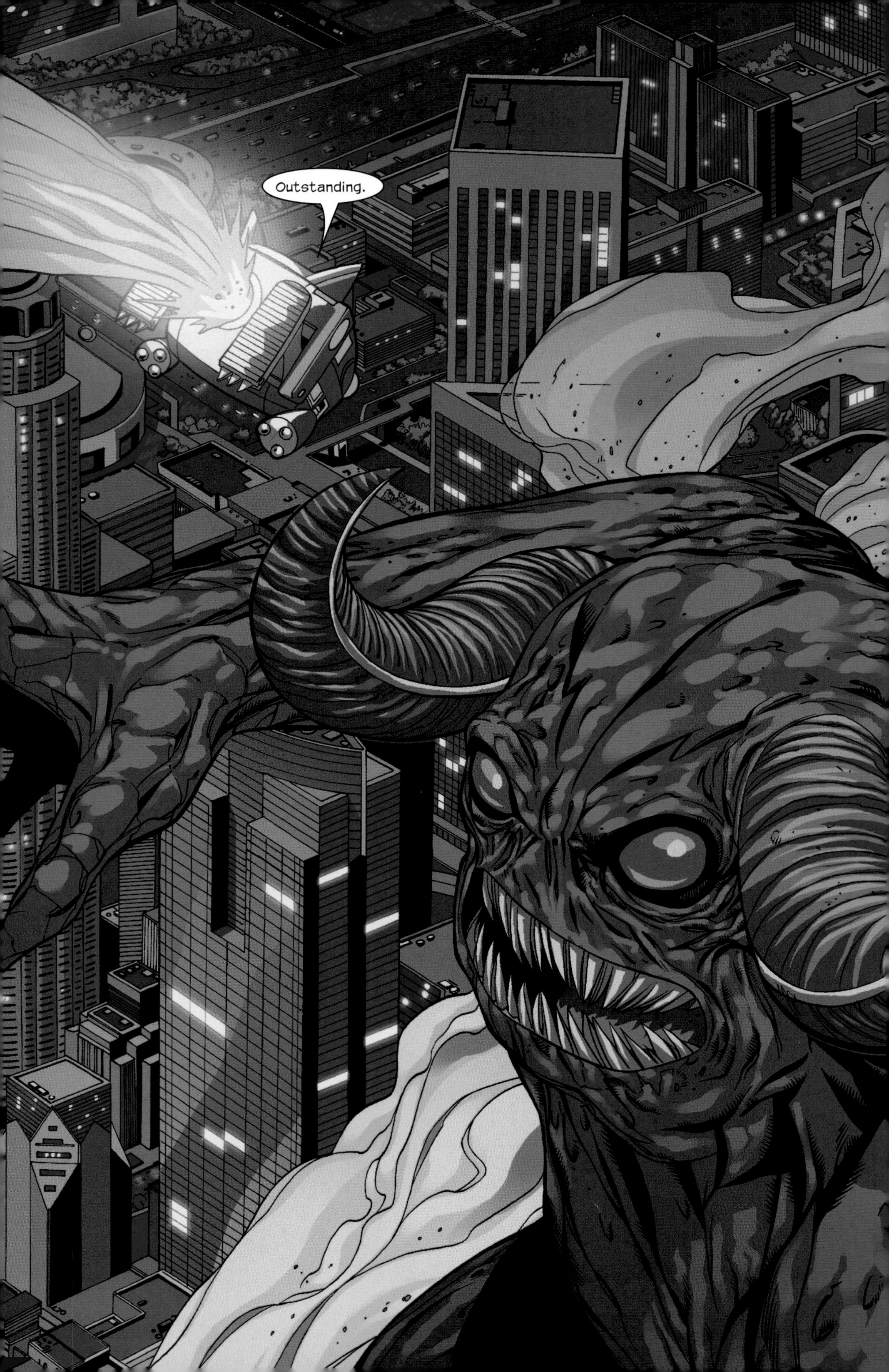
Outstanding.

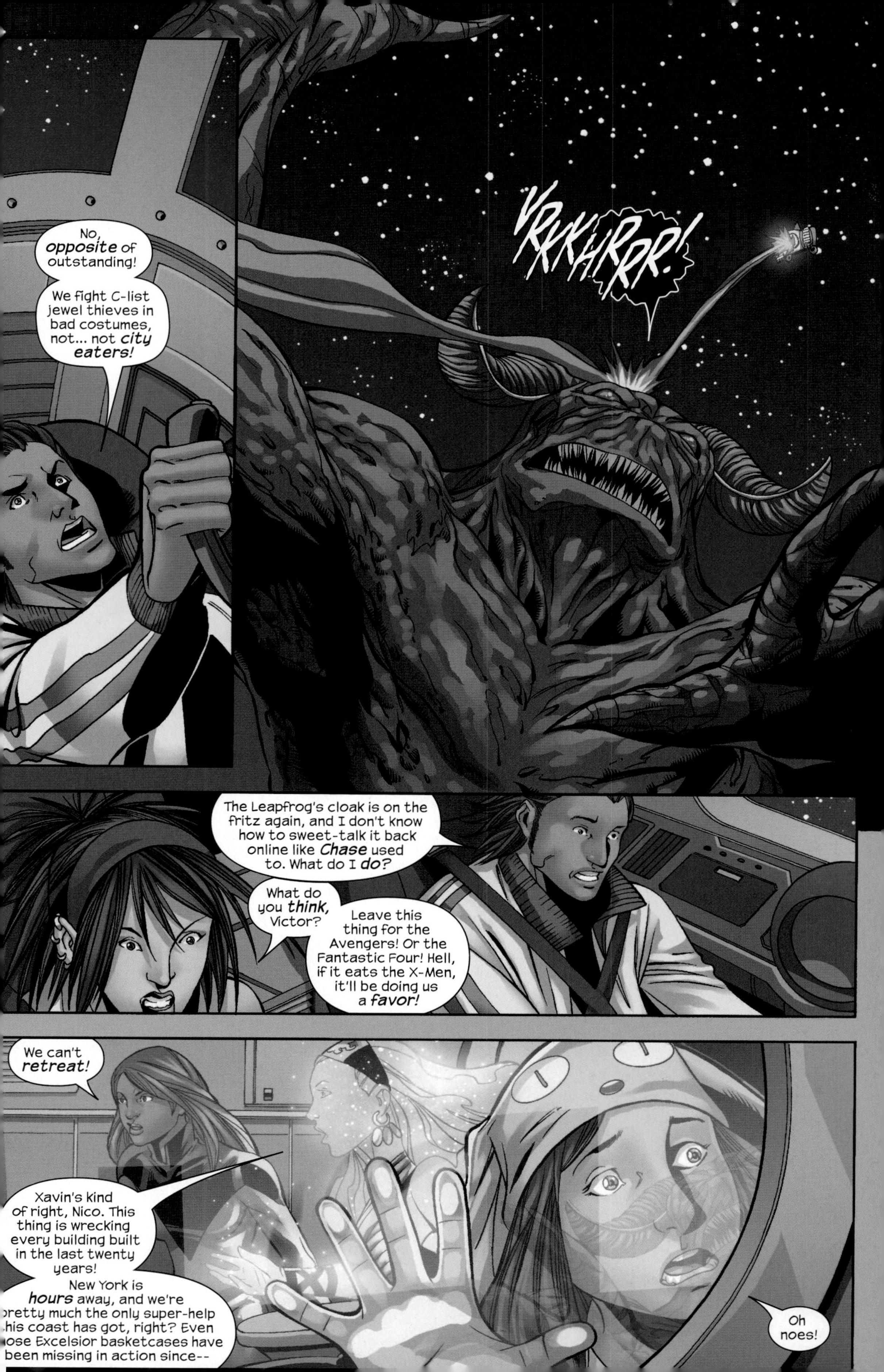

No, opposite of outstanding!
We fight C-list jewel thieves in bad costumes, not... not city eaters!
VRKKHRRR!
The Leapfrog's cloak is on the fritz again, and I don't know how to sweet-talk it back online like Chase used to. What do I do?
What do you think, Victor?
Leave this thing for the Avengers! Or the Fantastic Four! Hell, if it eats the X-Men, it'll be doing us a favor!
We can't retreat!
Xavin's kind of right, Nico. This thing is wrecking every building built in the last twenty years!
New York is hours away, and we're pretty much the only super-help this coast has got, right? Even those Excelsior basketcases have been missing in action since--
Oh noes!

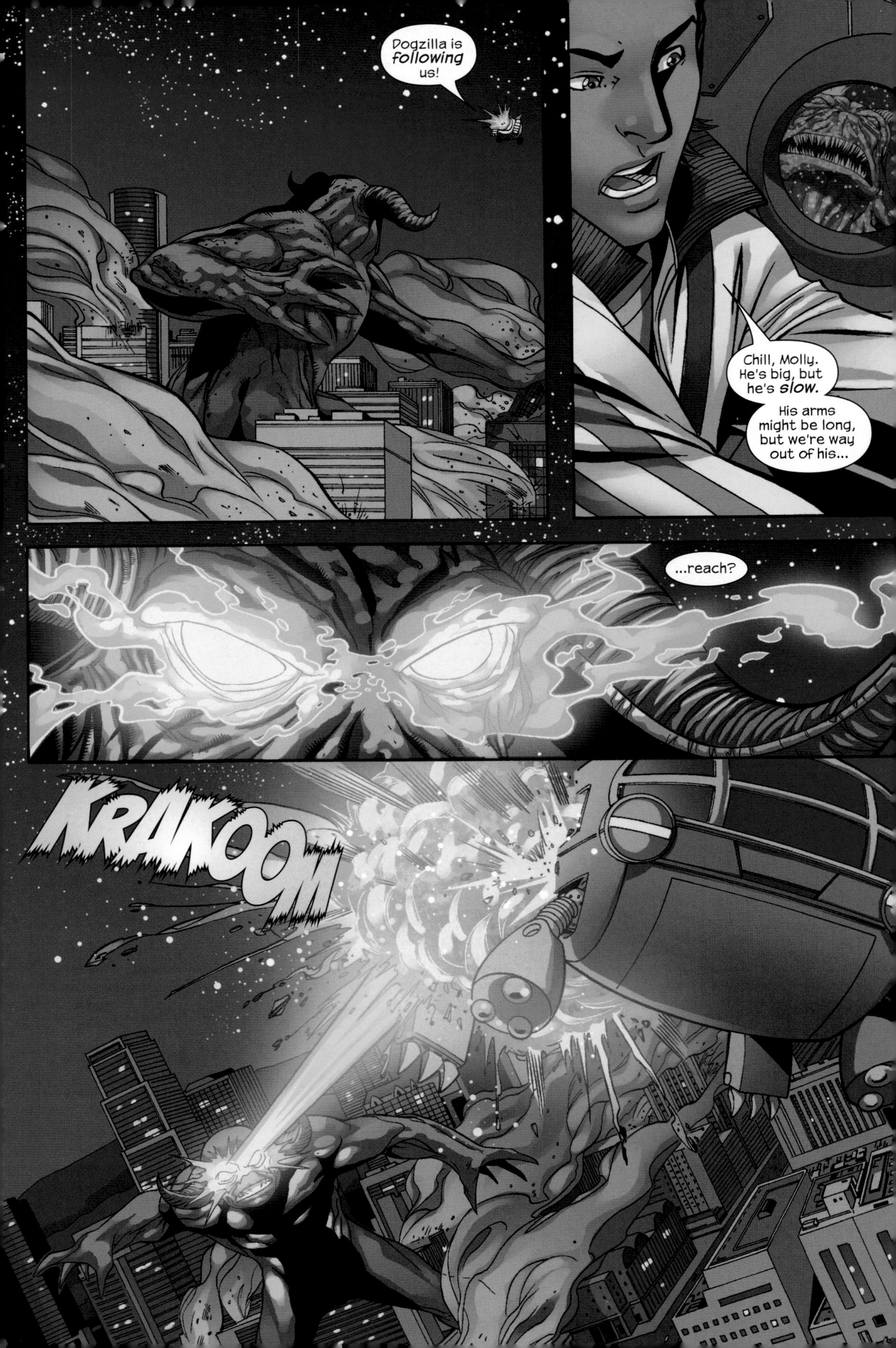
Dogzilla is following us!
Chill, Molly. He's big, but he's slow.
His arms might be long, but we're way out of his...
...reach?
KRAKOOM

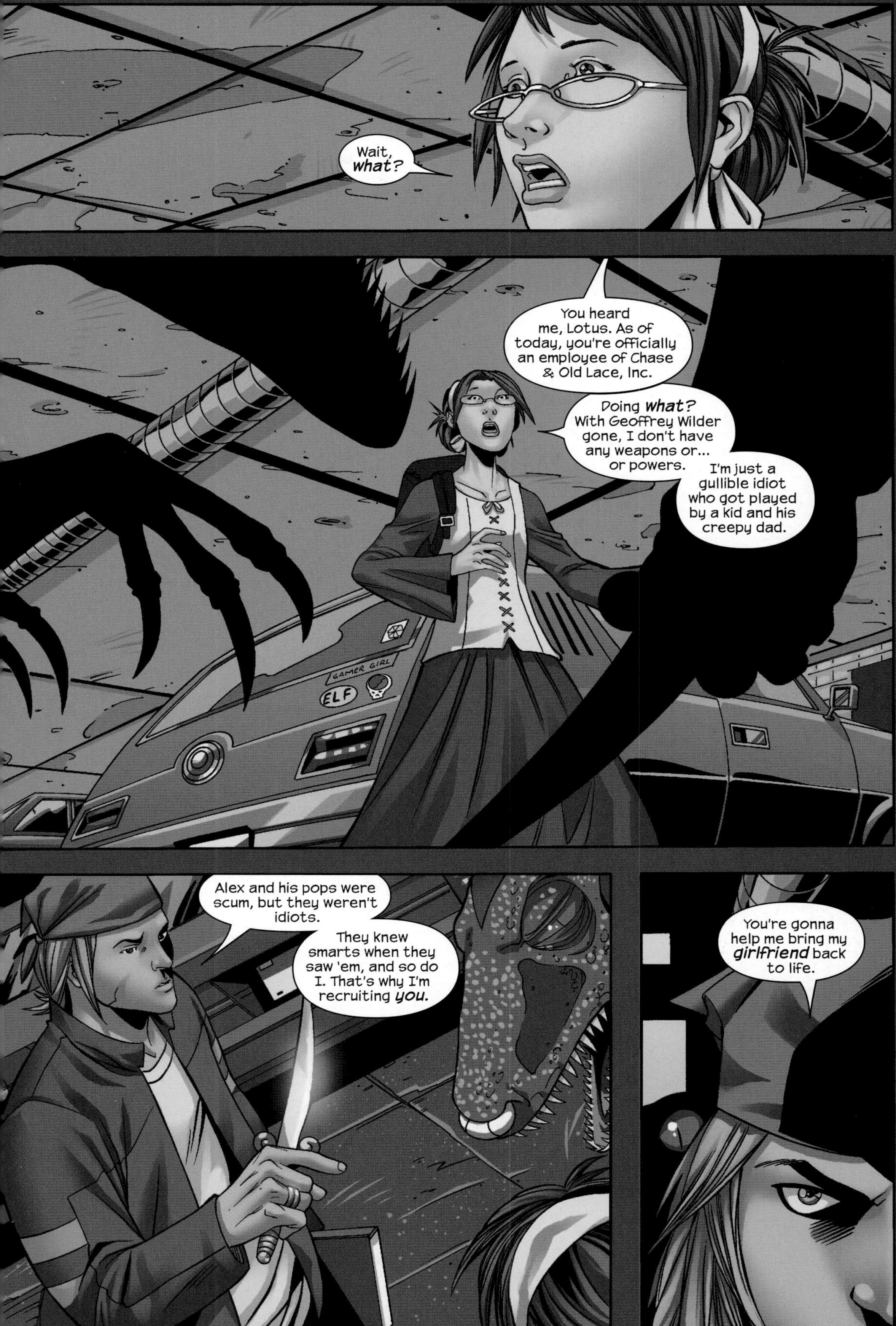
Wait, *what?*
You heard me, Lotus. As of today, you're officially an employee of Chase & Old Lace, Inc.
Doing *what?* With Geoffrey Wilder gone, I don't have any weapons or... or powers.
I'm just a gullible idiot who got played by a kid and his creepy dad.
GAMER GIRL
ELF
Alex and his pops were scum, but they weren't idiots.
They knew smarts when they saw 'em, and so do I. That's why I'm recruiting *you.*
You're gonna help me bring my *girlfriend* back to life.

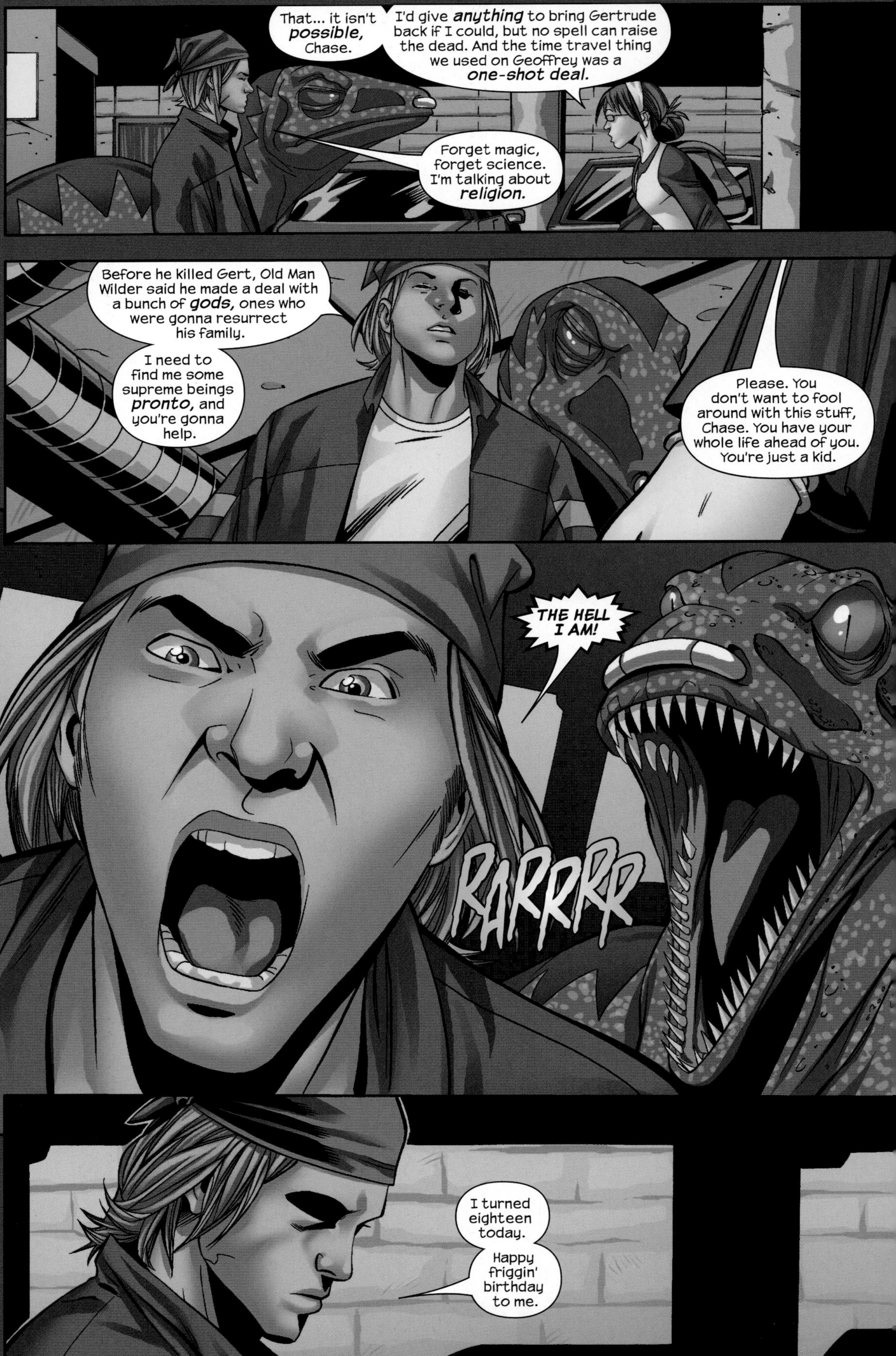

That... it isn't possible, Chase.
I'd give anything to bring Gertrude back if I could, but no spell can raise the dead. And the time travel thing we used on Geoffrey was a one-shot deal.
Forget magic, forget science. I'm talking about religion.
Before he killed Gert, Old Man Wilder said he made a deal with a bunch of gods, ones who were gonna resurrect his family.
I need to find me some supreme beings pronto, and you're gonna help.
Please. You don't want to fool around with this stuff, Chase. You have your whole life ahead of you. You're just a kid.
THE HELL I AM!
RARRRR
I turned eighteen today.
Happy friggin' birthday to me.

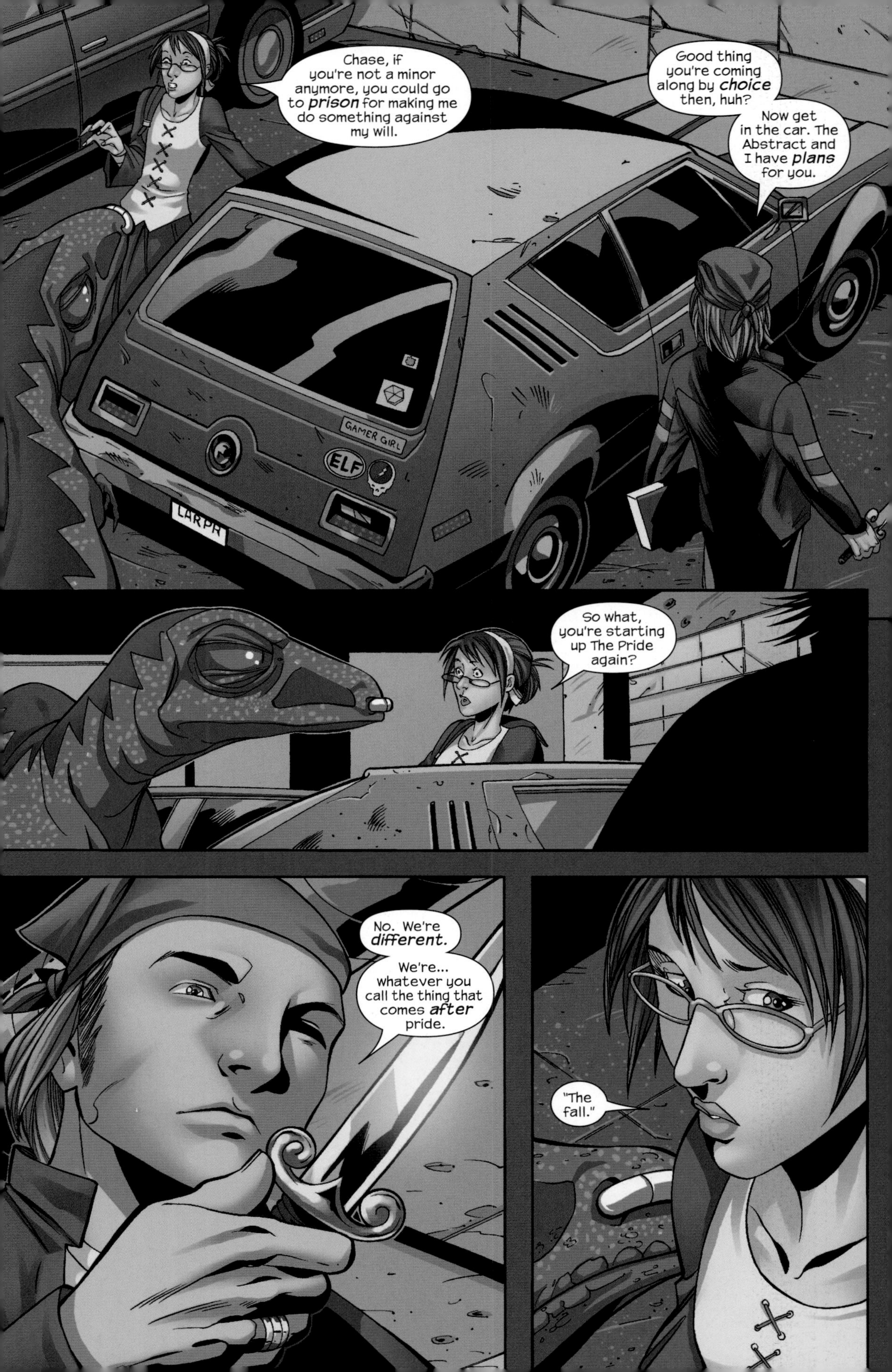

Chase, if you're not a minor anymore, you could go to *prison* for making me do something against my will.
Good thing you're coming along by *choice* then, huh?
Now get in the car. The Abstract and I have *plans* for you.
GAMER GIRL
ELF
LARPH
So what, you're starting up The Pride again?
No. We're *different.*
We're... whatever you call the thing that comes *after* pride.
"The fall."

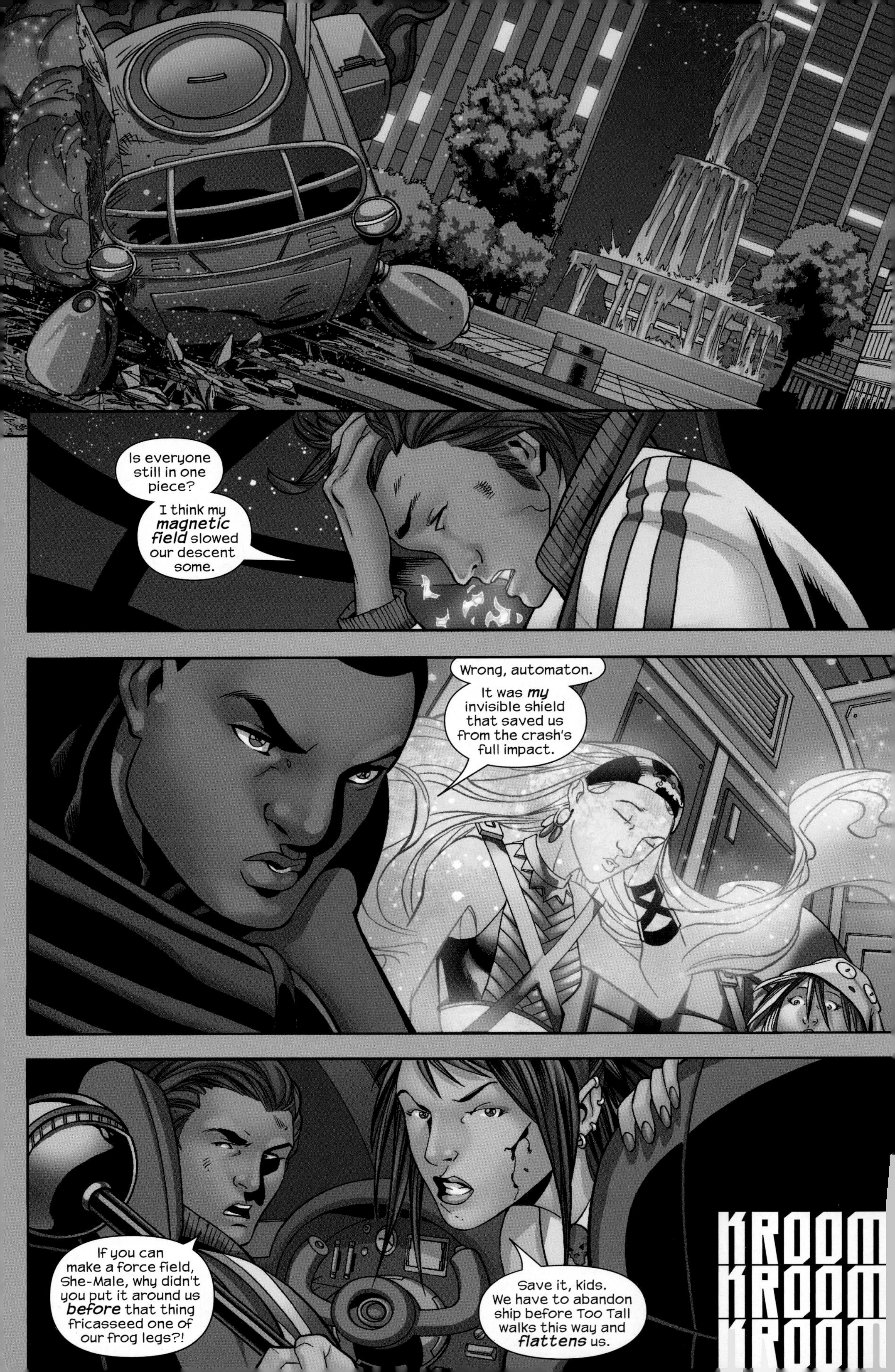
Is everyone still in one piece?
I think my *magnetic field* slowed our descent some.
Wrong, automaton.
It was *my* invisible shield that saved us from the crash's full impact.
If you can make a force field, She-Male, why didn't you put it around us *before* that thing fricasseed one of our frog legs?!
Save it, kids. We have to abandon ship before Too Tall walks this way and *flattens* us.
KROOM
KROOM
KROOM

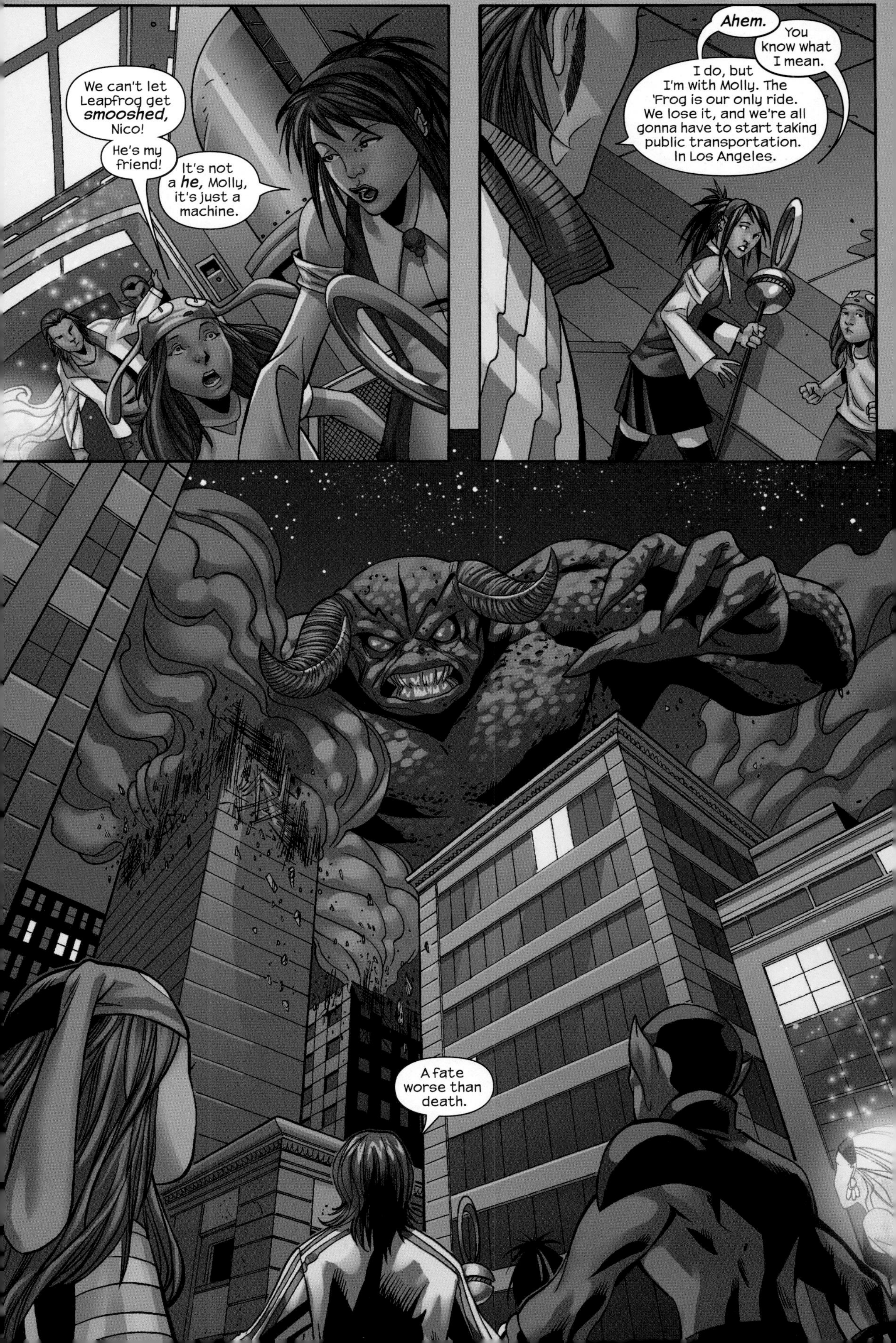

We can't let Leapfrog get smooshed, Nico!
He's my friend!
It's not a he, Molly, it's just a machine.
Ahem.
You know what I mean.
I do, but I'm with Molly. The 'Frog is our only ride. We lose it, and we're all gonna have to start taking public transportation. In Los Angeles.
A fate worse than death.

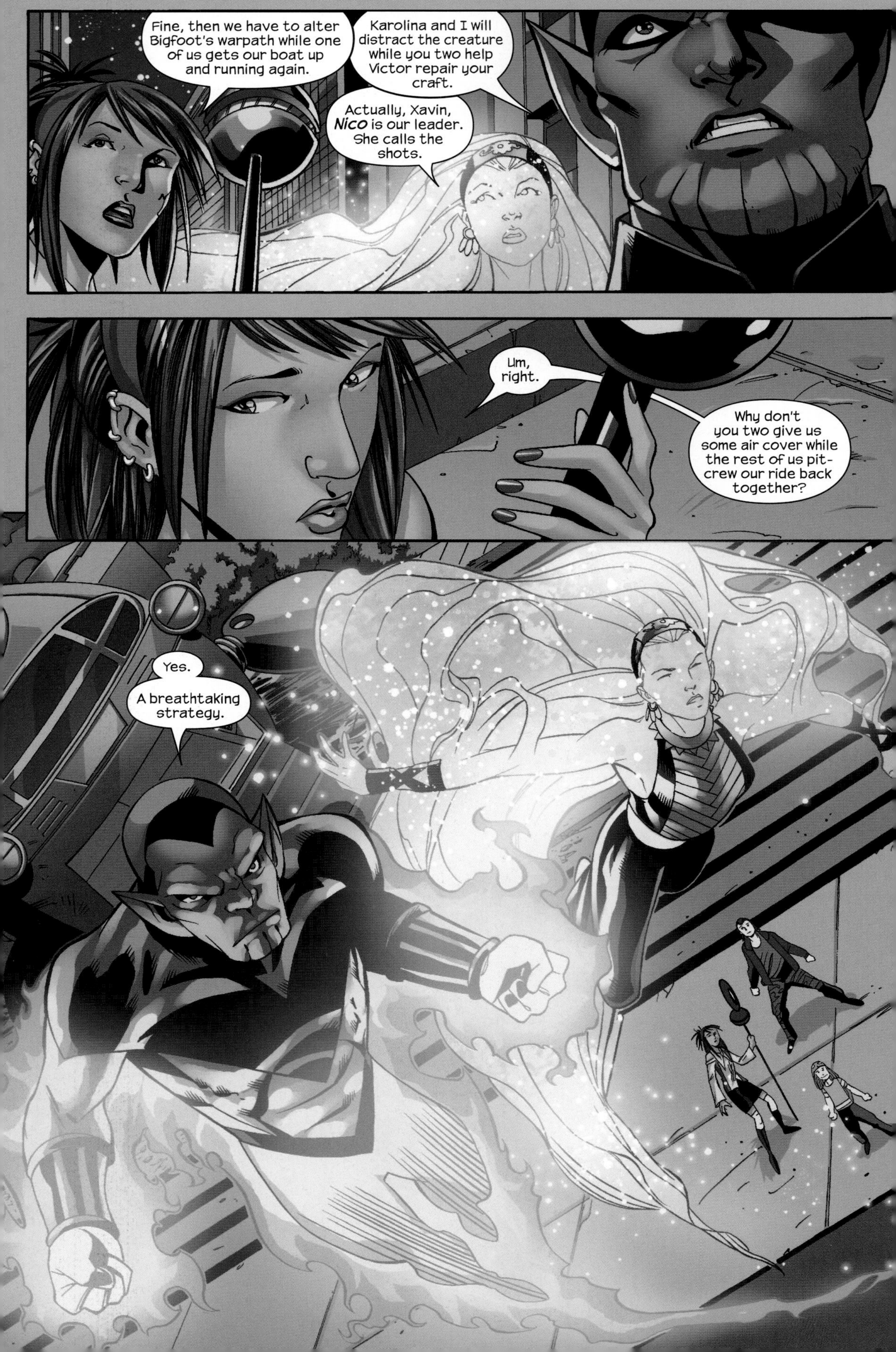

Fine, then we have to alter Bigfoot's warpath while one of us gets our boat up and running again.
Karolina and I will distract the creature while you two help Victor repair your craft.
Actually, Xavin, *Nico* is our leader. She calls the shots.
Um, right.
Why don't you two give us some air cover while the rest of us pit-crew our ride back together?
Yes.
A breathtaking strategy.

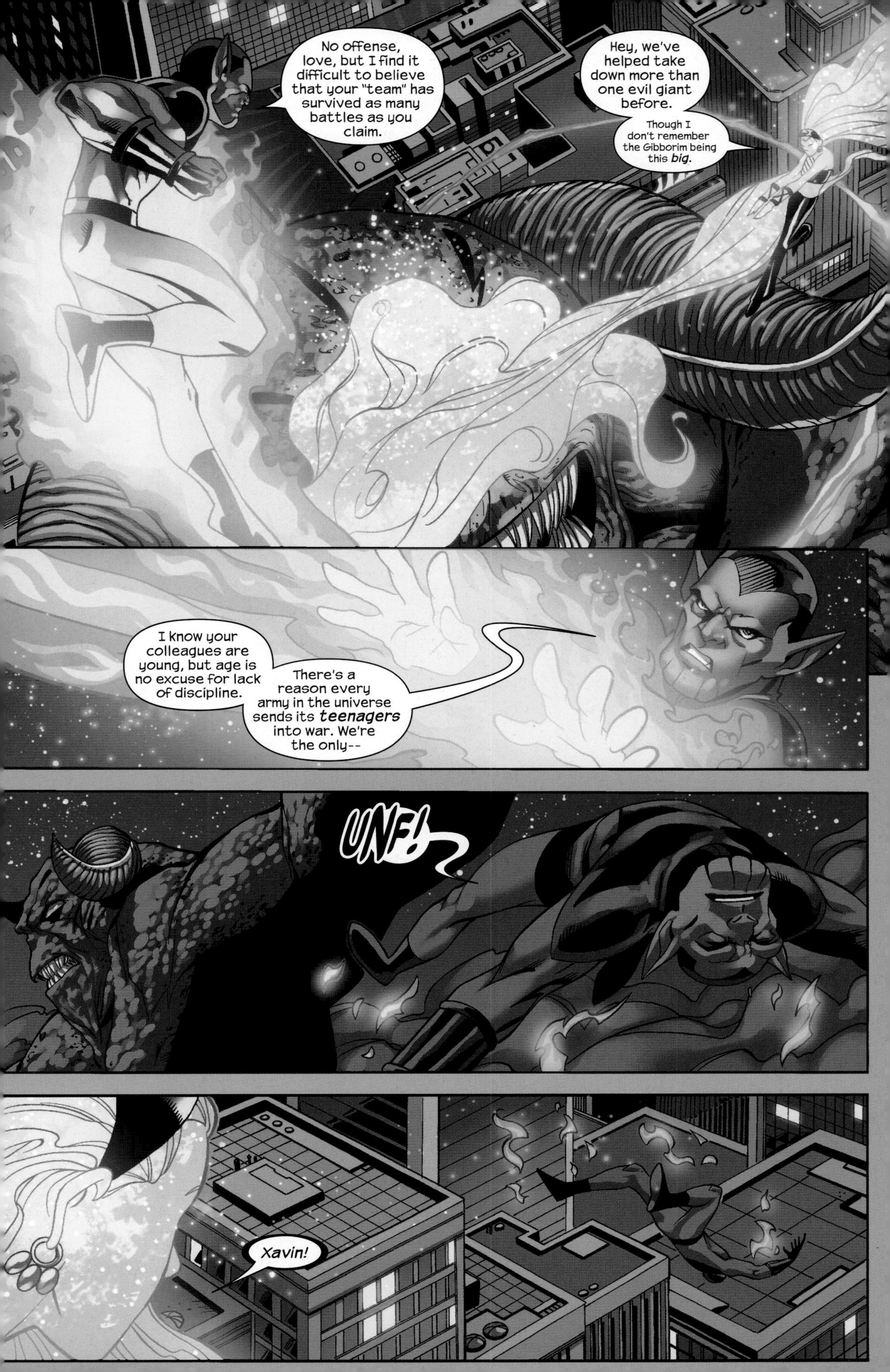
No offense, love, but I find it difficult to believe that your "team" has survived as many battles as you claim.
Hey, we've helped take down more than one evil giant before.
Though I don't remember the Gibborim being this *big.*
I know your colleagues are young, but age is no excuse for lack of discipline.
There's a reason every army in the universe sends its *teenagers* into war. We're the only--
UNF!
Xavin!

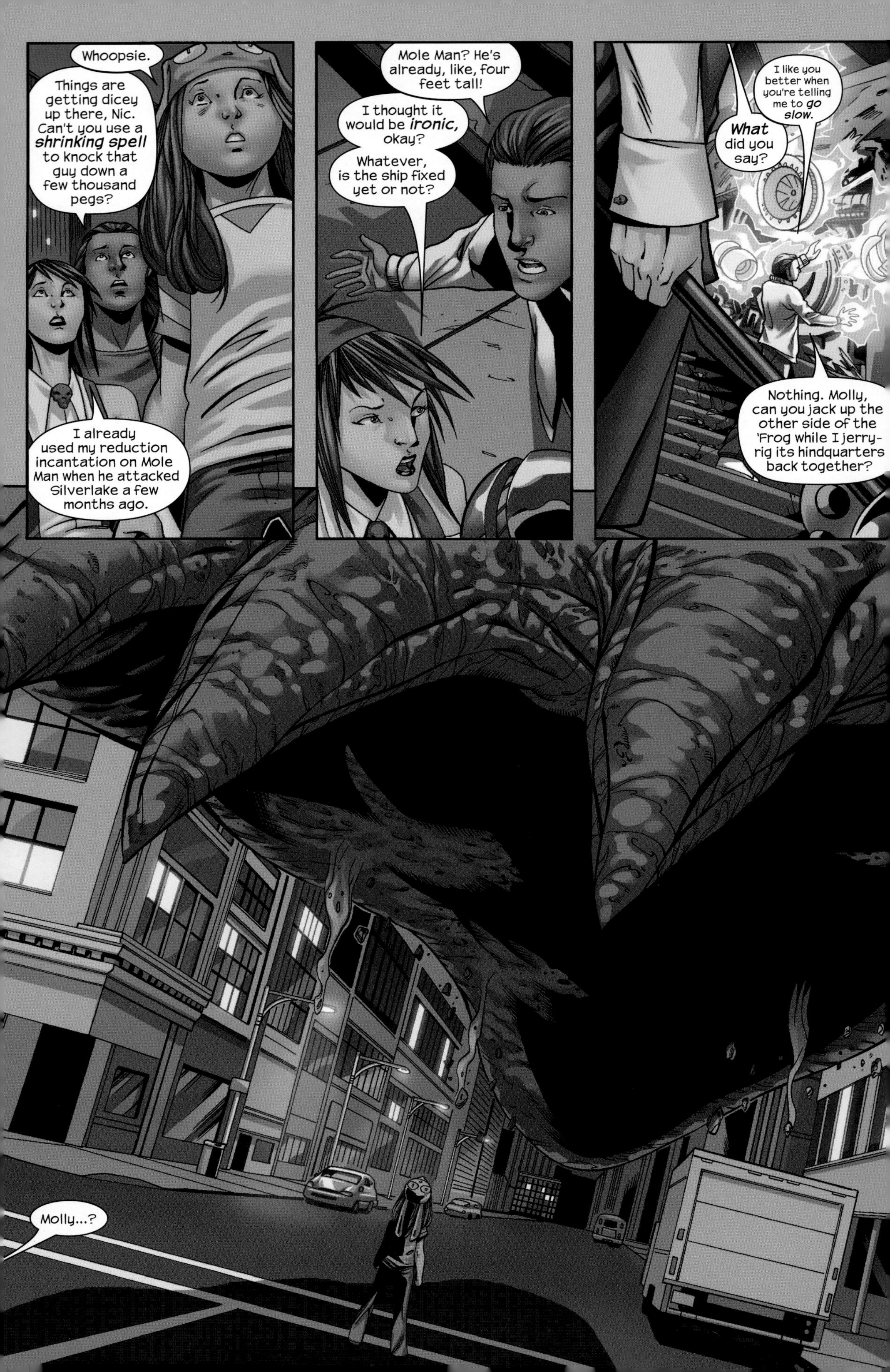

Whoopsie.
Things are getting dicey up there, Nic. Can't you use a shrinking spell to knock that guy down a few thousand pegs?
I already used my reduction incantation on Mole Man when he attacked Silverlake a few months ago.
Mole Man? He's already, like, four feet tall!
I thought it would be ironic, okay?
Whatever, is the ship fixed yet or not?
I like you better when you're telling me to go slow.
What did you say?
Nothing. Molly, can you jack up the other side of the 'Frog while I jerry-rig its hindquarters back together?
Molly...?

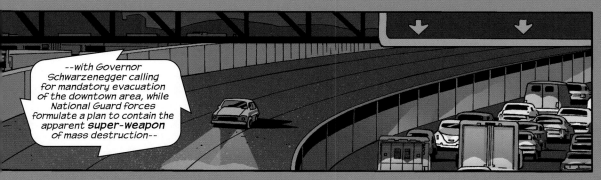

--with Governor Schwarzenegger calling for mandatory evacuation of the downtown area, while National Guard forces formulate a plan to contain the apparent *super-weapon* of mass destruction--

Guess that explains why no one is paying attention to the hatchback with the *dinosaur* in it.

Don't worry, radio always exaggerates stuff.

Just another night in L.A.

Chase, can I ask you a question? When you were little, what did you want to be when you grew up?

I don't know, bounty hunter or something. What do you care?

You remember that old super hero, Mockingbird? When I was a girl, I dreamed of being just like her someday. But instead, I got duped into becoming a *villain*.

You see what I'm getting at, right?

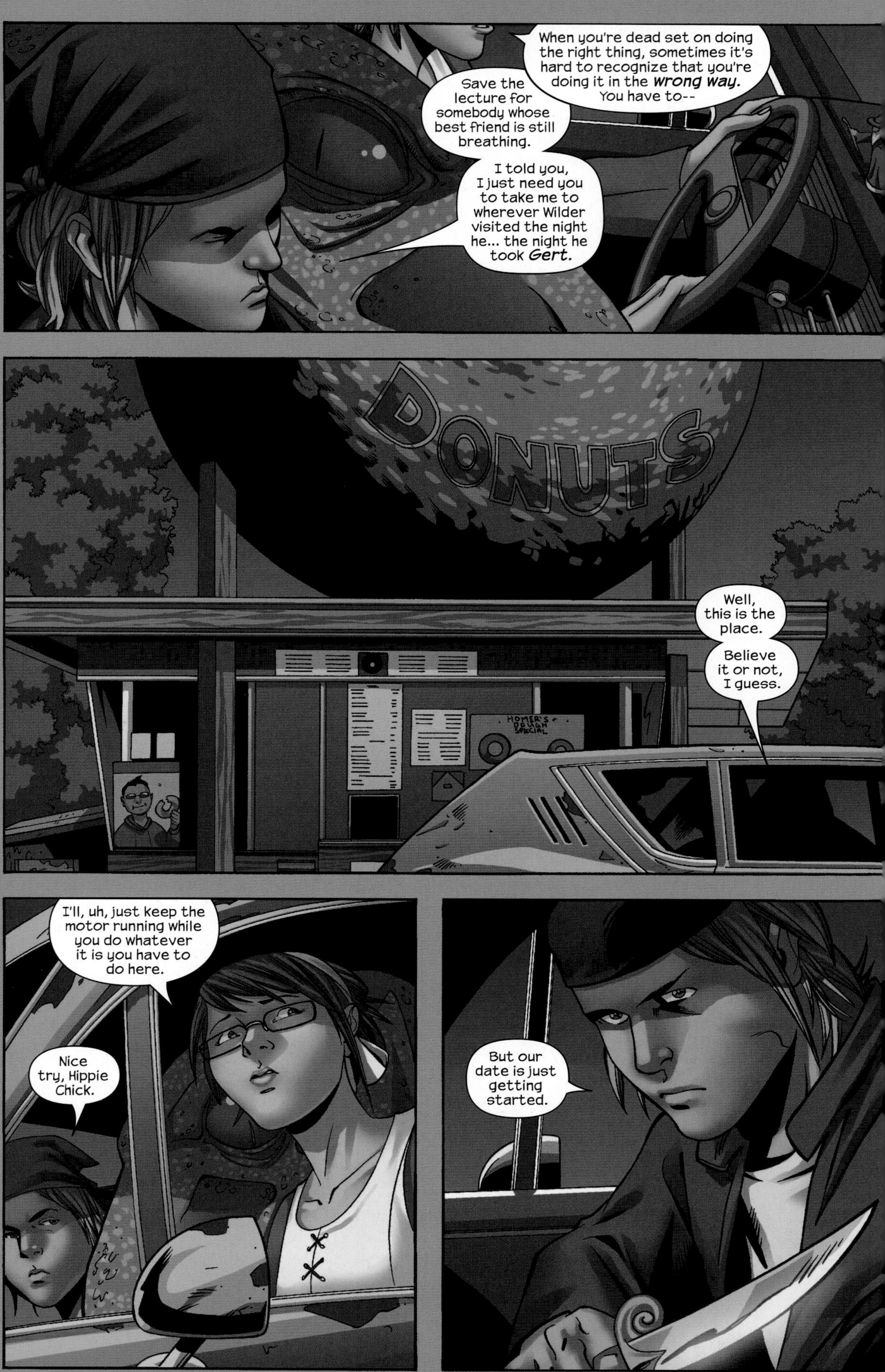
When you're dead set on doing the right thing, sometimes it's hard to recognize that you're doing it in the *wrong way.* You have to--
Save the lecture for somebody whose best friend is still breathing.
I told you, I just need you to take me to wherever Wilder visited the night he... the night he took *Gert.*
DONUTS
HOMER'S DOUGH SPECIAL
Well, this is the place.
Believe it or not, I guess.
I'll, uh, just keep the motor running while you do whatever it is you have to do here.
Nice try, Hippie Chick.
But our date is just getting started.

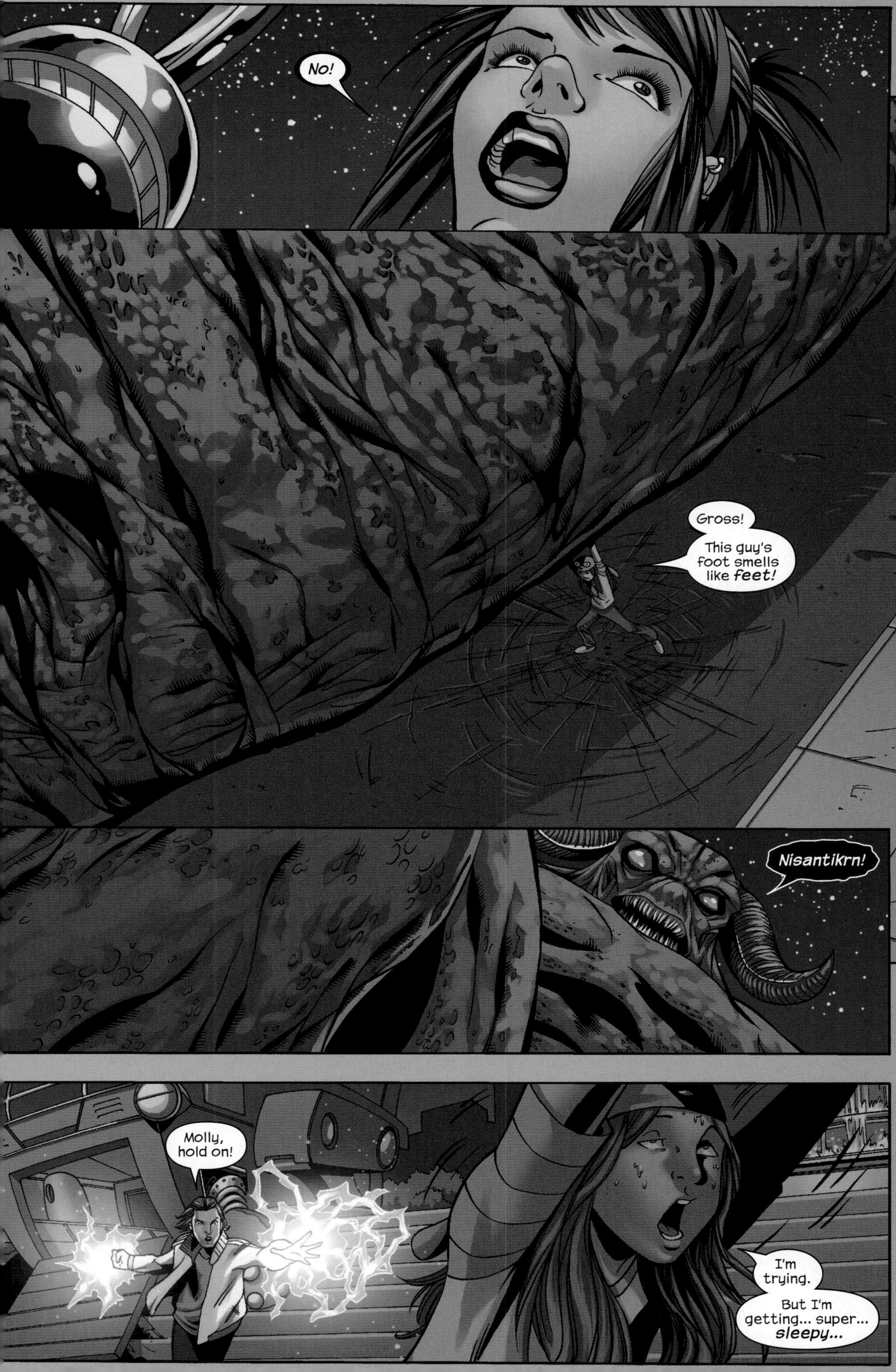
No!
Gross!
This guy's foot smells like feet!
Nisantikrn!
Molly, hold on!
I'm trying.
But I'm getting... super... sleepy...

I'm on it.

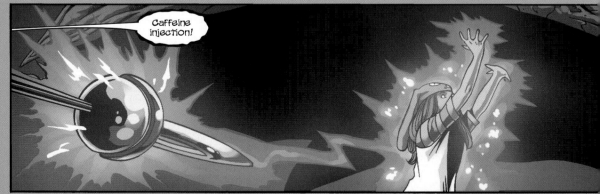

Caffeine injection!

Heh. It's like my heart is having a pizza party.

ÄHHOOOOO!

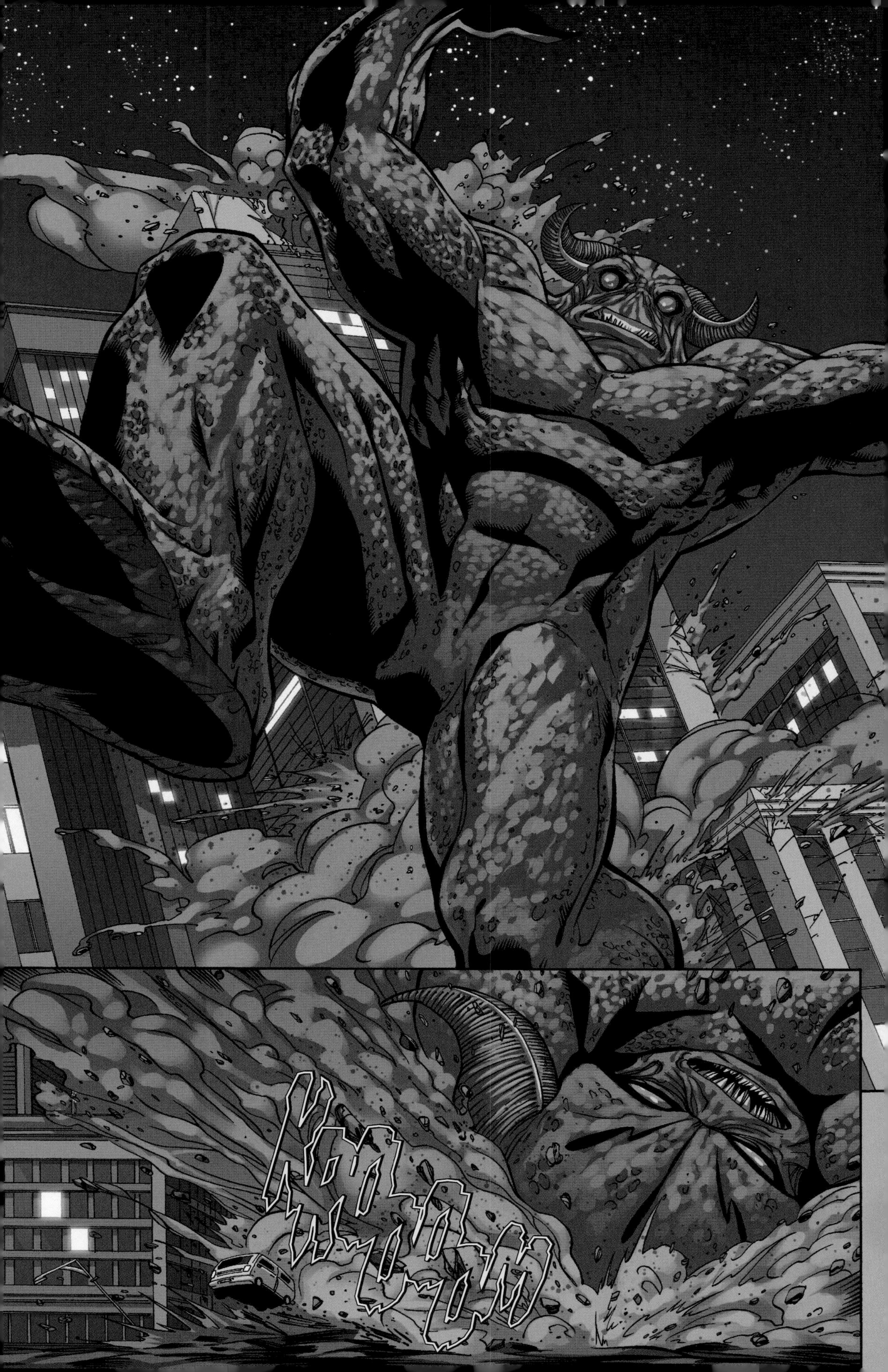

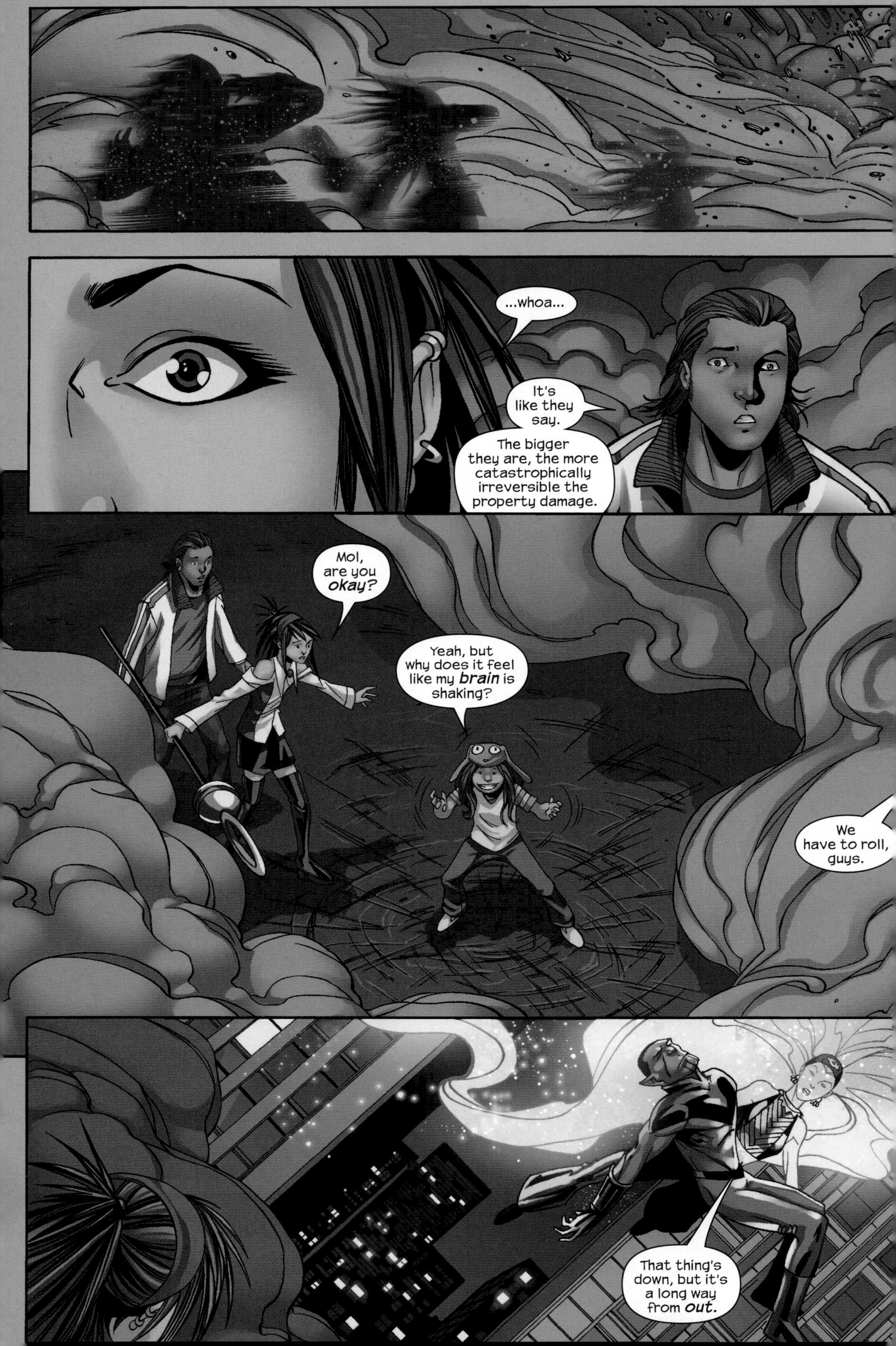
...whoa...
It's like they say.
The bigger they are, the more catastrophically irreversible the property damage.
Mol, are you okay?
Yeah, but why does it feel like my brain is shaking?
We have to roll, guys.
That thing's down, but it's a long way from out.

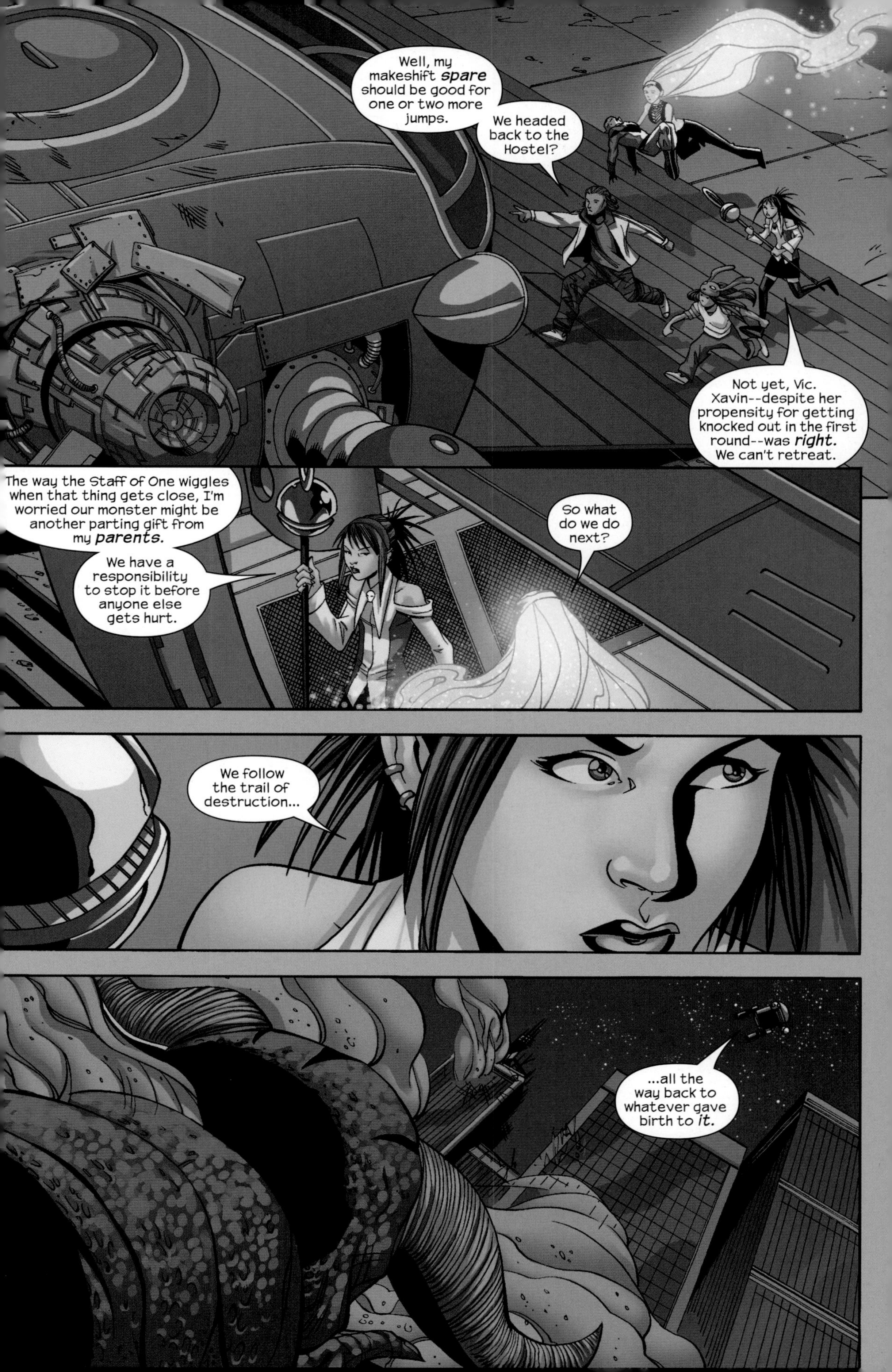
Well, my makeshift *spare* should be good for one or two more jumps.
We headed back to the Hostel?
Not yet, Vic. Xavin--despite her propensity for getting knocked out in the first round--was *right.* We can't retreat.
The way the Staff of One wiggles when that thing gets close, I'm worried our monster might be another parting gift from my *parents.*
We have a responsibility to stop it before anyone else gets hurt.
So what do we do next?
We follow the trail of destruction...
...all the way back to whatever gave birth to *it.*

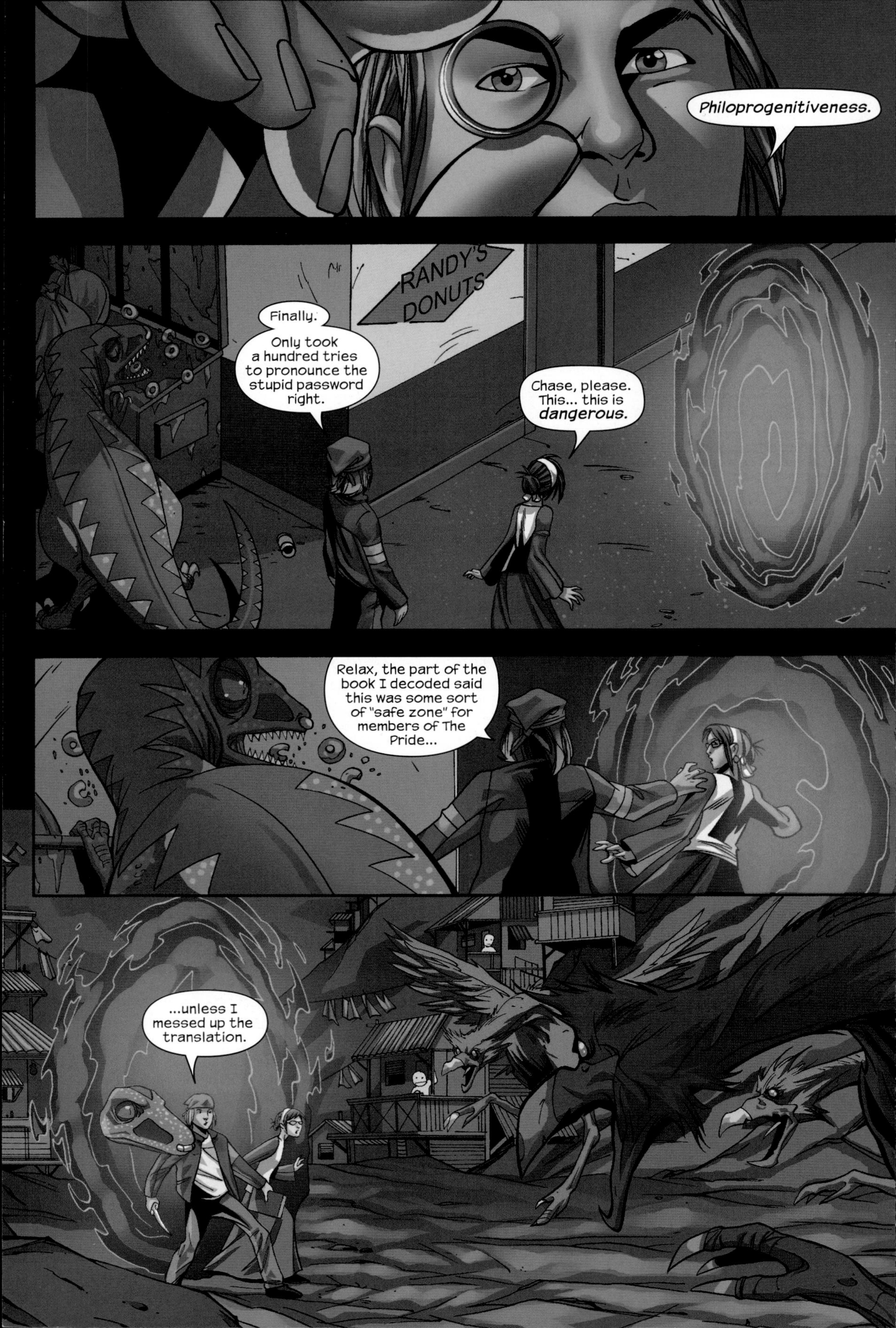
Philoprogenitiveness.
RANDY'S DONUTS
Finally.
Only took a hundred tries to pronounce the stupid password right.
Chase, please. This... this is *dangerous.*
Relax, the part of the book I decoded said this was some sort of "safe zone" for members of The Pride...
...unless I messed up the translation.

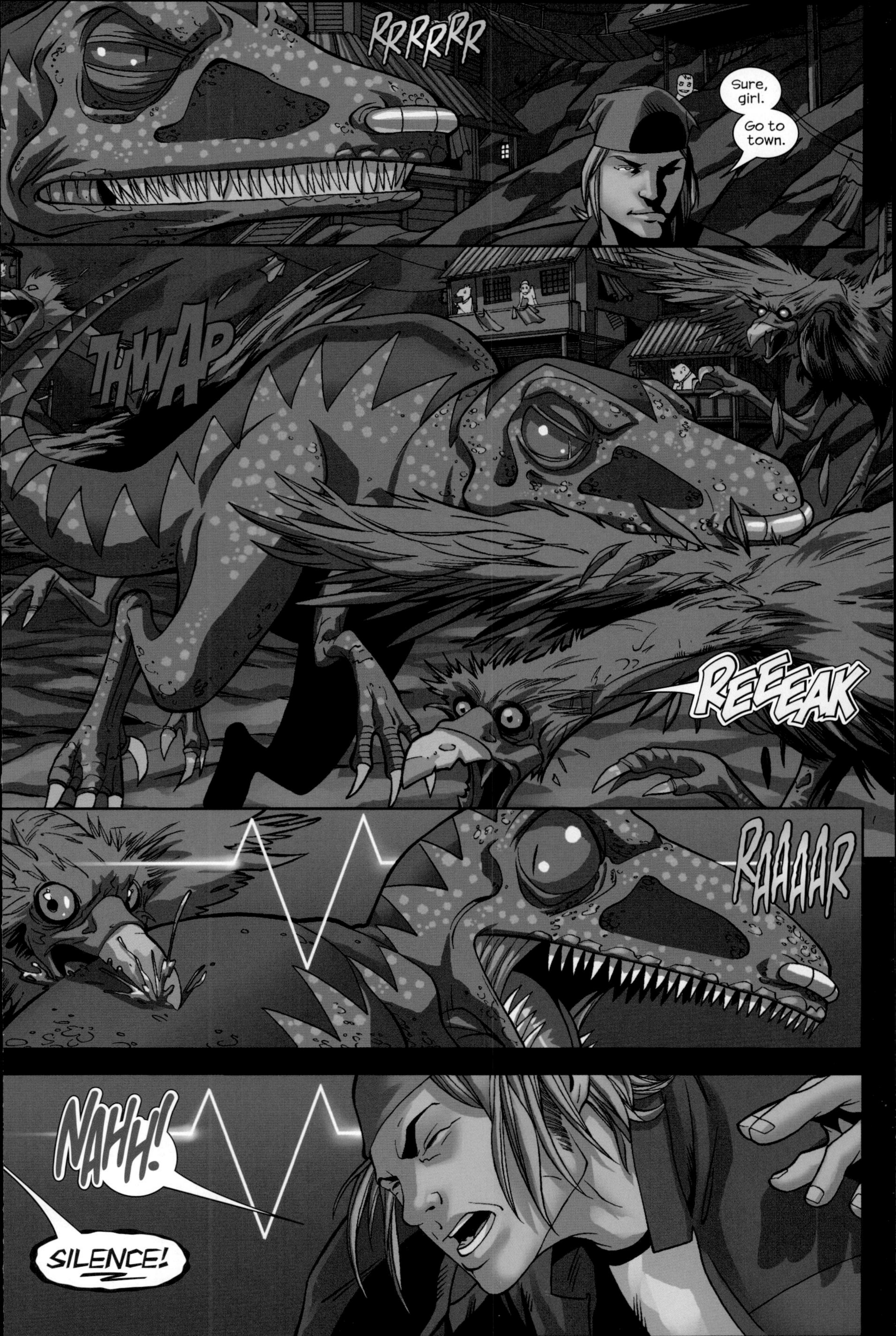
RRRRRR
Sure, girl.
Go to town.
THWAP
REEEAK
RAAAAR
NAHH!
SILENCE!

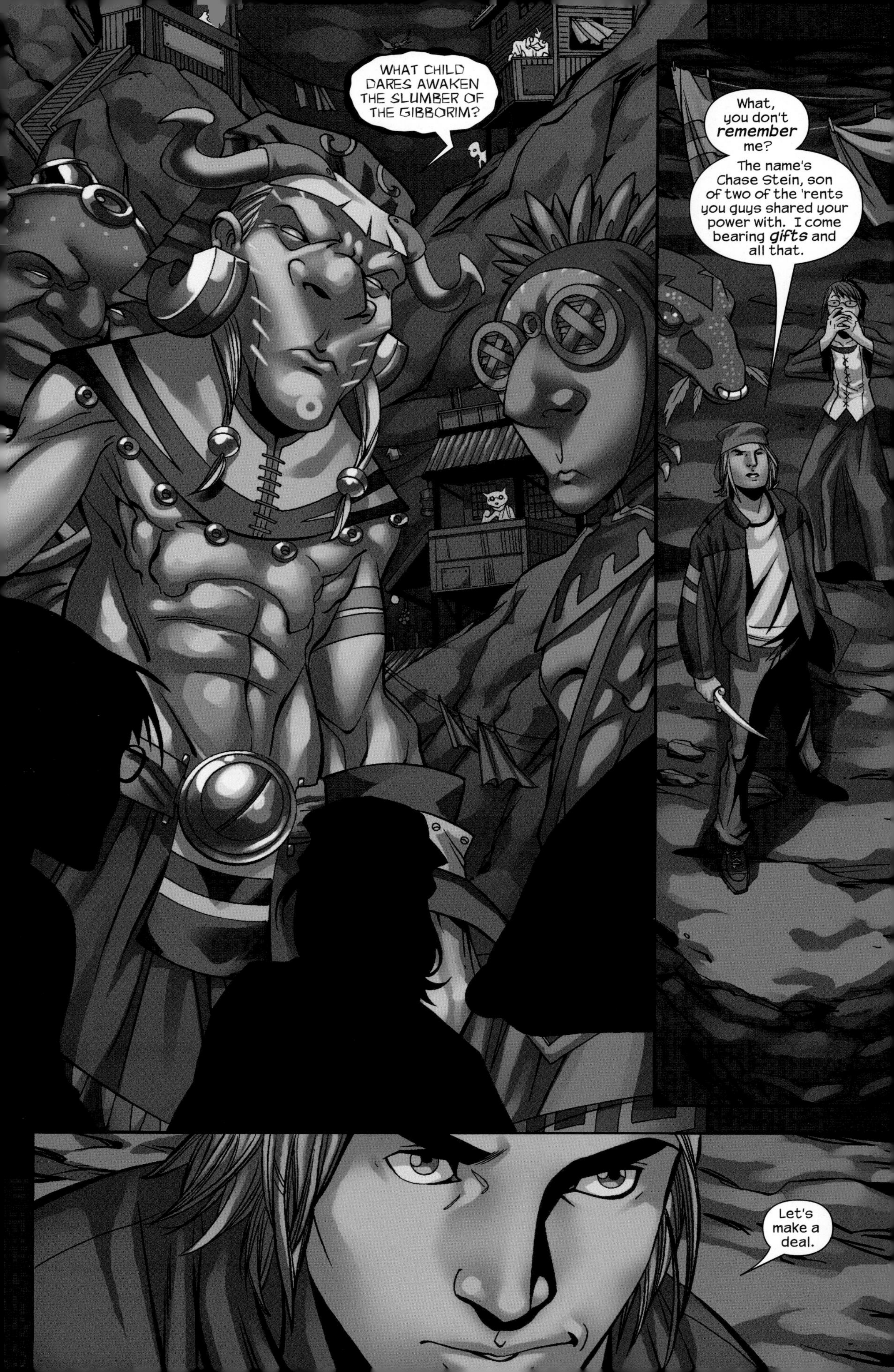
WHAT CHILD DARES AWAKEN THE SLUMBER OF THE GIBBORIM?
What, you don't **remember** me?
The name's Chase Stein, son of two of the 'rents you guys shared your power with. I come bearing ***gifts*** and all that.
Let's make a deal.

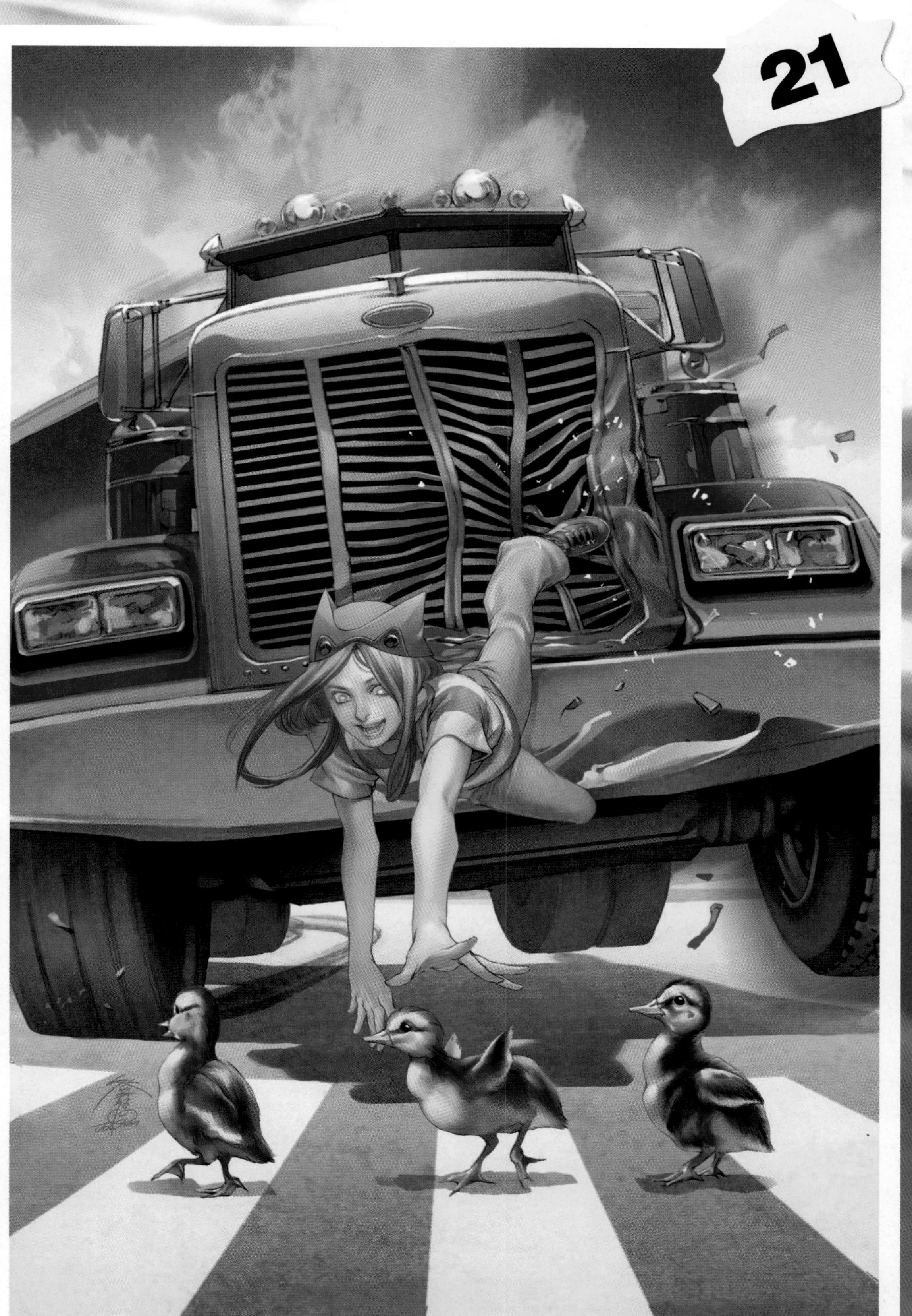
21

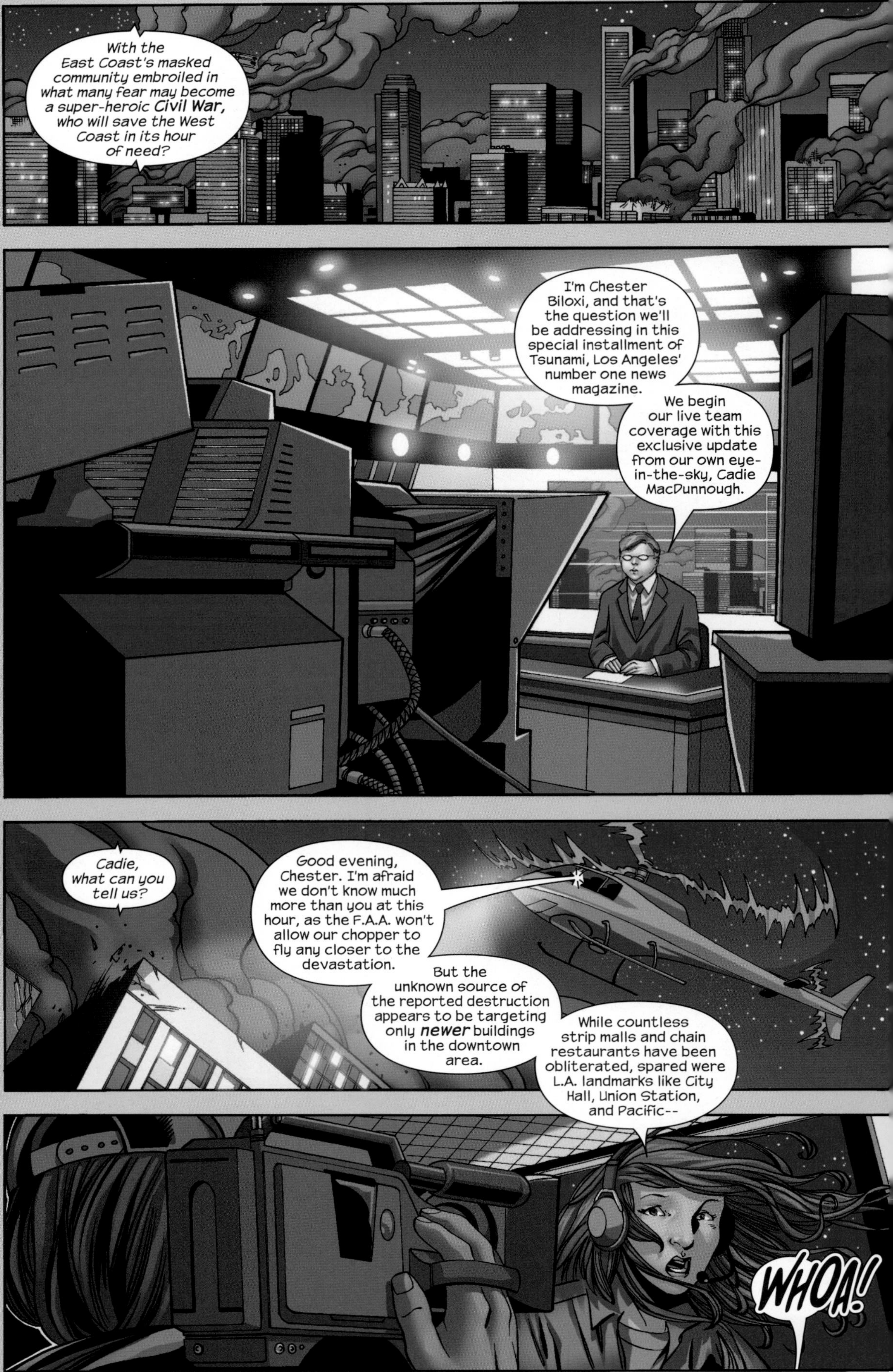
With the East Coast's masked community embroiled in what many fear may become a super-heroic Civil War, who will save the West Coast in its hour of need?
I'm Chester Biloxi, and that's the question we'll be addressing in this special installment of Tsunami, Los Angeles' number one news magazine.
We begin our live team coverage with this exclusive update from our own eye-in-the-sky, Cadie MacDunnough.
Cadie, what can you tell us?
Good evening, Chester. I'm afraid we don't know much more than you at this hour, as the F.A.A. won't allow our chopper to fly any closer to the devastation.
But the unknown source of the reported destruction appears to be targeting only newer buildings in the downtown area.
While countless strip malls and chain restaurants have been obliterated, spared were L.A. landmarks like City Hall, Union Station, and Pacific--
WHOA!

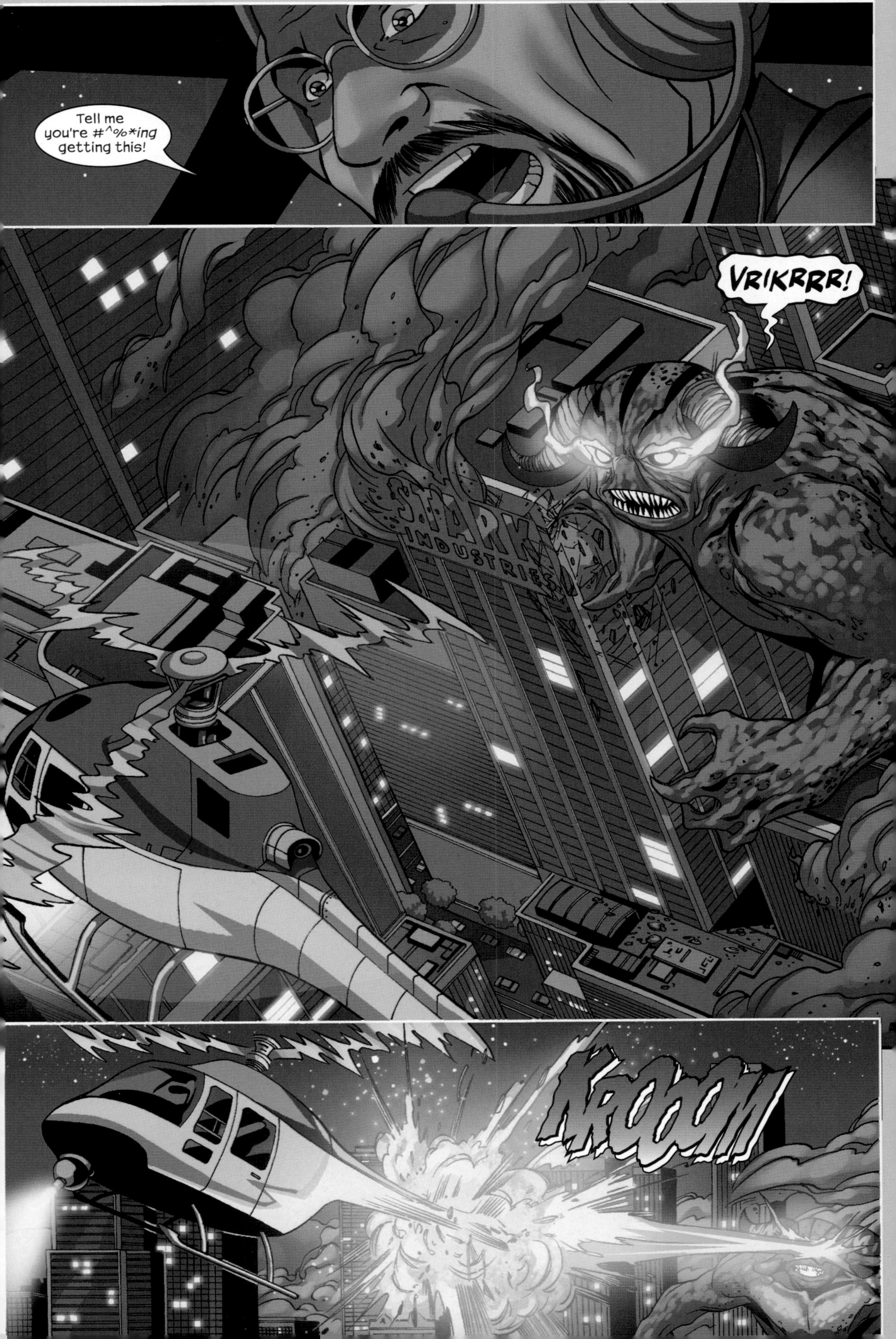

Tell me you're #^%*ing getting this!
VRIKRRR!
STARK INDUSTRIES
KRAKOOM

AHHH!

Cadie, are you...?

Chester, I'm not sure if we're still broadcasting, but our helicopter is... is *losing altitude*.

If this gets out, remind the heroes of this country that we need them!

It's time for them to stop acting like *children* and get back to--

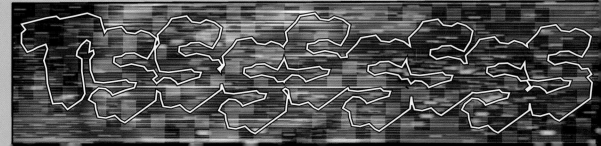

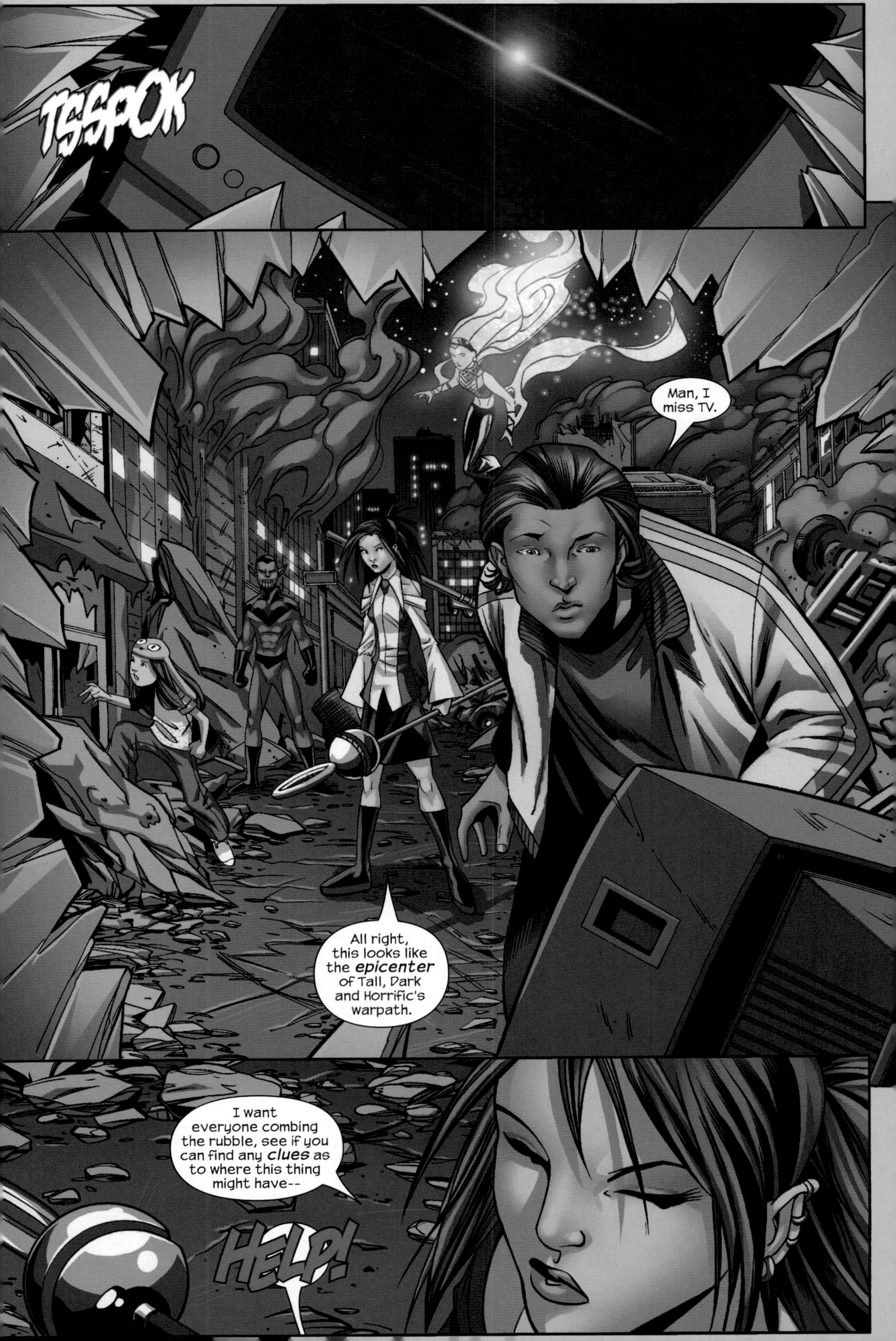
TSSPOK
Man, I miss TV.
All right, this looks like the epicenter of Tall, Dark and Horrific's warpath.
I want everyone combing the rubble, see if you can find any clues as to where this thing might have--
HELP!

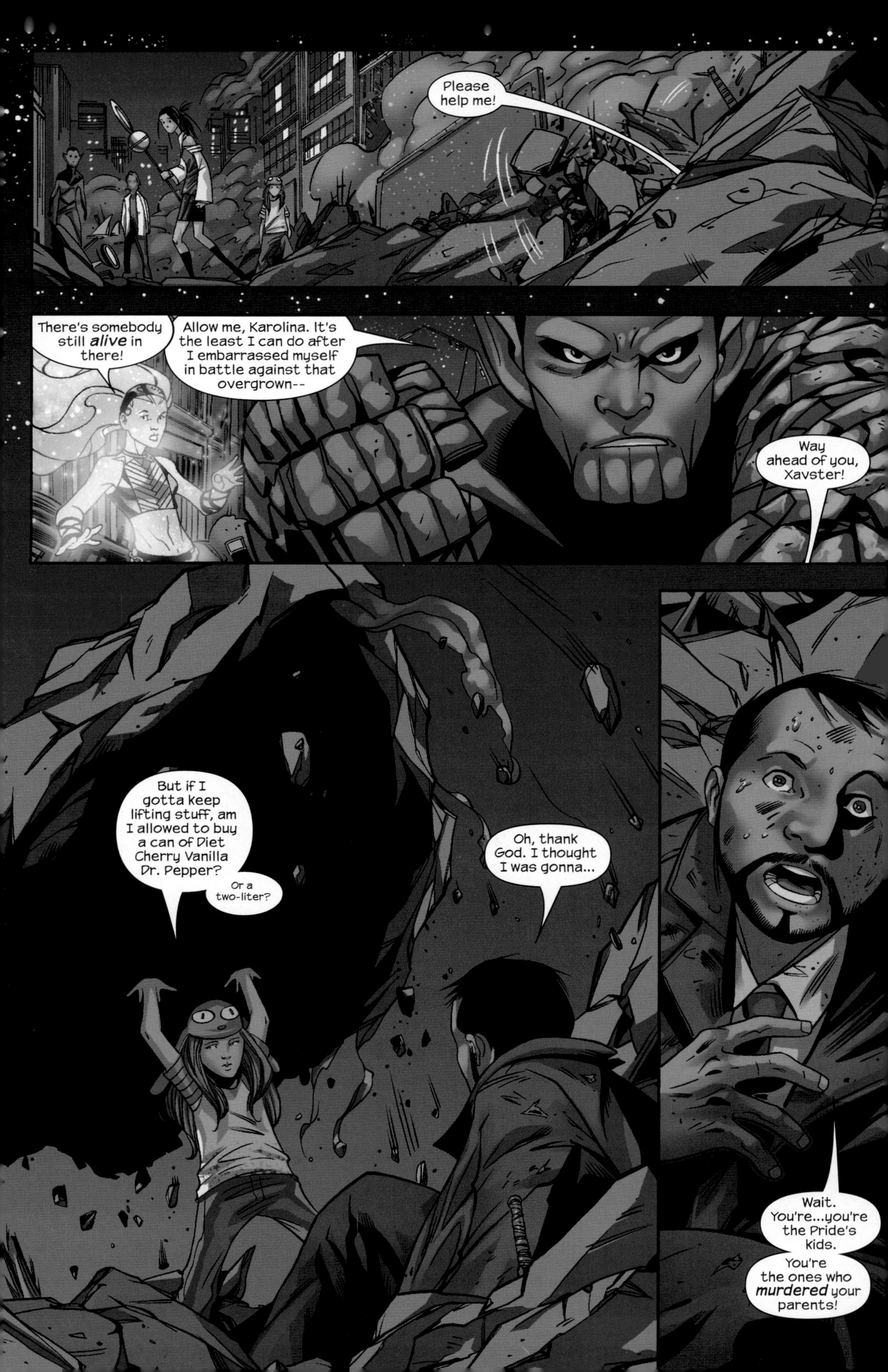
Please help me!
There's somebody still *alive* in there!
Allow me, Karolina. It's the least I can do after I embarrassed myself in battle against that overgrown--
Way ahead of you, Xavster!
But if I gotta keep lifting stuff, am I allowed to buy a can of Diet Cherry Vanilla Dr. Pepper?
Or a two-liter?
Oh, thank God. I thought I was gonna...
Wait. You're...you're the Pride's kids.
You're the ones who *murdered* your parents!

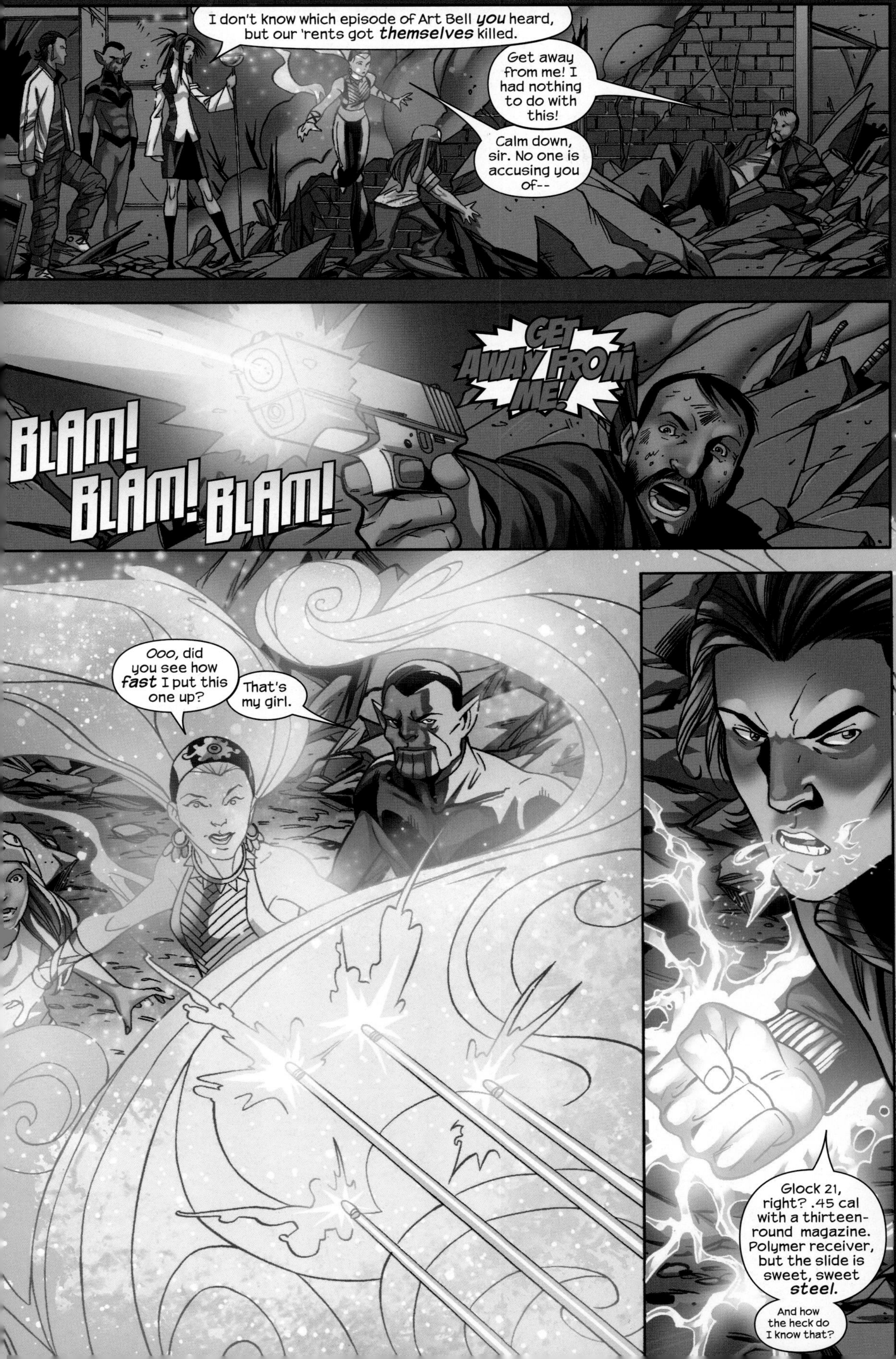

I don't know which episode of Art Bell *you* heard, but our 'rents got *themselves* killed.
Get away from me! I had nothing to do with this!
Calm down, sir. No one is accusing you of--
GET AWAY FROM ME!
BLAM! BLAM! BLAM!
Ooo, did you see how *fast* I put this one up?
That's my girl.
Glock 21, right? .45 cal with a thirteen-round magazine. Polymer receiver, but the slide is sweet, sweet *steel.*
And how the heck do I know that?

AHHHH!

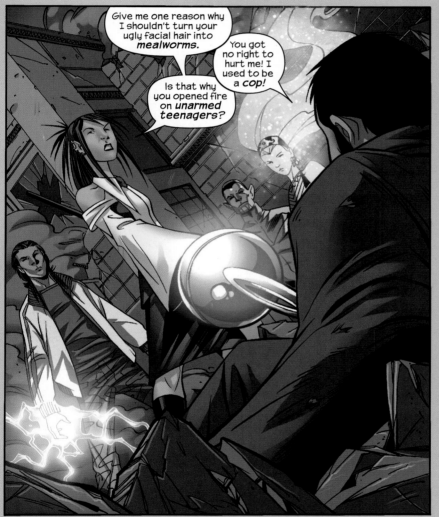

Give me one reason why I shouldn't turn your ugly facial hair into *mealworms*.

You got no right to hurt me! I used to be a *cop!*

Is that why you opened fire on *unarmed teenagers?*

Gotta love the L.A.P.D.

It's not my fault!

I didn't turn the old guy into that monster; the magical doodad I nicked from one of your *evil folks* did!

Which "old guy" are you rambling about?

Walters. Geezer who's been running this *antiques joint* since the dawn of time.

Is this him?

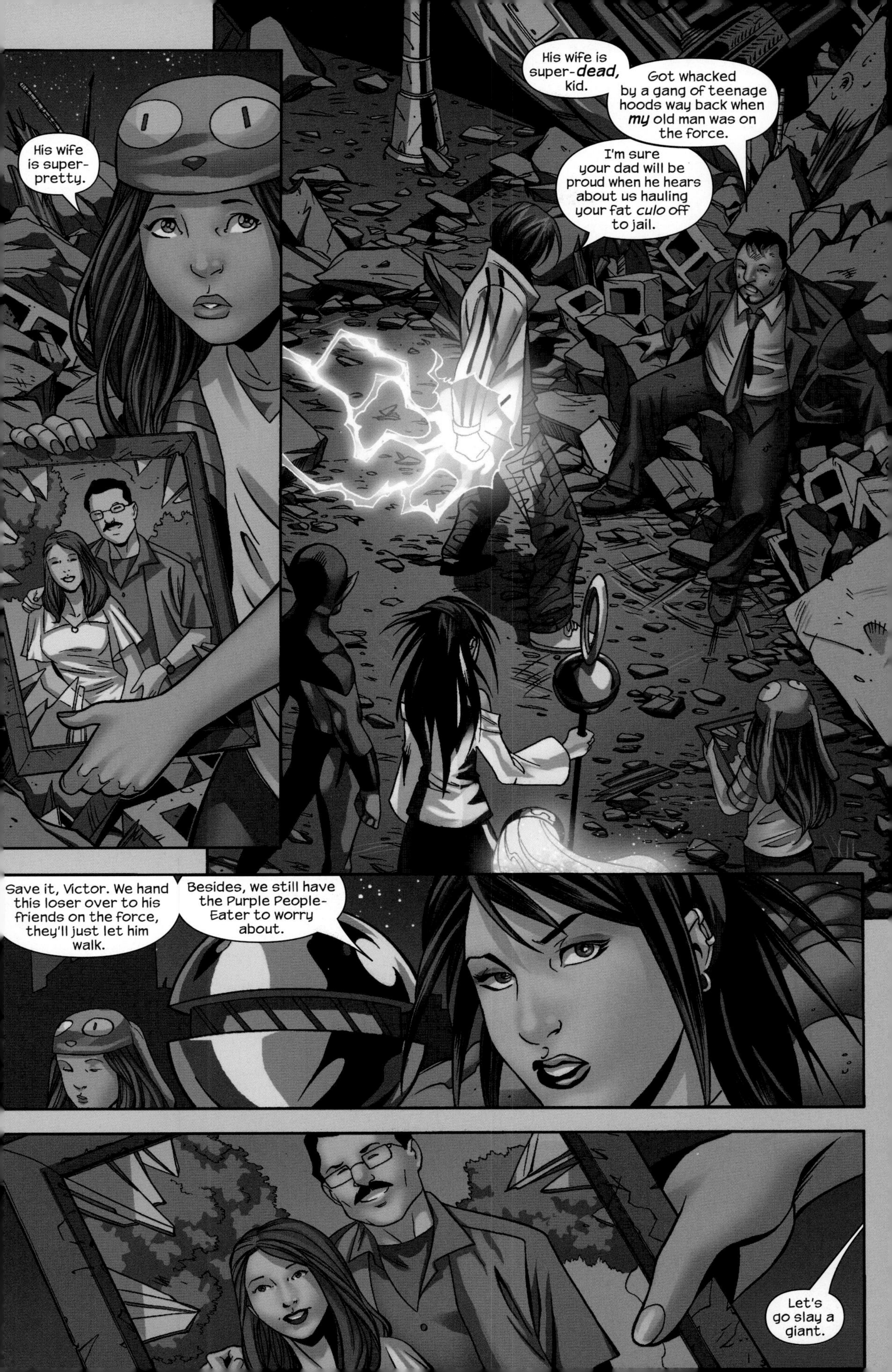
His wife is super-pretty.
His wife is super-*dead*, kid.
Got whacked by a gang of teenage hoods way back when *my* old man was on the force.
I'm sure your dad will be proud when he hears about us hauling your fat *culo* off to jail.
Save it, Victor. We hand this loser over to his friends on the force, they'll just let him walk.
Besides, we still have the Purple People-Eater to worry about.
Let's go slay a giant.

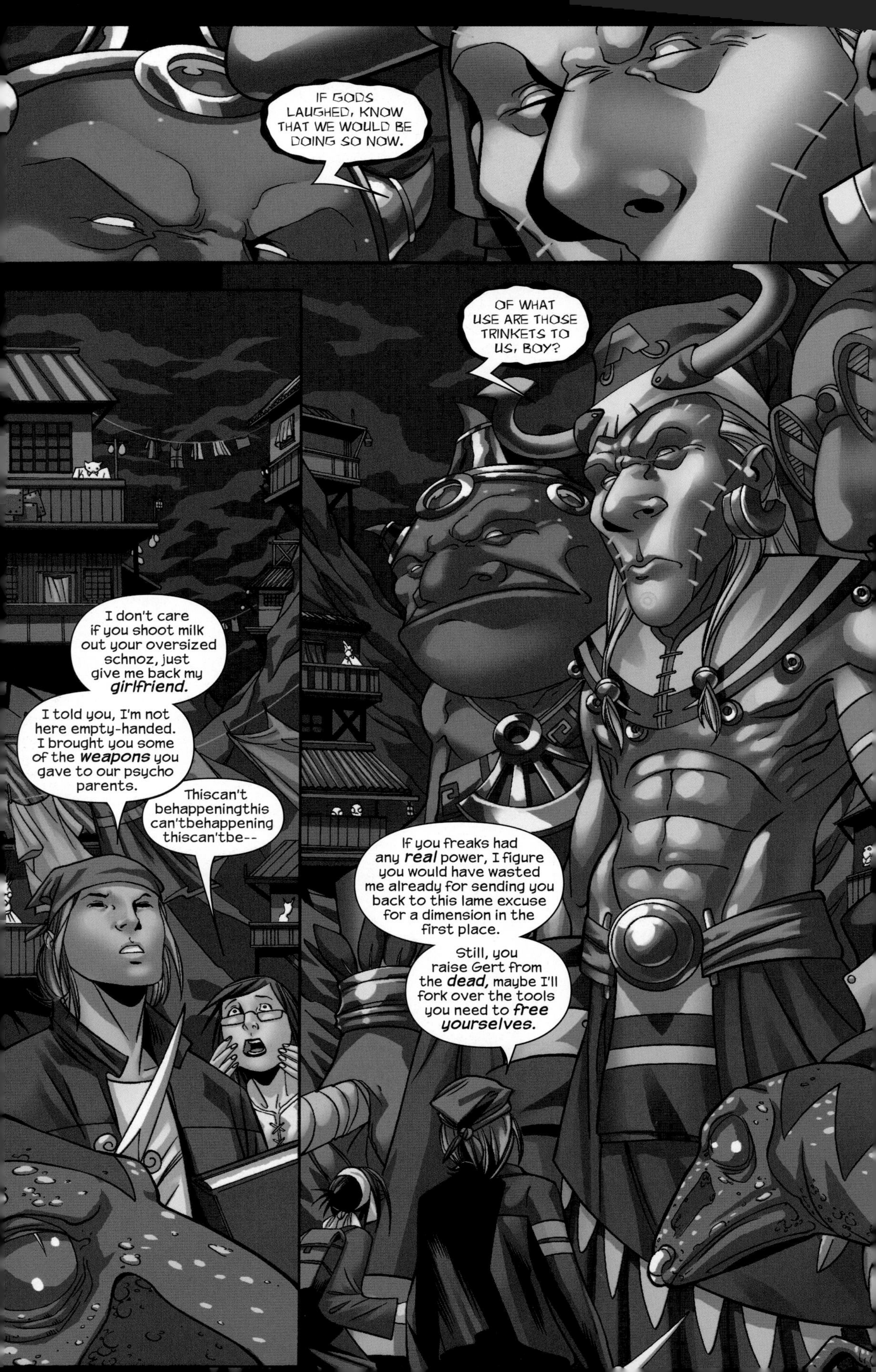
IF GODS LAUGHED, KNOW THAT WE WOULD BE DOING SO NOW.
OF WHAT USE ARE THOSE TRINKETS TO US, BOY?
I don't care if you shoot milk out your oversized schnoz, just give me back my *girlfriend.*
I told you, I'm not here empty-handed. I brought you some of the *weapons* you gave to our psycho parents.
Thiscan't behappeningthis can'tbehappening thiscan'tbe--
If you freaks had any *real* power, I figure you would have wasted me already for sending you back to this lame excuse for a dimension in the first place.
Still, you raise Gert from the *dead,* maybe I'll fork over the tools you need to *free yourselves.*

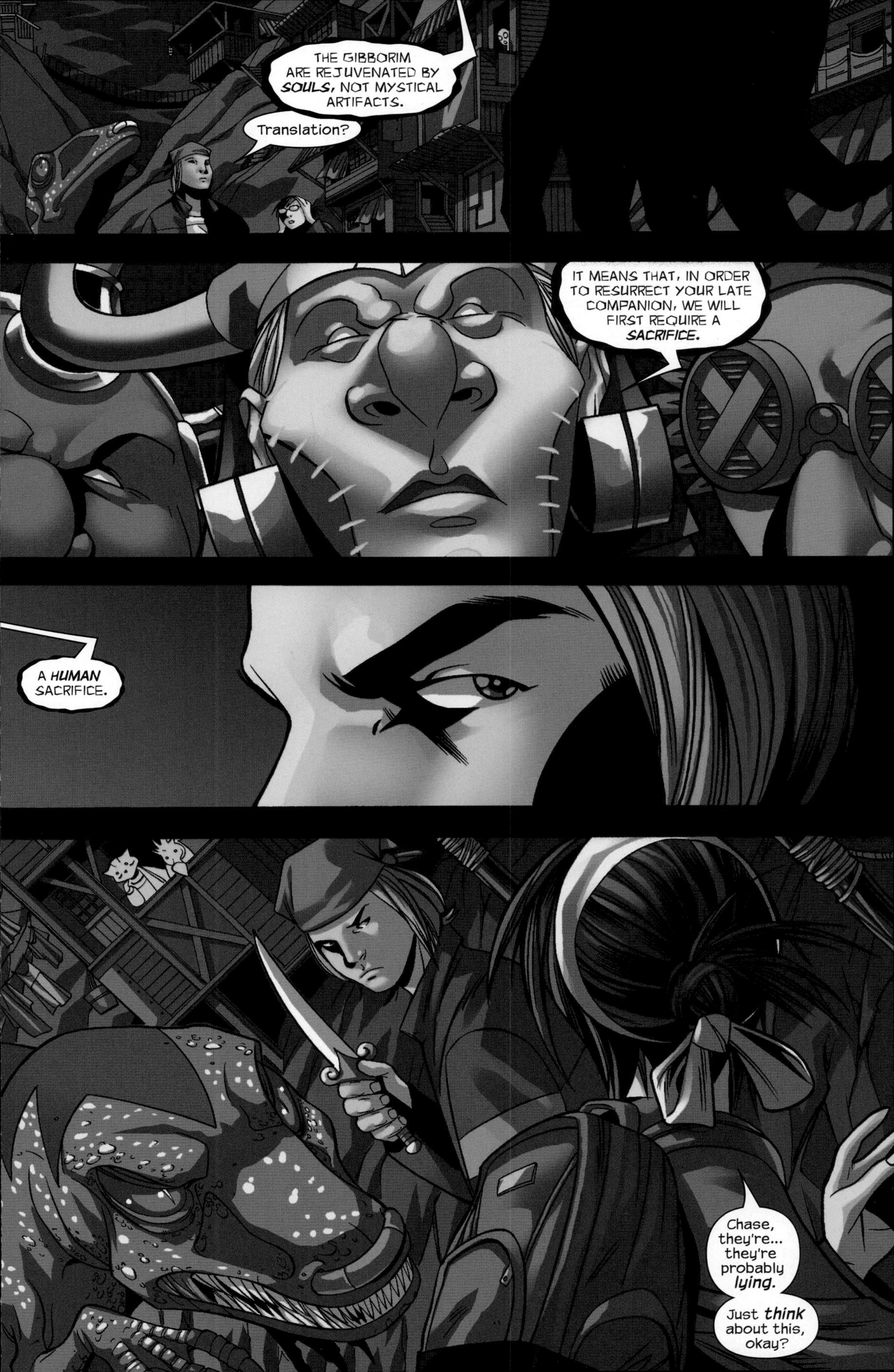
THE GIBBORIM ARE REJUVENATED BY *SOULS*, NOT MYSTICAL ARTIFACTS.
Translation?
IT MEANS THAT, IN ORDER TO RESURRECT YOUR LATE COMPANION, WE WILL FIRST REQUIRE A *SACRIFICE*.
A *HUMAN* SACRIFICE.
Chase, they're... they're probably *lying*.
Just *think* about this, okay?

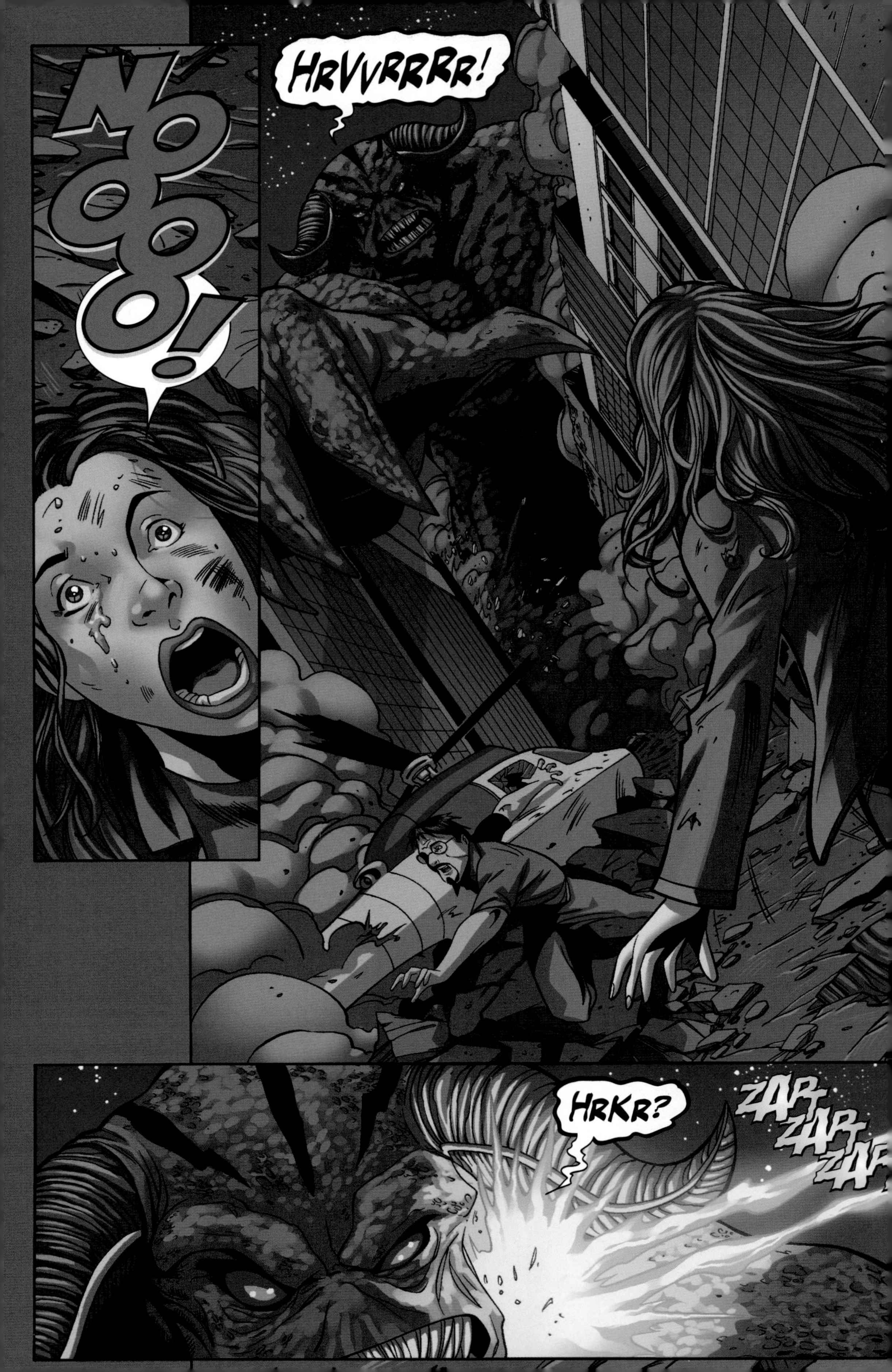
NOOOO!
HRVVRRRR!
HRKR?
ZAP ZAP ZAP

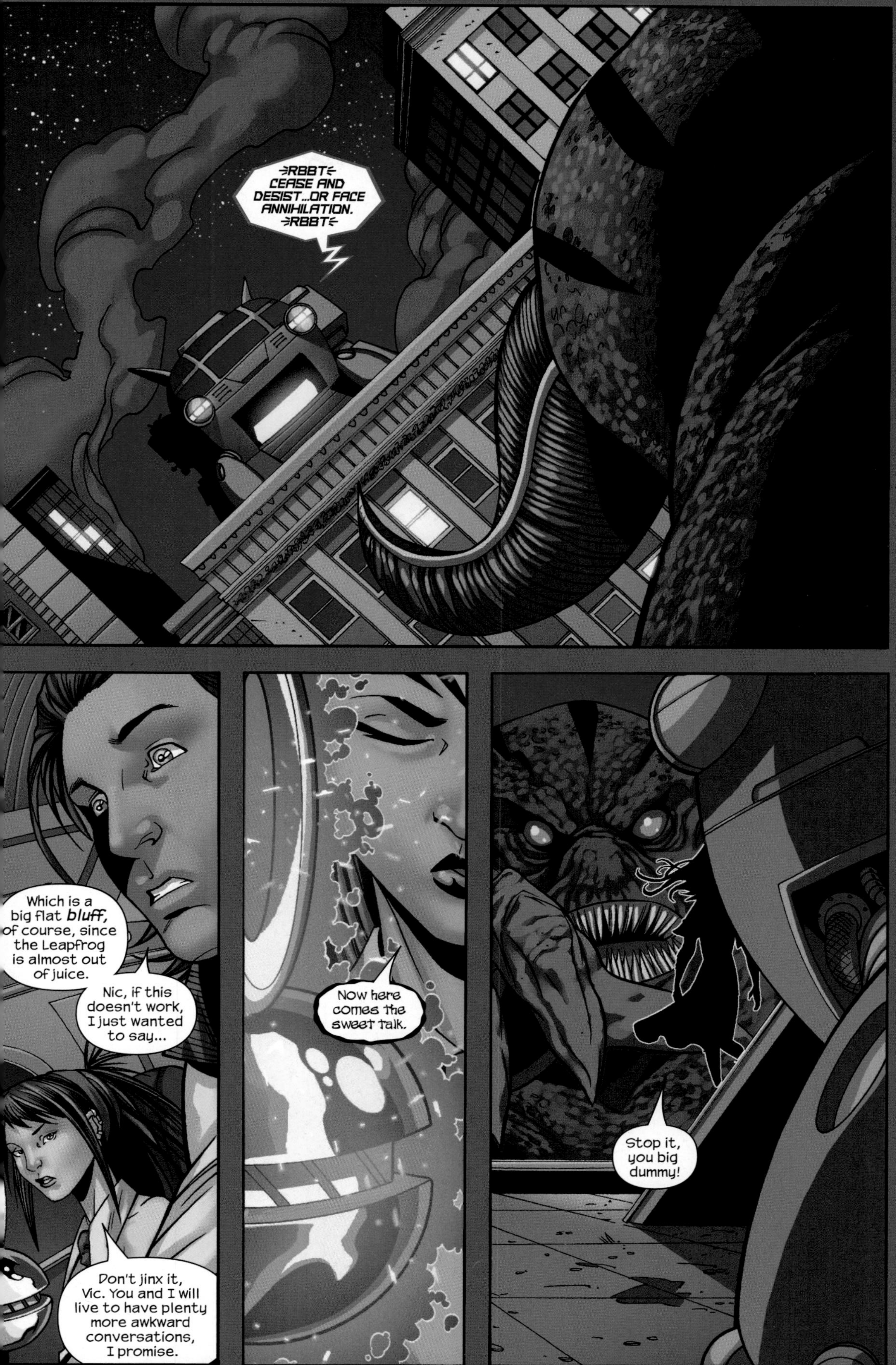

=RBBT= CEASE AND DESIST...OR FACE ANNIHILATION. =RBBT=
Which is a big flat *bluff,* of course, since the Leapfrog is almost out of juice.
Nic, if this doesn't work, I just wanted to say...
Don't jinx it, Vic. You and I will live to have plenty more awkward conversations, I promise.
Now here comes the sweet talk.
Stop it, you big dummy!

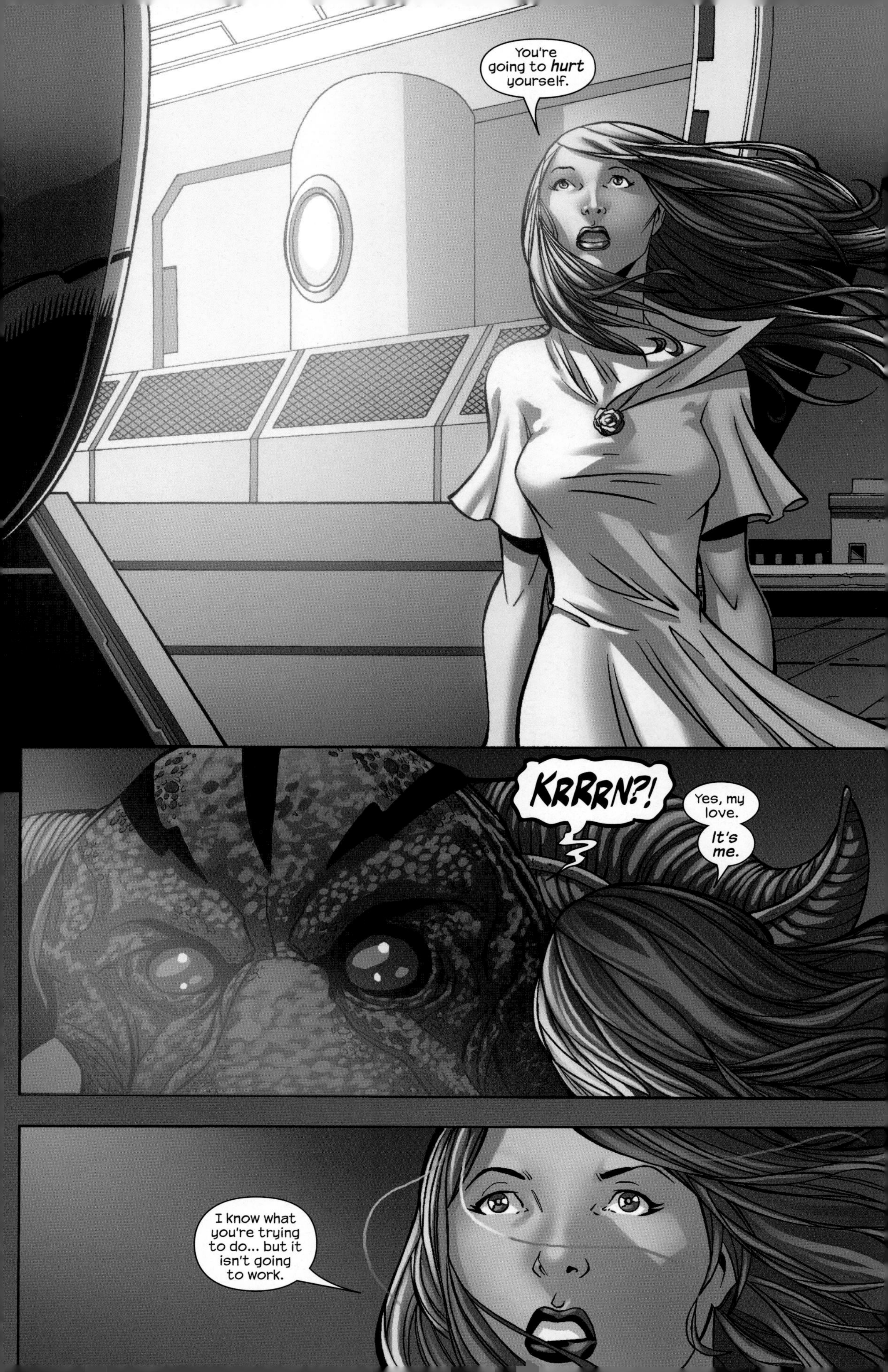
You're going to *hurt* yourself.
KRRRN?!
Yes, my love.
It's me.
I know what you're trying to do... but it isn't going to work.

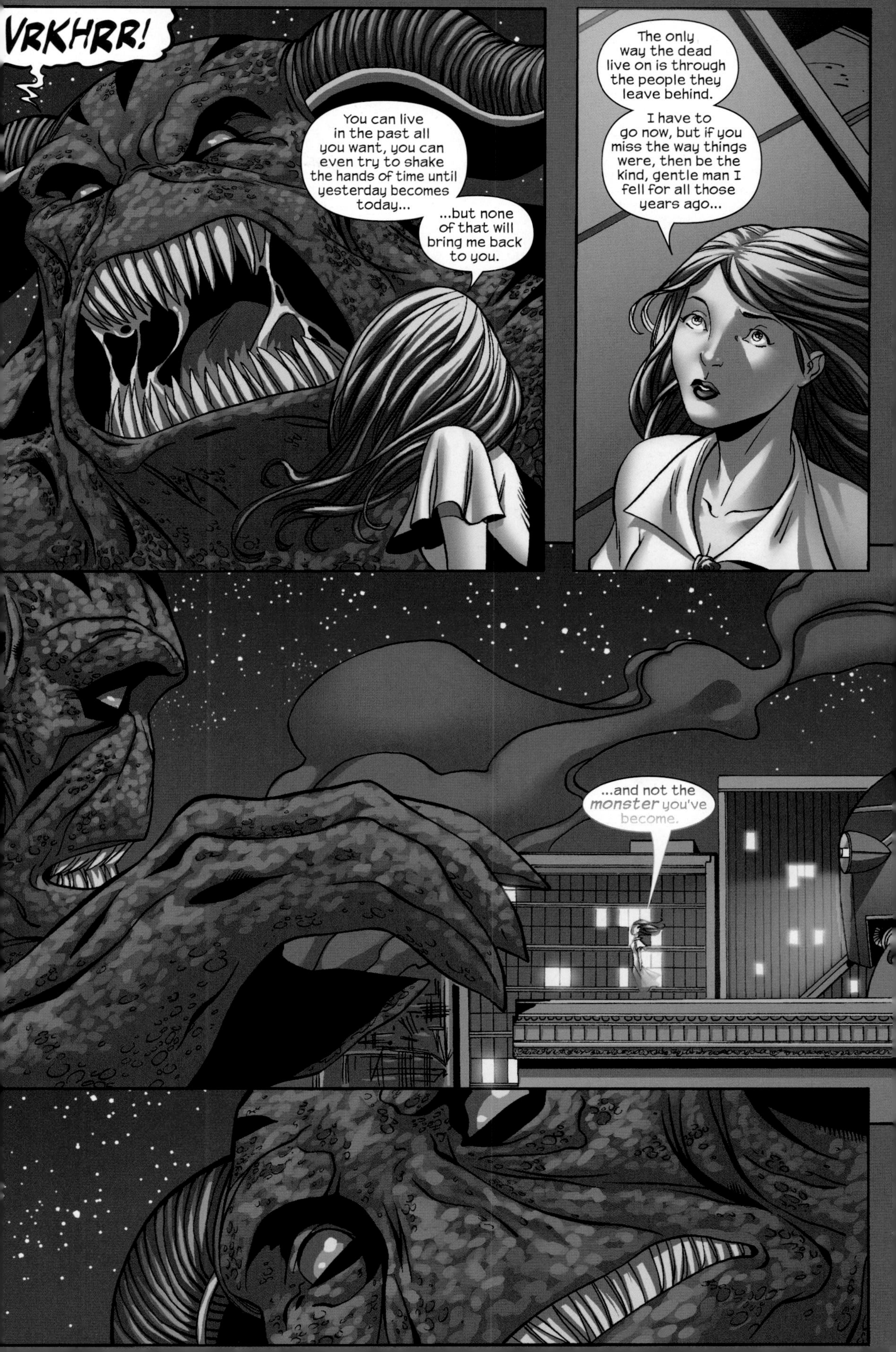
VRKHRR!
You can live in the past all you want, you can even try to shake the hands of time until yesterday becomes today...
...but none of that will bring me back to you.
The only way the dead live on is through the people they leave behind.
I have to go now, but if you miss the way things were, then be the kind, gentle man I fell for all those years ago...
...and not the *monster* you've become.

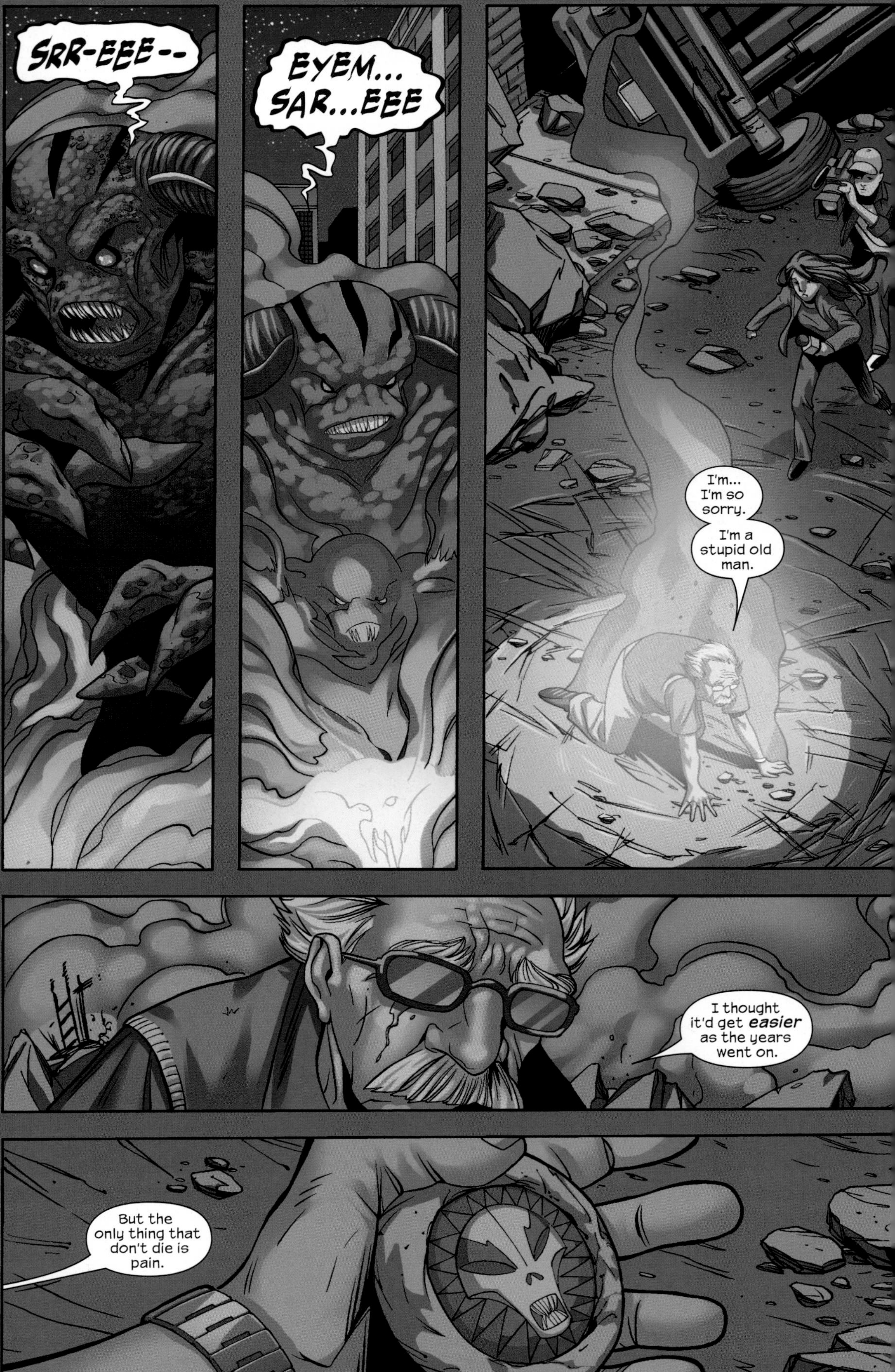
SRR-EEE--
EYEM... SAR...EEE
I'm... I'm so sorry.
I'm a stupid old man.
I thought it'd get *easier* as the years went on.
But the only thing that don't die is pain.

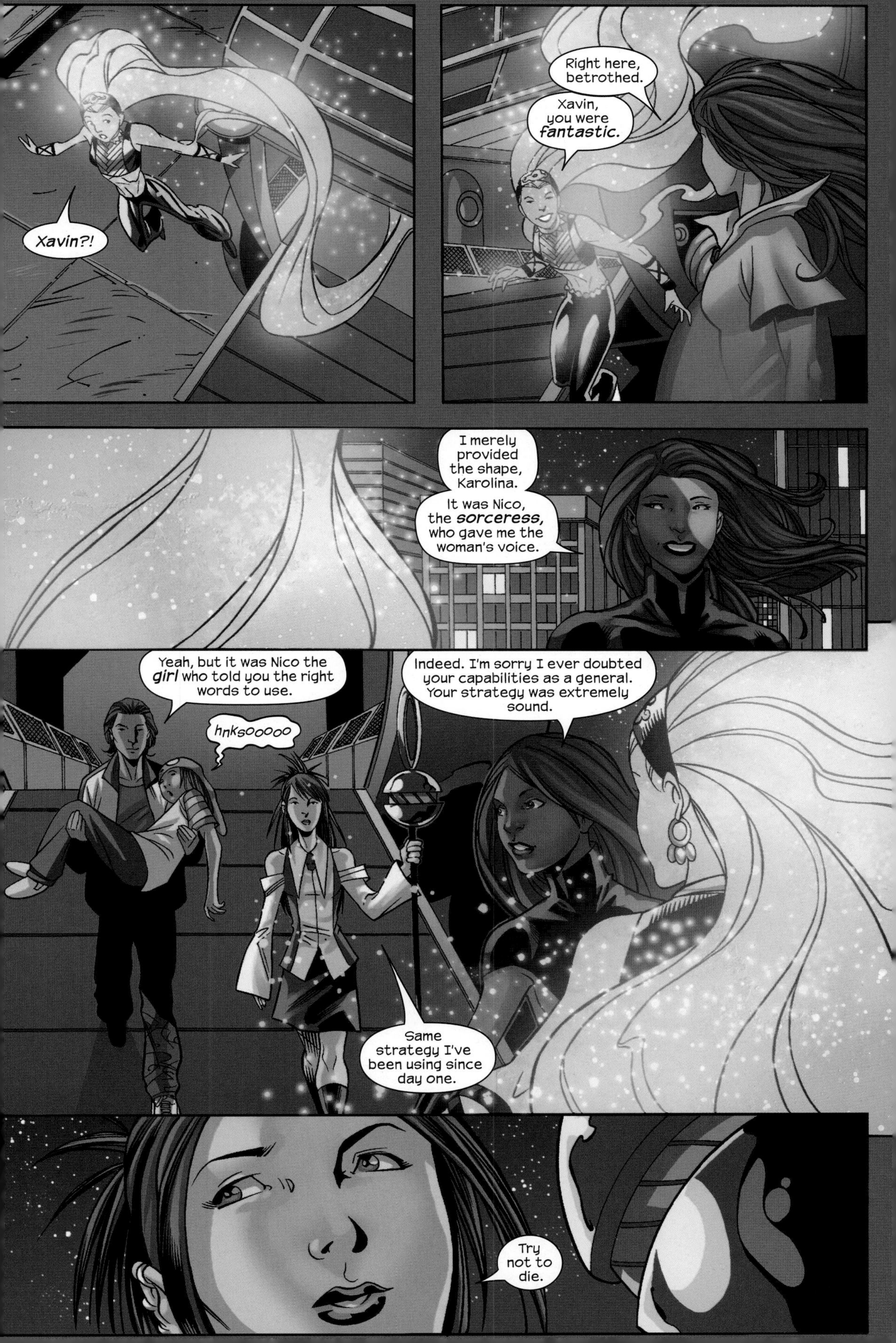
Xavin?!
Right here, betrothed.
Xavin, you were *fantastic.*
I merely provided the shape, Karolina.
It was Nico, the ***sorceress,*** who gave me the woman's voice.
Yeah, but it was Nico the ***girl*** who told you the right words to use.
hnksooooo
Indeed. I'm sorry I ever doubted your capabilities as a general. Your strategy was extremely sound.
Same strategy I've been using since day one.
Try not to die.

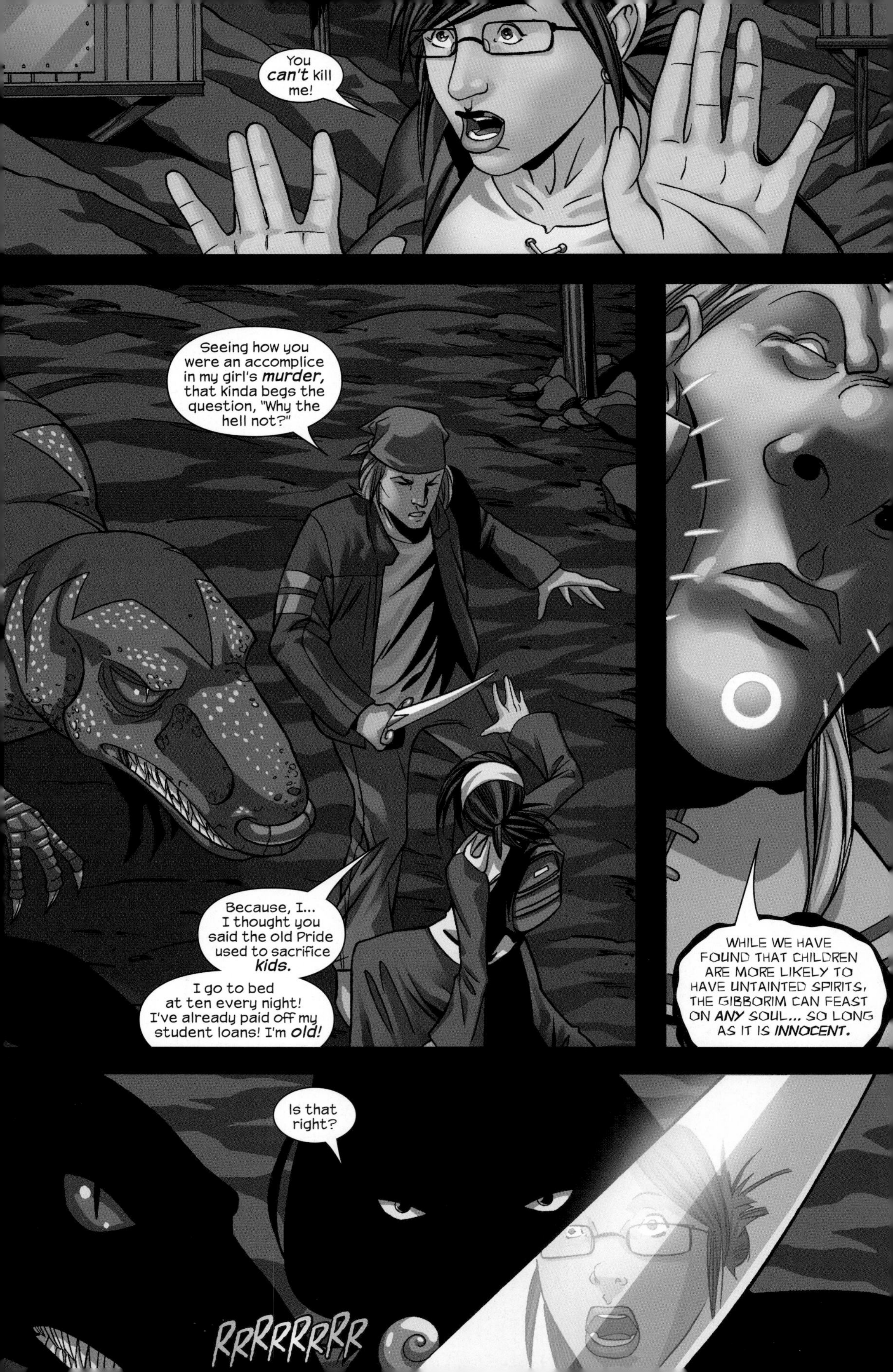
You can't kill me!
Seeing how you were an accomplice in my girl's murder, that kinda begs the question, "Why the hell not?"
Because, I... I thought you said the old Pride used to sacrifice kids.
I go to bed at ten every night! I've already paid off my student loans! I'm old!
WHILE WE HAVE FOUND THAT CHILDREN ARE MORE LIKELY TO HAVE UNTAINTED SPIRITS, THE GIBBORIM CAN FEAST ON ANY SOUL... SO LONG AS IT IS INNOCENT.
Is that right?
RRRRRRRR

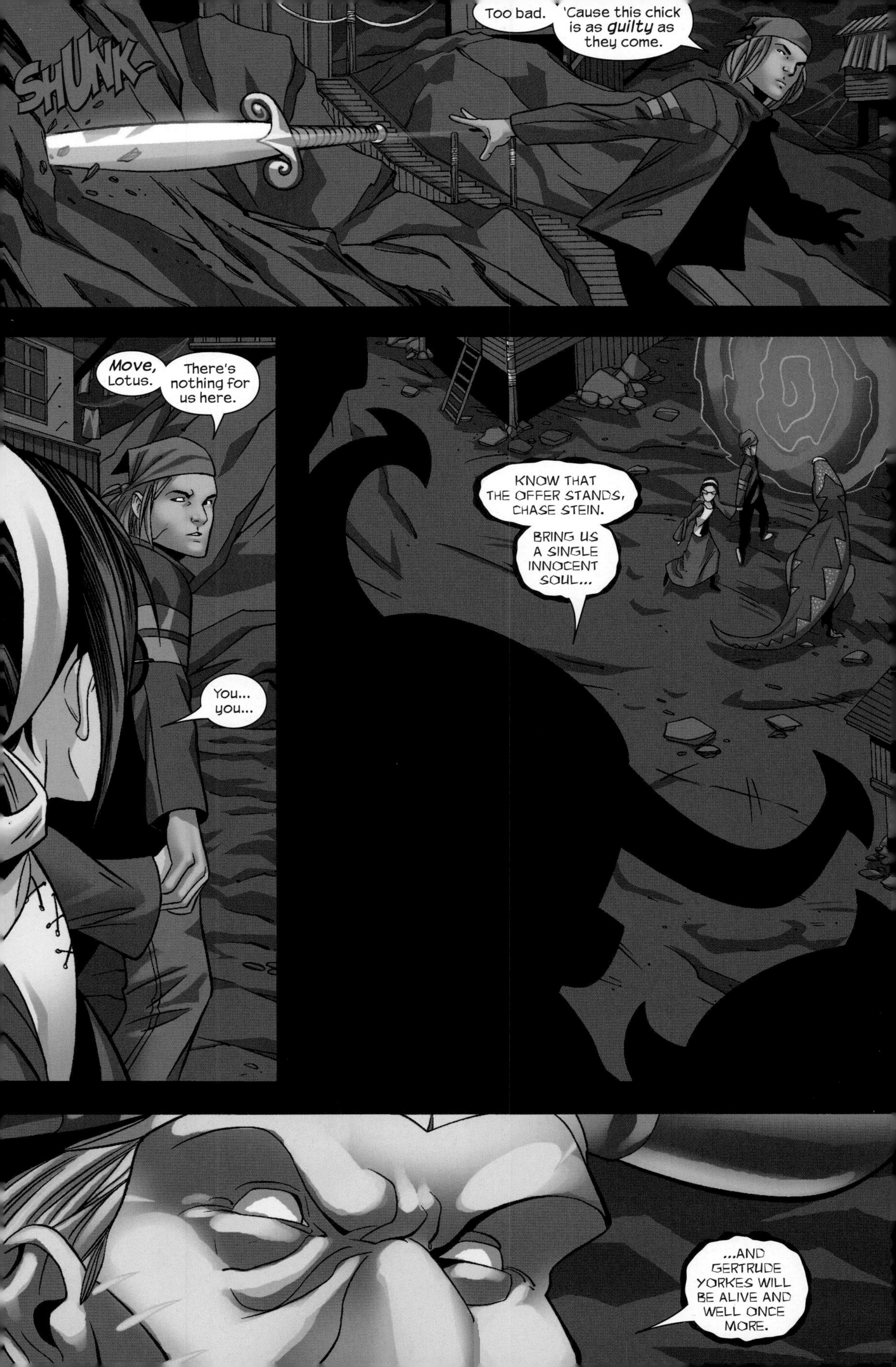
SHUNK
Too bad.
'Cause this chick is as *guilty* as they come.
Move, Lotus.
There's nothing for us here.
You... you...
KNOW THAT THE OFFER STANDS, CHASE STEIN.
BRING US A SINGLE INNOCENT SOUL...
...AND GERTRUDE YORKES WILL BE ALIVE AND WELL ONCE MORE.

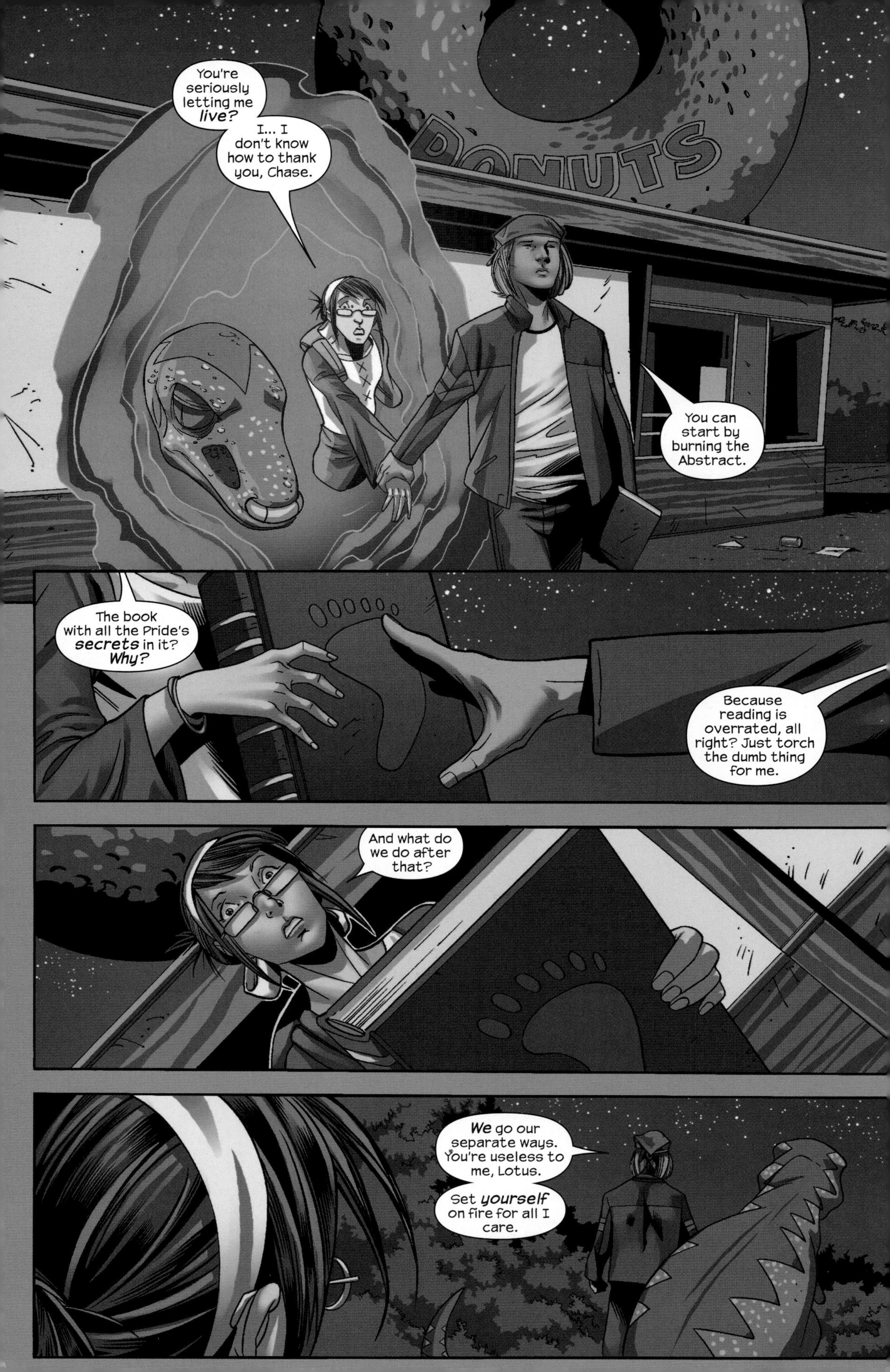
DONUTS
You're seriously letting me *live?*
I... I don't know how to thank you, Chase.
You can start by burning the Abstract.
The book with all the Pride's *secrets* in it? *Why?*
Because reading is overrated, all right? Just torch the dumb thing for me.
And what do we do after that?
We go our separate ways. You're useless to me, Lotus.
Set *yourself* on fire for all I care.

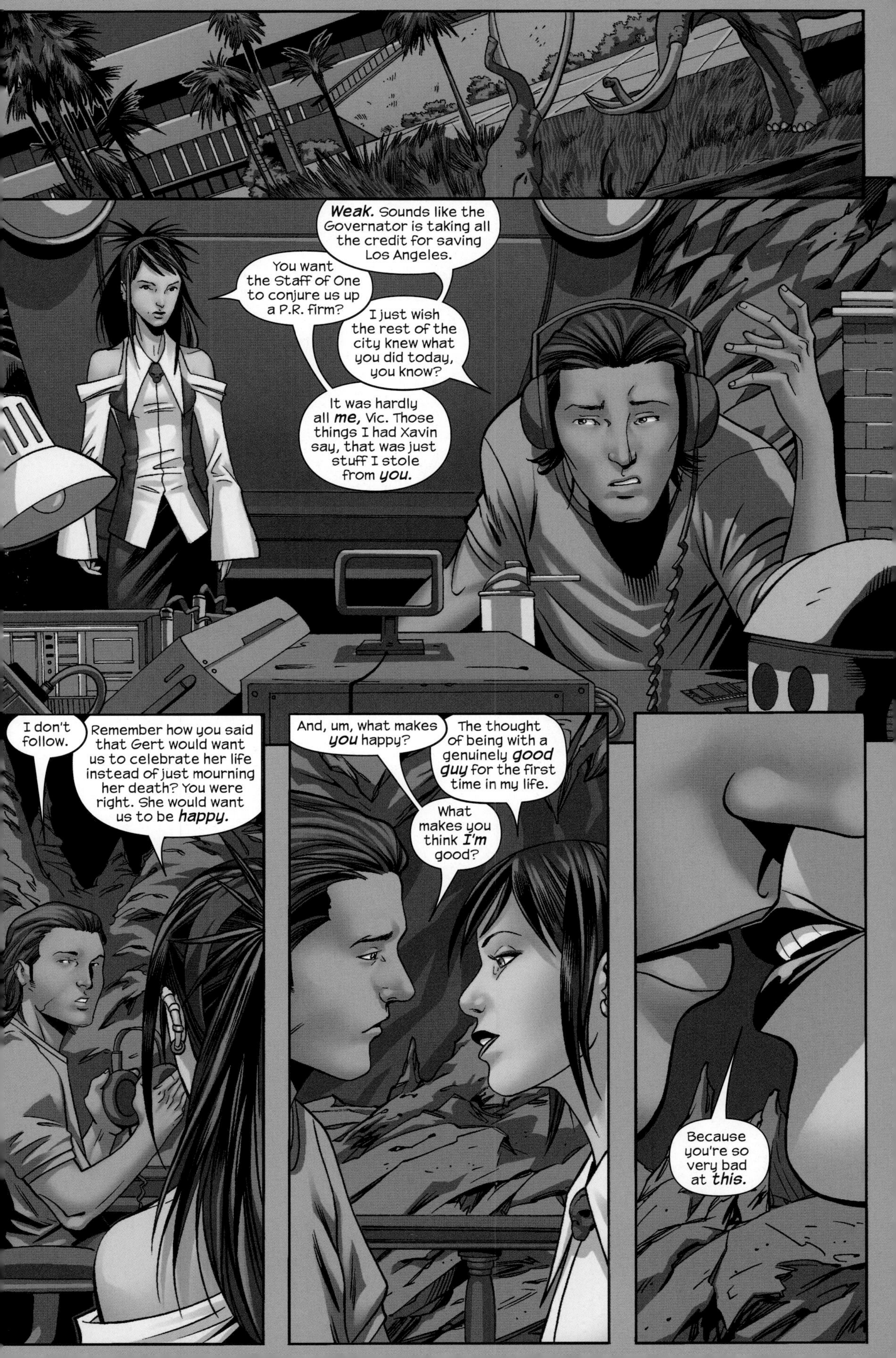
Weak. Sounds like the Governator is taking all the credit for saving Los Angeles.
You want the Staff of One to conjure us up a P.R. firm?
I just wish the rest of the city knew what you did today, you know?
It was hardly all me, Vic. Those things I had Xavin say, that was just stuff I stole from you.
I don't follow.
Remember how you said that Gert would want us to celebrate her life instead of just mourning her death? You were right. She would want us to be happy.
And, um, what makes you happy?
The thought of being with a genuinely good guy for the first time in my life.
What makes you think I'm good?
Because you're so very bad at this.

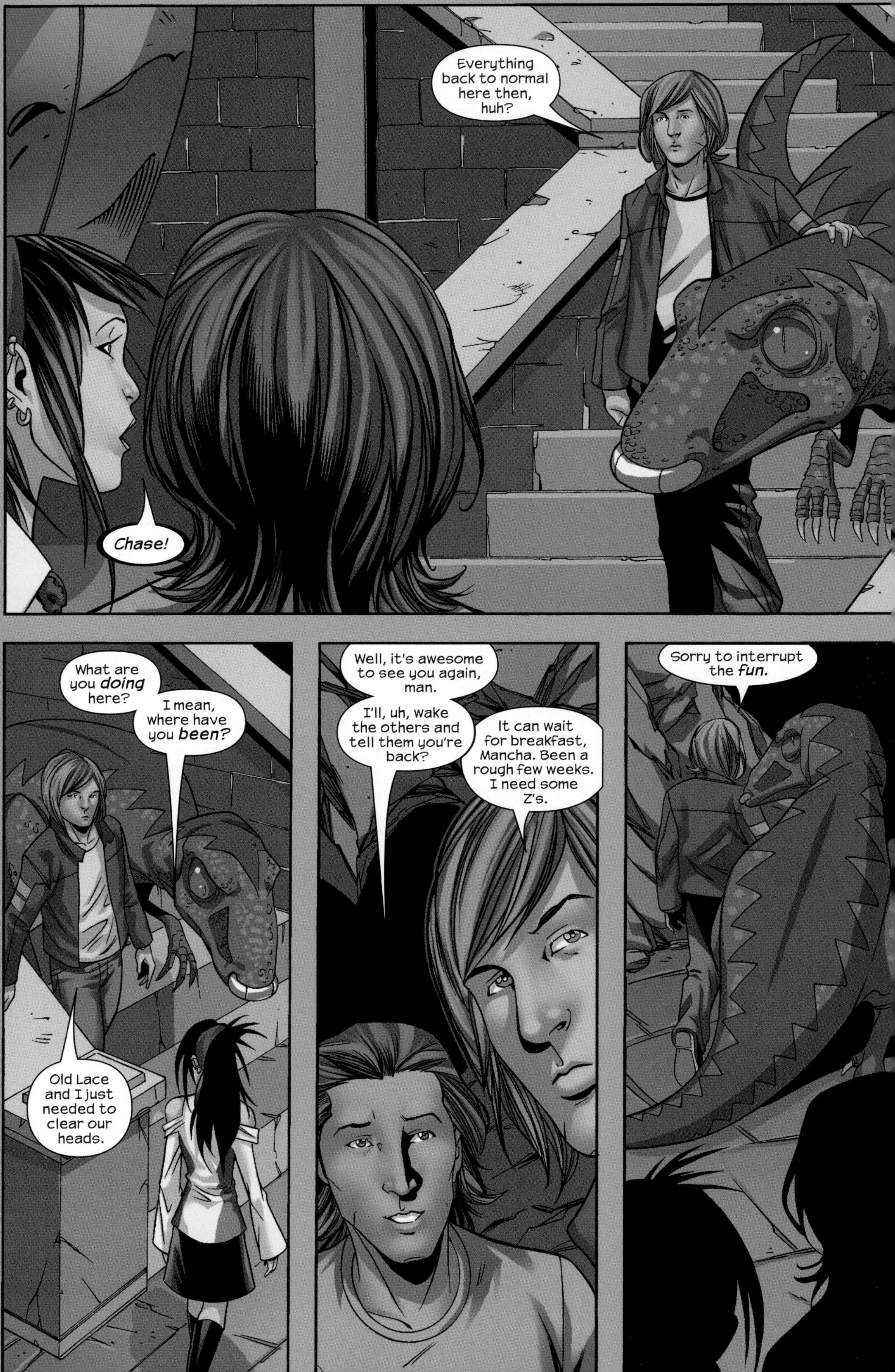
Everything back to normal here then, huh?
Chase!
What are you doing here?
I mean, where have you been?
Old Lace and I just needed to clear our heads.
Well, it's awesome to see you again, man.
I'll, uh, wake the others and tell them you're back?
It can wait for breakfast, Mancha. Been a rough few weeks. I need some Z's.
Sorry to interrupt the fun.

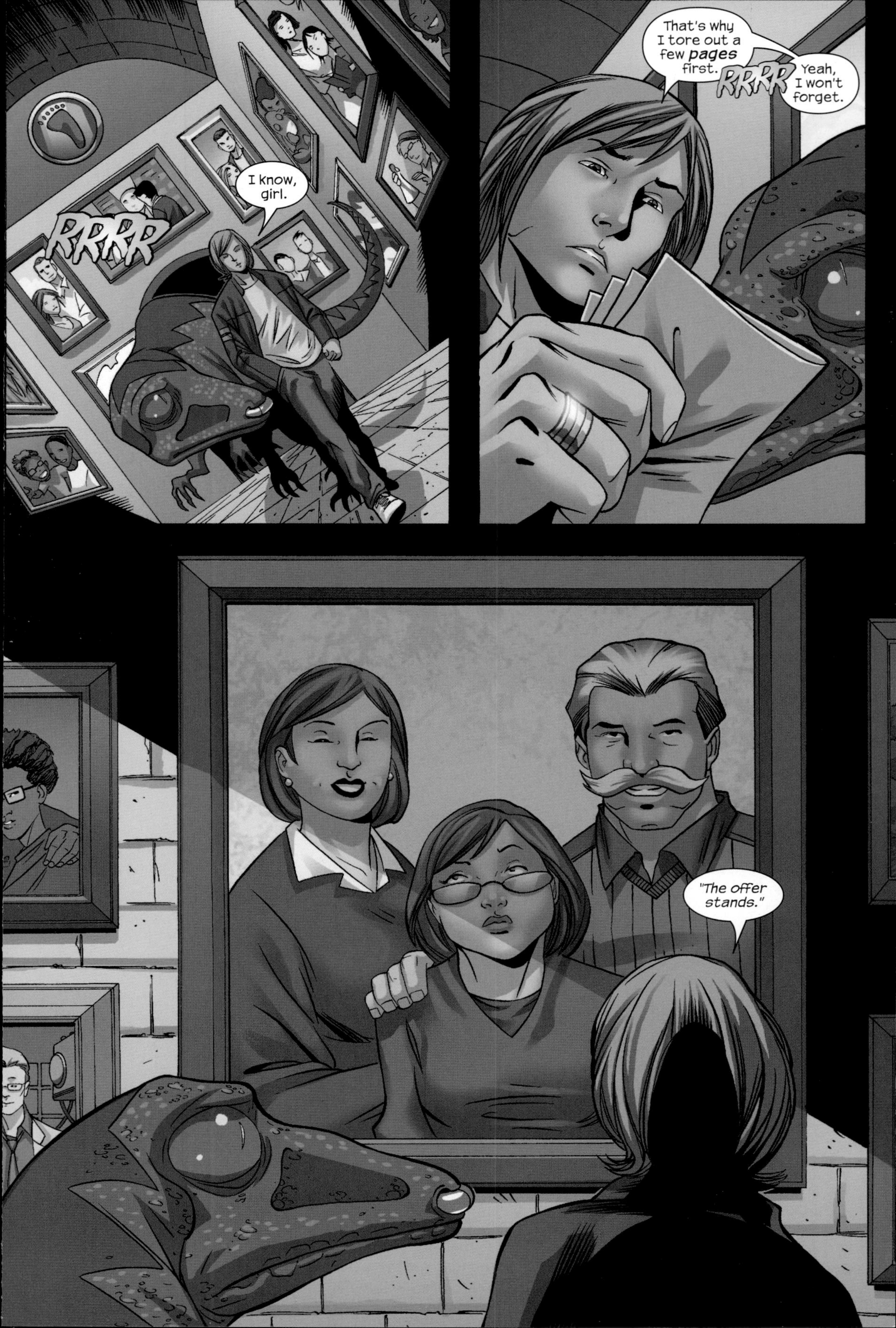
RRRR
I know, girl.
That's why I tore out a few *pages* first.
RRRR
Yeah, I won't forget.
"The offer stands."

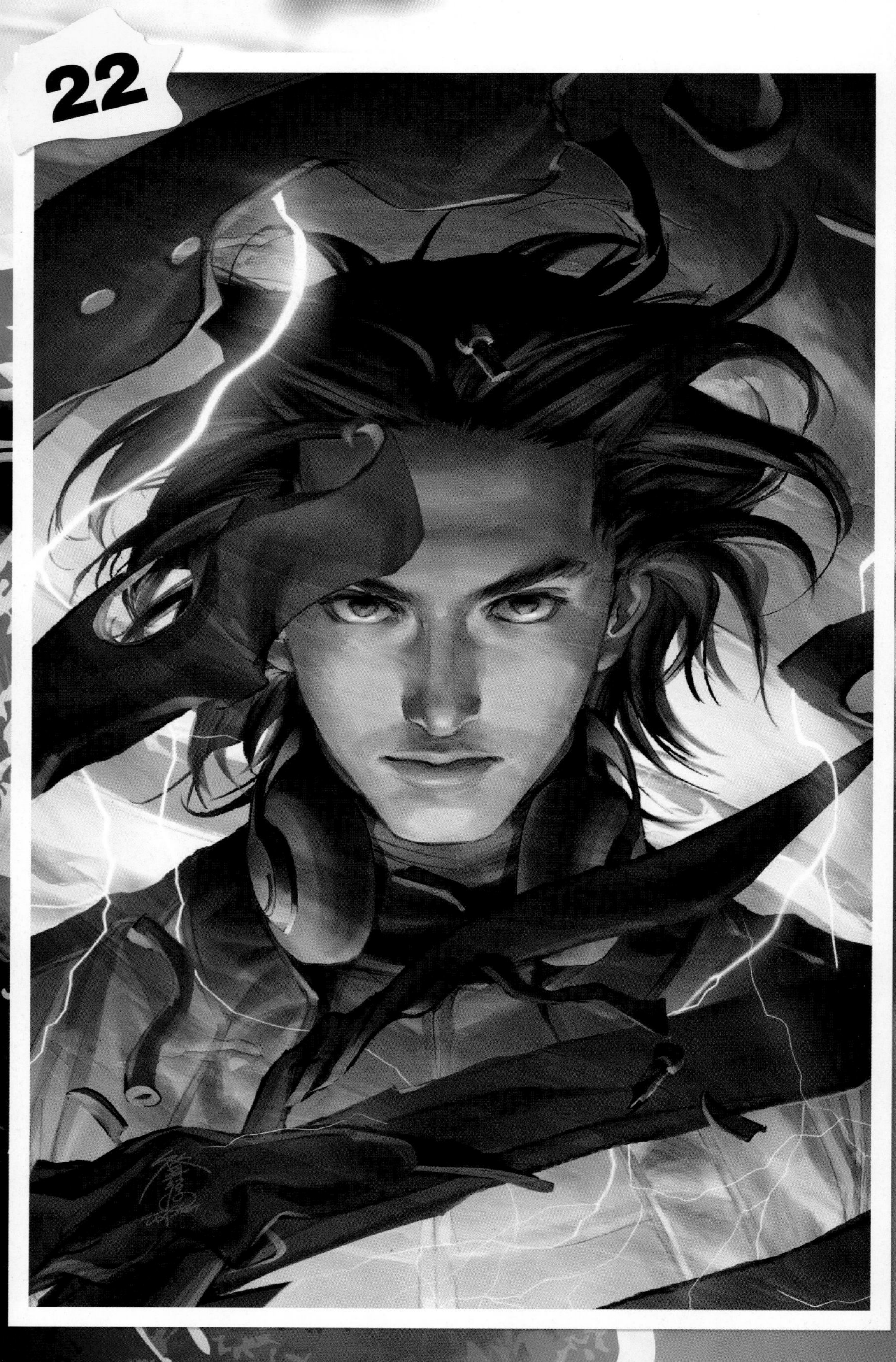
22

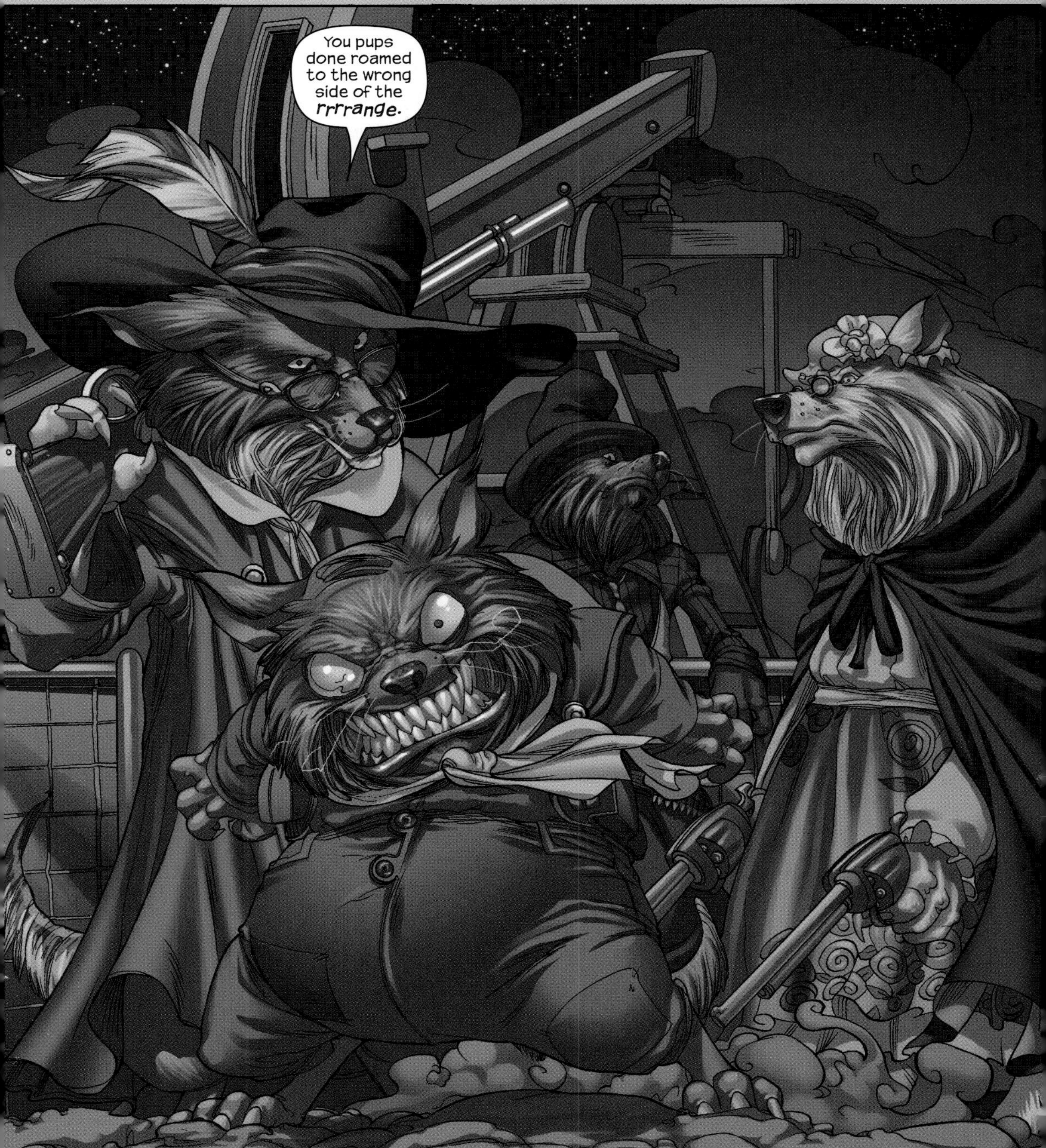
You pups done roamed to the wrong side of the rrrrange.

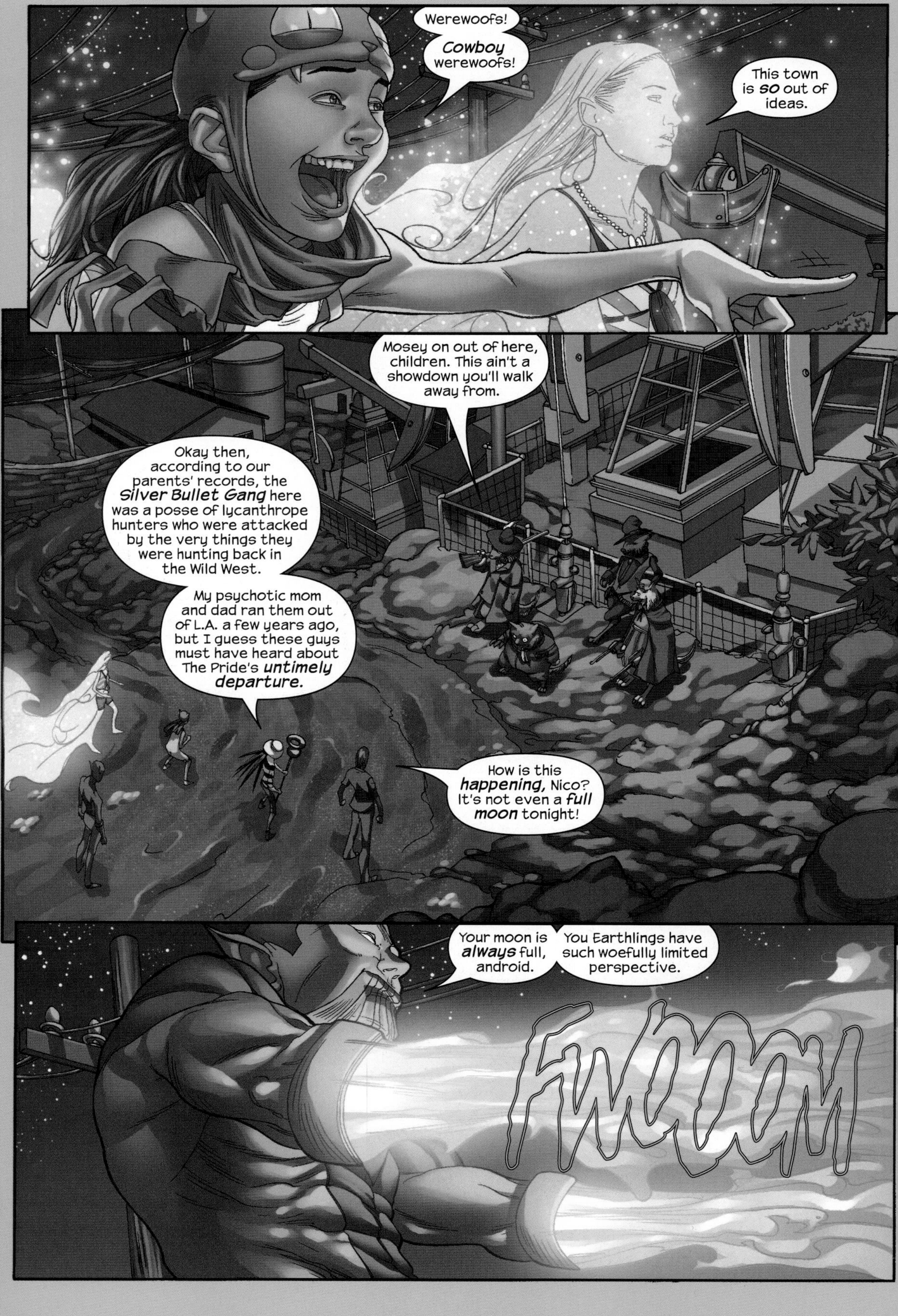
Werewoofs!
Cowboy werewoofs!
This town is SO out of ideas.
Mosey on out of here, children. This ain't a showdown you'll walk away from.
Okay then, according to our parents' records, the Silver Bullet Gang here was a posse of lycanthrope hunters who were attacked by the very things they were hunting back in the Wild West.
My psychotic mom and dad ran them out of L.A. a few years ago, but I guess these guys must have heard about The Pride's untimely departure.
How is this happening, Nico? It's not even a full moon tonight!
Your moon is always full, android.
You Earthlings have such woefully limited perspective.
FWOOOM

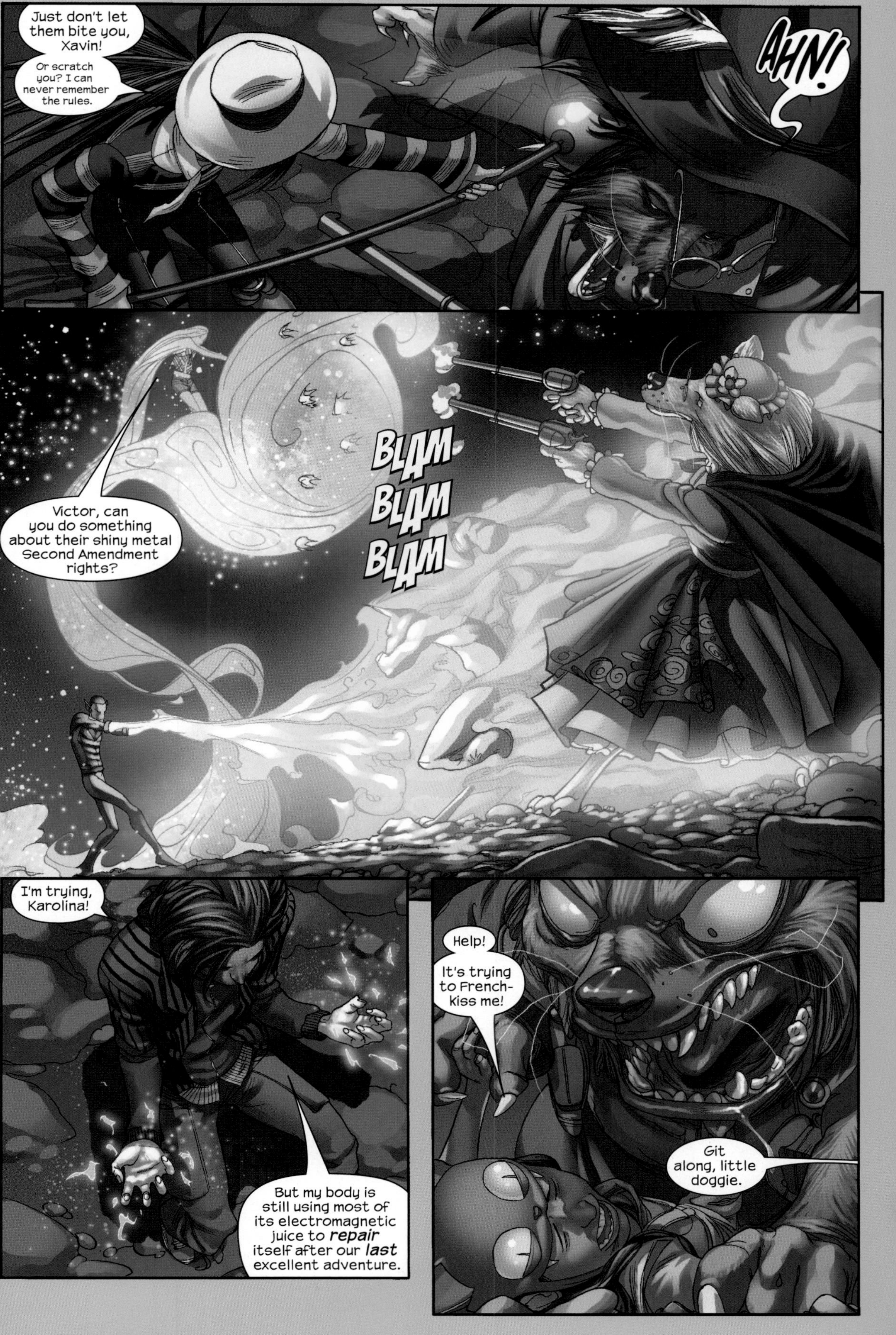
Just don't let them bite you, Xavin!
Or scratch you? I can never remember the rules.
AHN!
Victor, can you do something about their shiny metal Second Amendment rights?
BLAM
BLAM
BLAM
I'm trying, Karolina!
But my body is still using most of its electromagnetic juice to *repair* itself after our *last* excellent adventure.
Help!
It's trying to French-kiss me!
Git along, little doggie.

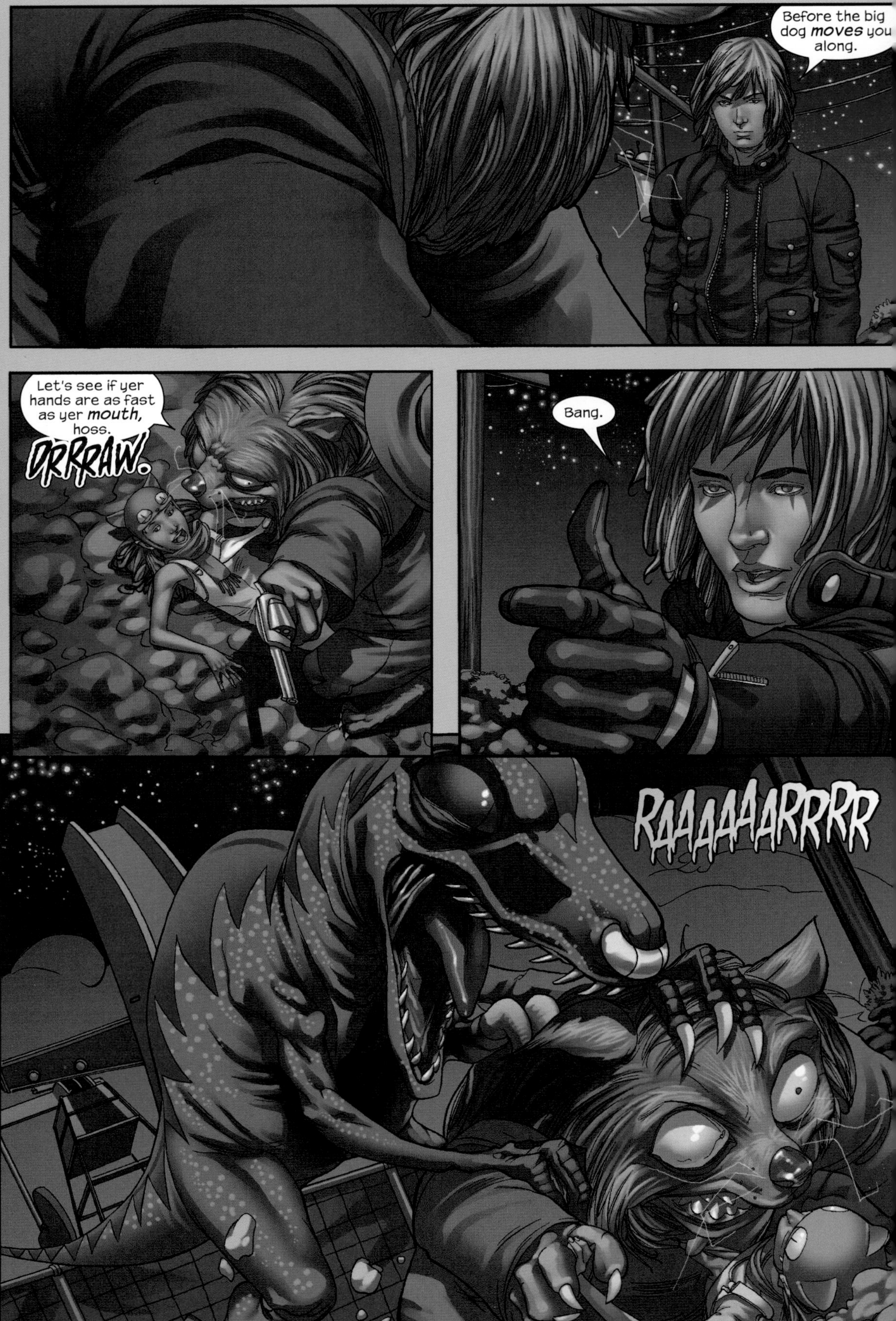
Before the big dog *moves* you along.
Let's see if yer hands are as fast as yer *mouth,* hoss.
DRRRAW.
Bang.
RAAAAAARRRR

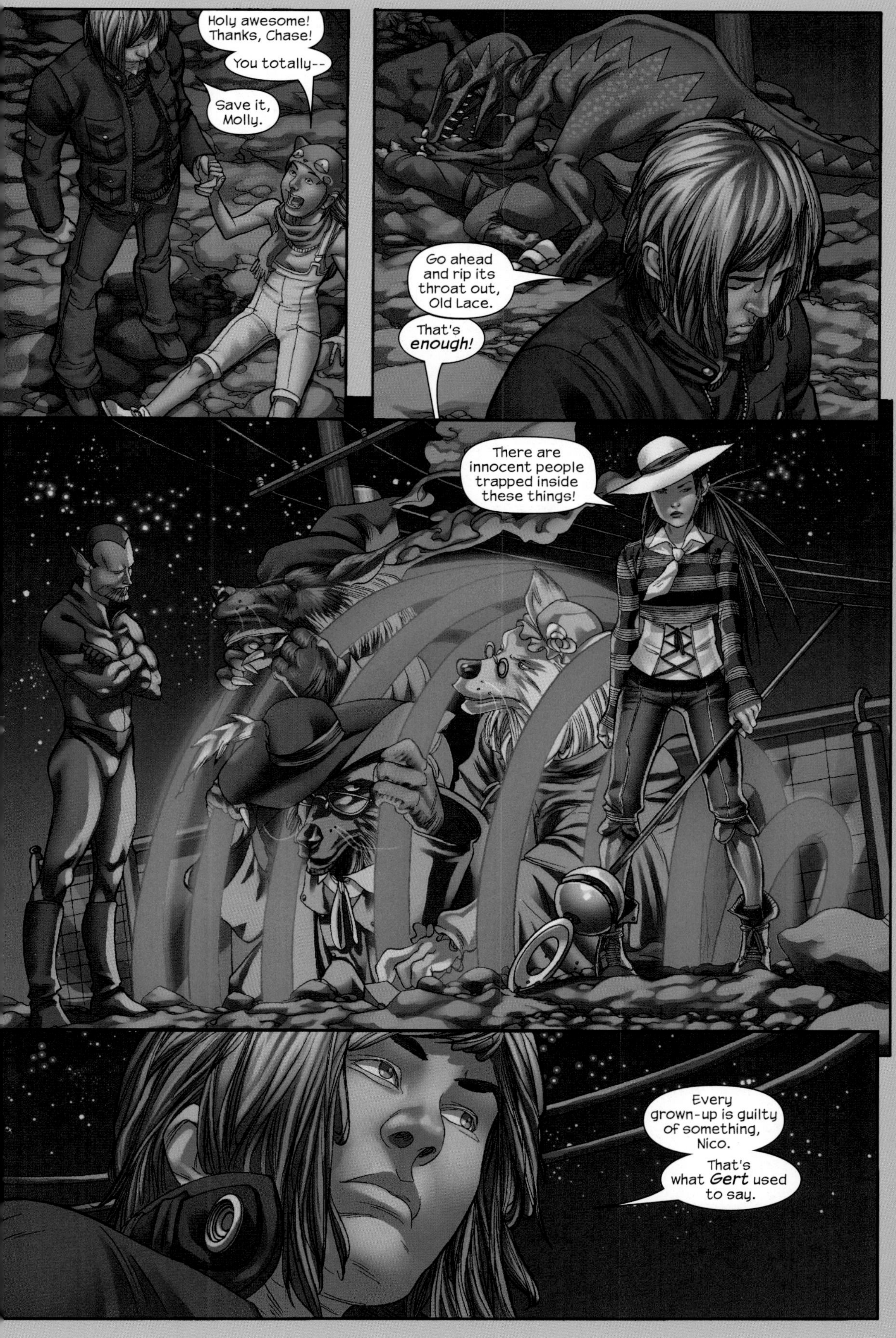
Holy awesome! Thanks, Chase!
You totally--
Save it, Molly.
Go ahead and rip its throat out, Old Lace.
That's *enough!*
There are innocent people trapped inside these things!
Every grown-up is guilty of something, Nico.
That's what *Gert* used to say.

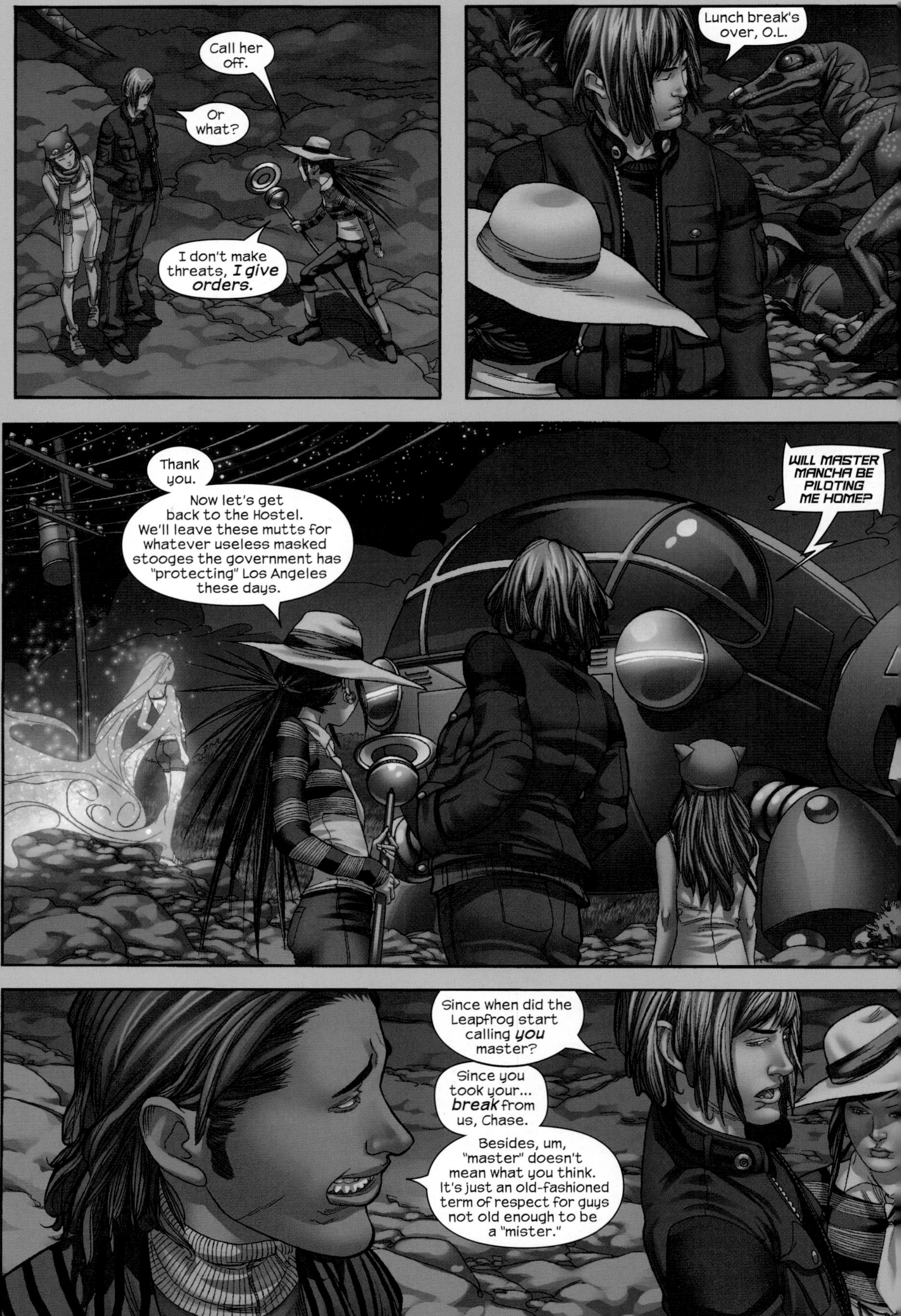
Call her off.
Or what?
I don't make threats, *I give orders.*
Lunch break's over, O.L.
Thank you.
Now let's get back to the Hostel. We'll leave these mutts for whatever useless masked stooges the government has "protecting" Los Angeles these days.
WILL MASTER MANCHA BE PILOTING ME HOME?
Since when did the Leapfrog start calling *you* master?
Since you took your... *break* from us, Chase.
Besides, um, "master" doesn't mean what you think. It's just an old-fashioned term of respect for guys not old enough to be a "mister."

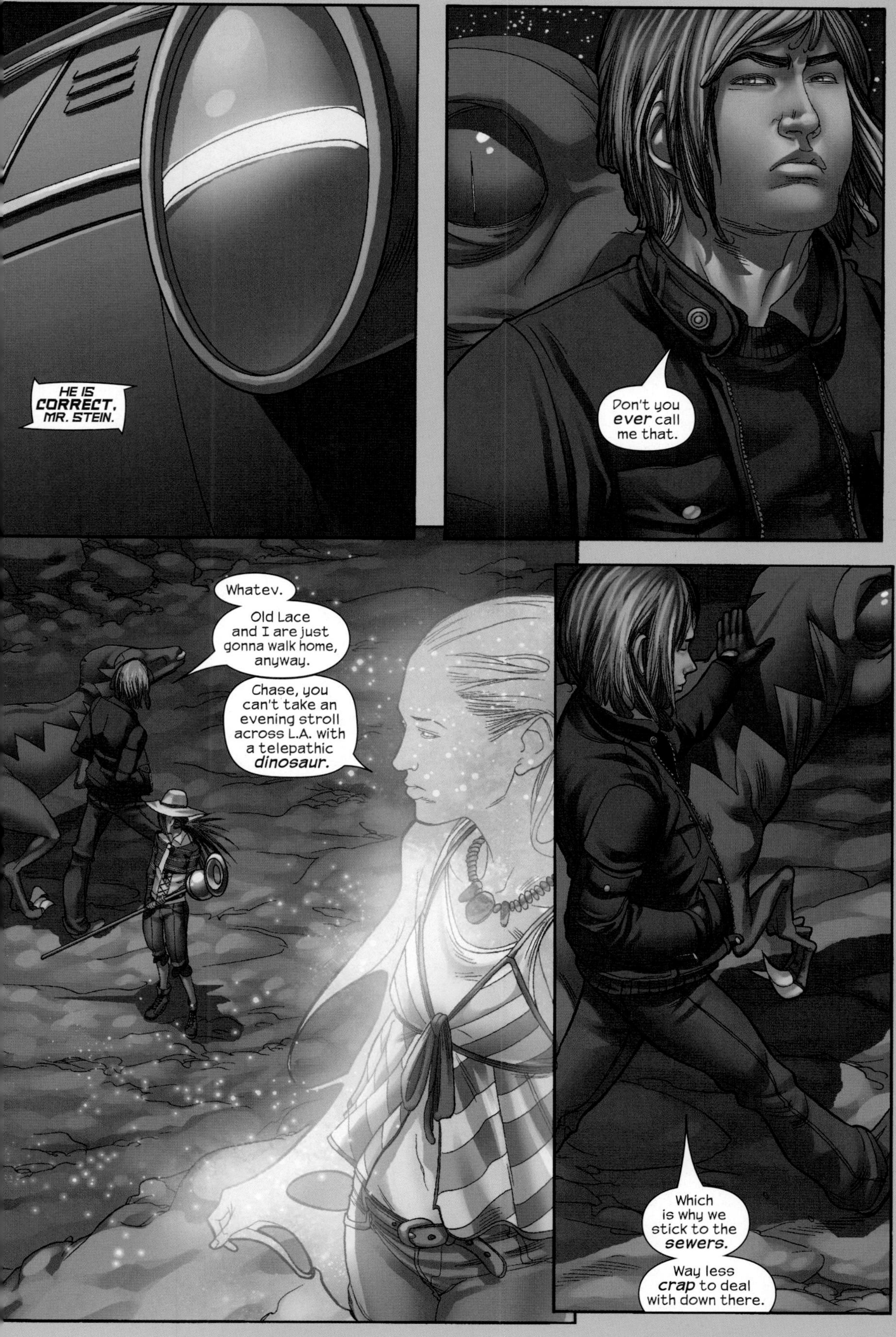
HE IS CORRECT, MR. STEIN.
Don't you ever call me that.
Whatev.
Old Lace and I are just gonna walk home, anyway.
Chase, you can't take an evening stroll across L.A. with a telepathic dinosaur.
Which is why we stick to the sewers.
Way less crap to deal with down there.

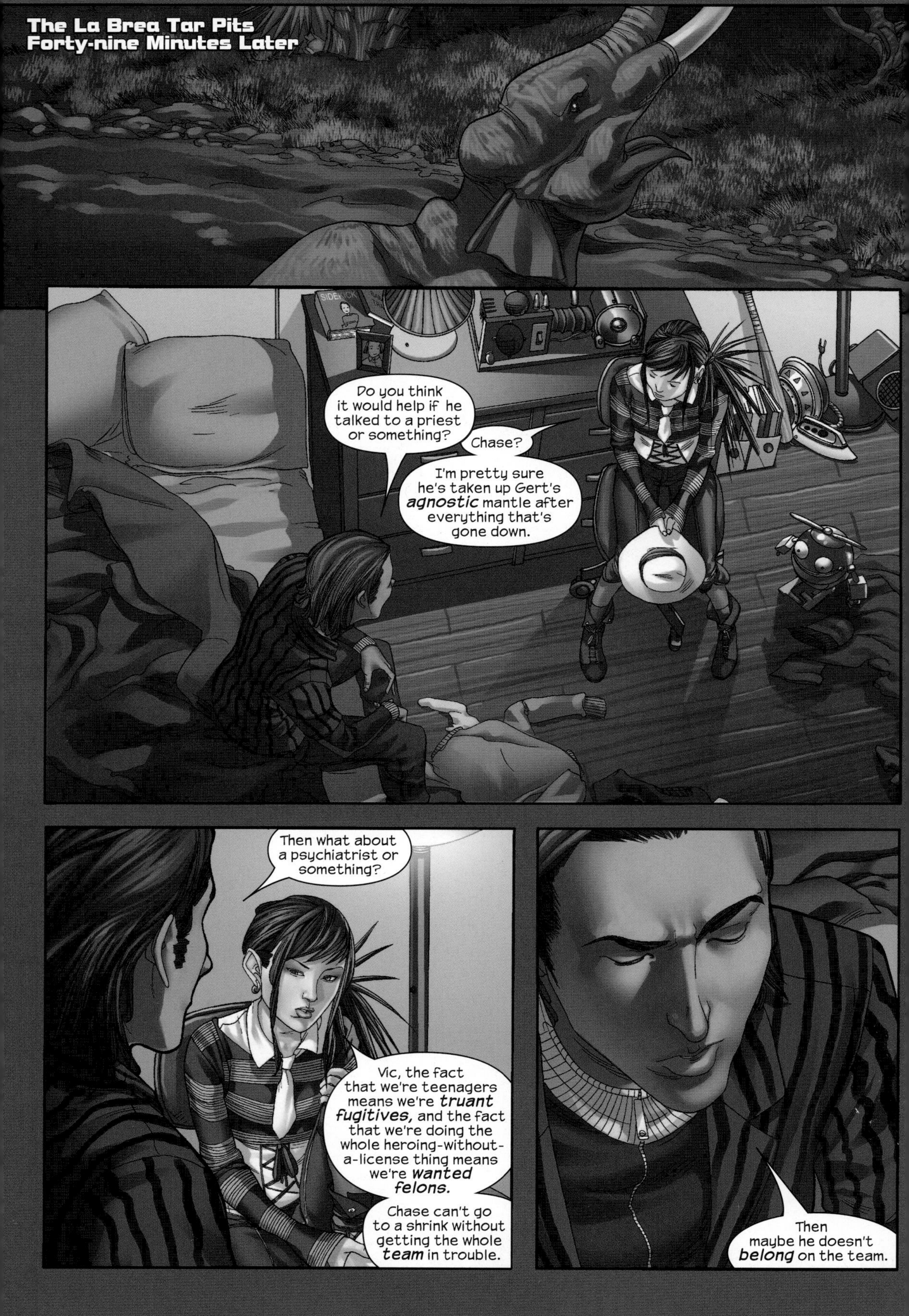
The La Brea Tar Pits
Forty-nine Minutes Later
SIDEKICK
Do you think it would help if he talked to a priest or something?
Chase?
I'm pretty sure he's taken up Gert's *agnostic* mantle after everything that's gone down.
Then what about a psychiatrist or something?
Vic, the fact that we're teenagers means we're *truant fugitives,* and the fact that we're doing the whole heroing-without-a-license thing means we're *wanted felons.*
Chase can't go to a shrink without getting the whole *team* in trouble.
Then maybe he doesn't *belong* on the team.

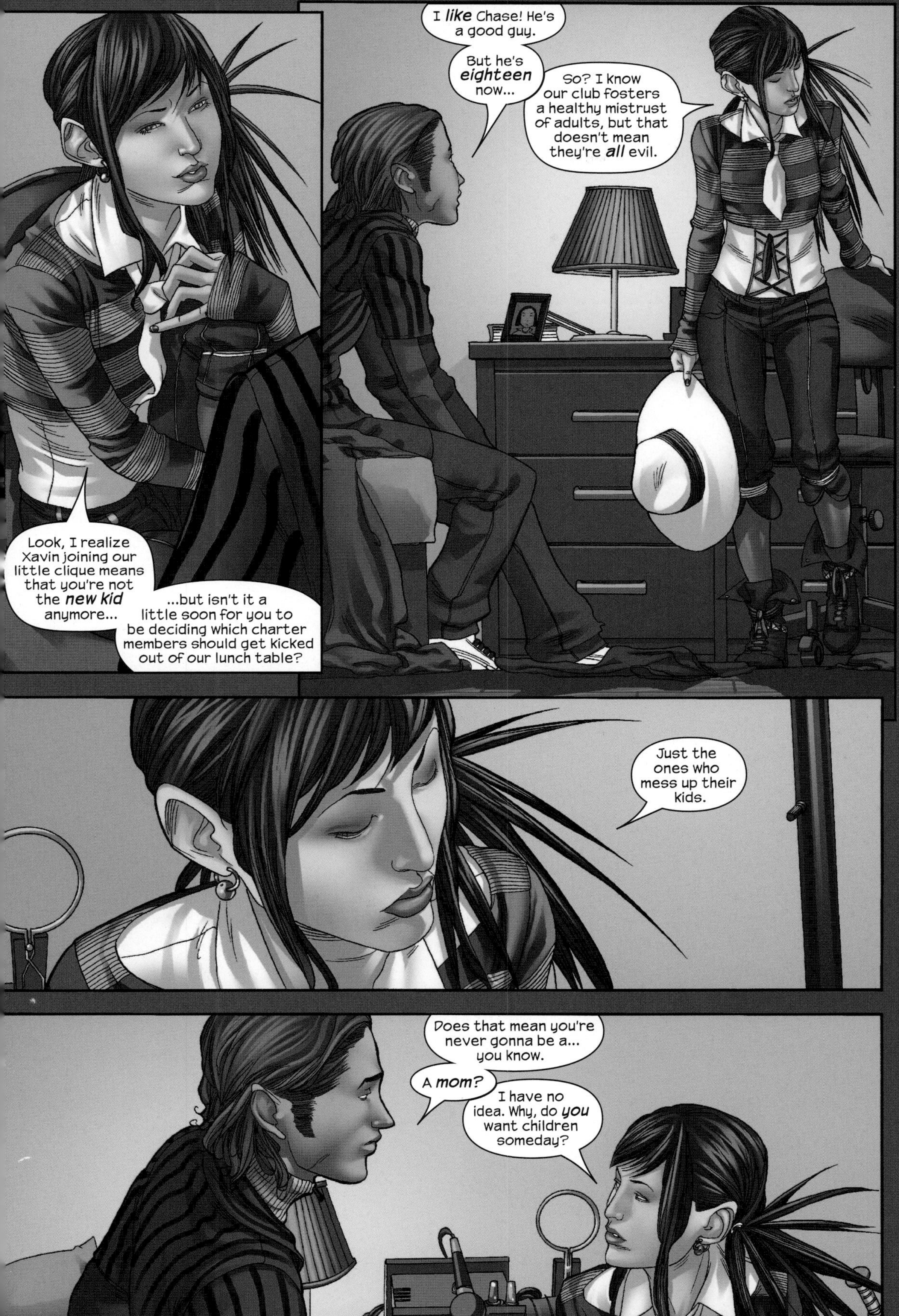
Look, I realize Xavin joining our little clique means that you're not the new kid anymore...
...but isn't it a little soon for you to be deciding which charter members should get kicked out of our lunch table?
I like Chase! He's a good guy.
But he's eighteen now...
So? I know our club fosters a healthy mistrust of adults, but that doesn't mean they're all evil.
Just the ones who mess up their kids.
Does that mean you're never gonna be a... you know.
A mom?
I have no idea. Why, do you want children someday?

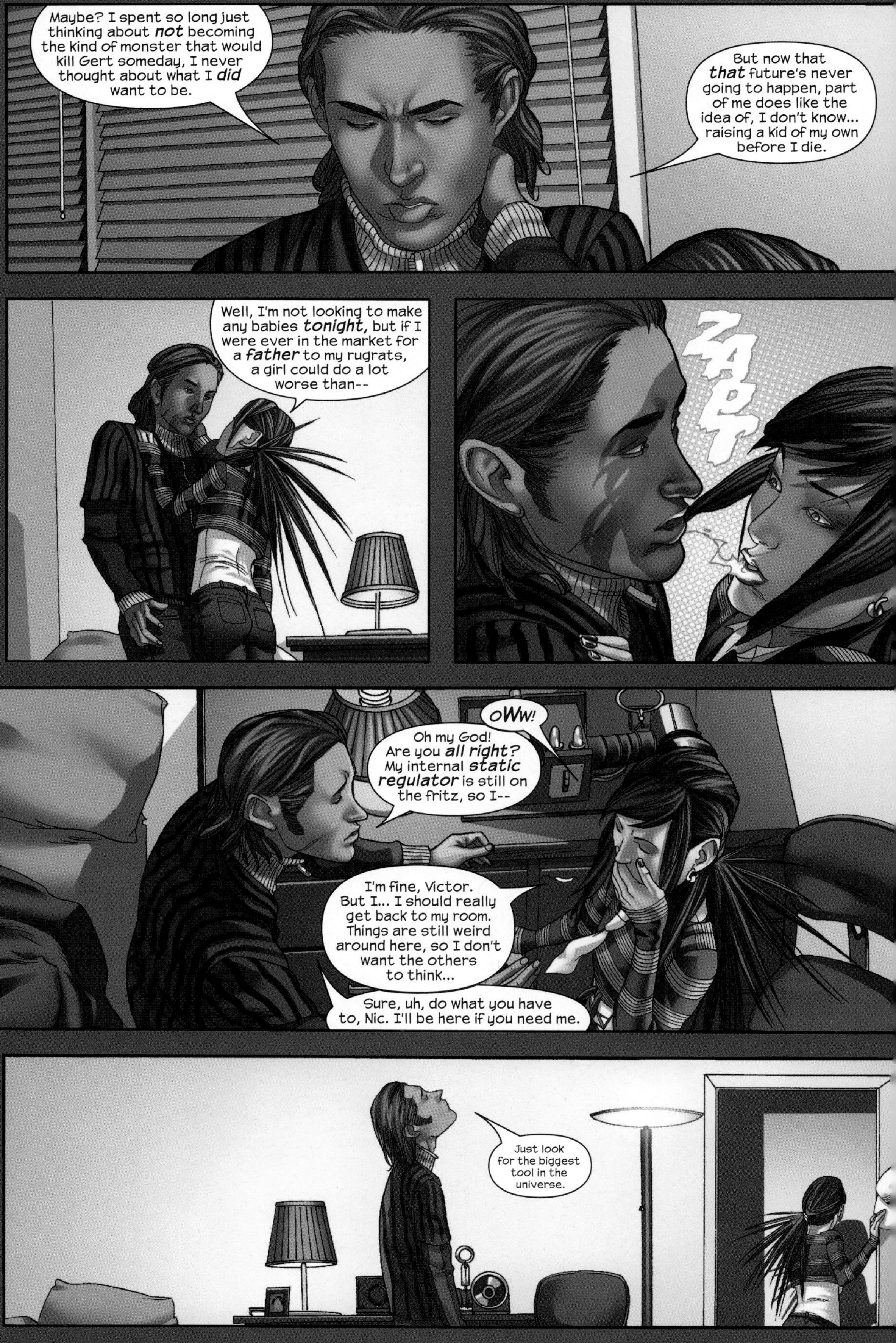
Maybe? I spent so long just thinking about **not** becoming the kind of monster that would kill Gert someday, I never thought about what I **did** want to be.
But now that **that** future's never going to happen, part of me does like the idea of, I don't know... raising a kid of my own before I die.
Well, I'm not looking to make any babies **tonight**, but if I were ever in the market for a **father** to my rugrats, a girl could do a lot worse than--
ZAPT
OWW!
Oh my God! Are you **all right**? My internal **static regulator** is still on the fritz, so I--
I'm fine, Victor. But I... I should really get back to my room. Things are still weird around here, so I don't want the others to think...
Sure, uh, do what you have to, Nic. I'll be here if you need me.
Just look for the biggest tool in the universe.

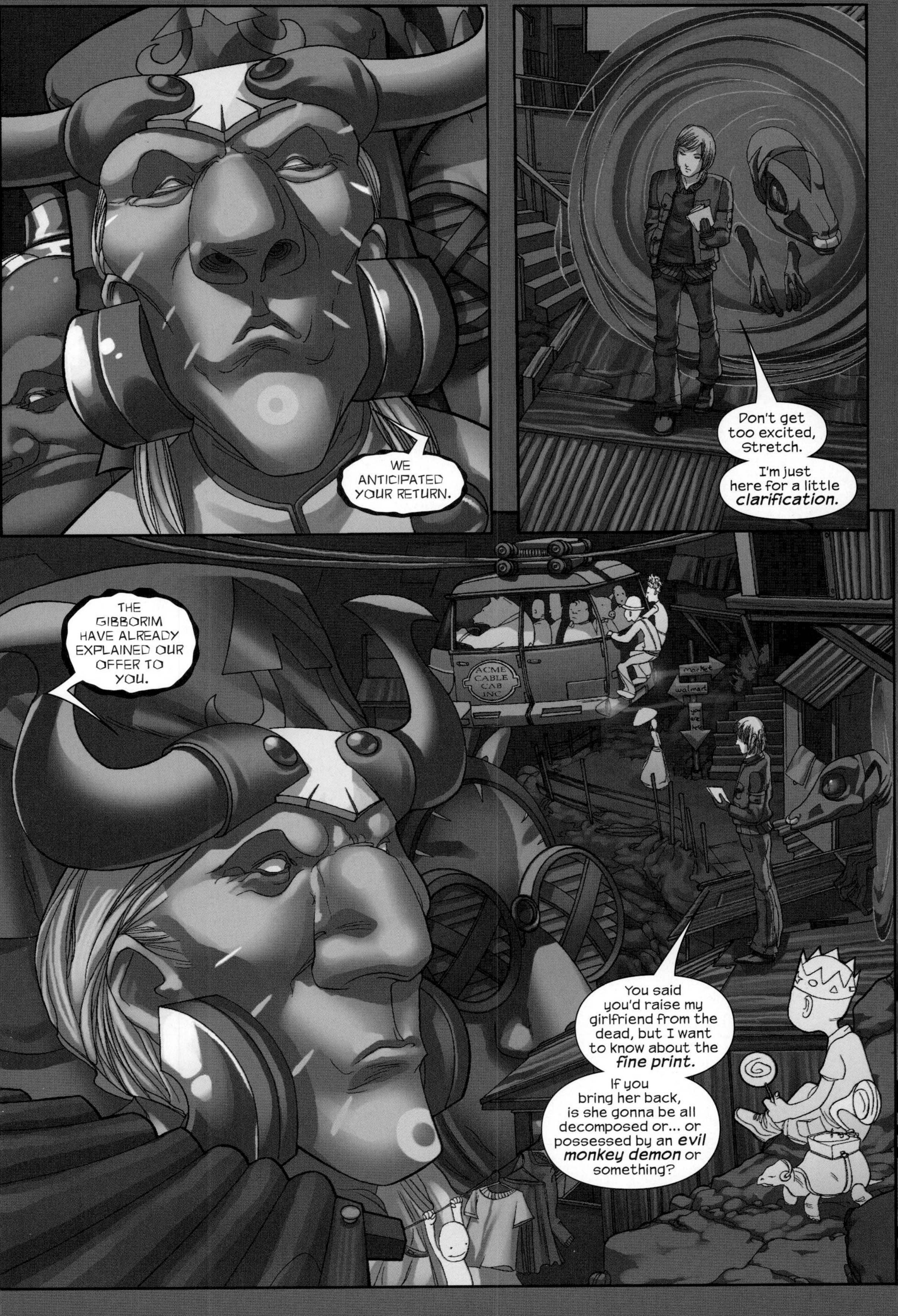
WE ANTICIPATED YOUR RETURN.
Don't get too excited, Stretch.
I'm just here for a little *clarification.*
THE GIBBORIM HAVE ALREADY EXPLAINED OUR OFFER TO *YOU.*
ACME CABLE CAB INC
market
walmart
You said you'd raise my girlfriend from the dead, but I want to know about the *fine print.*
If you bring her back, is she gonna be all decomposed or... or possessed by an *evil monkey demon* or something?

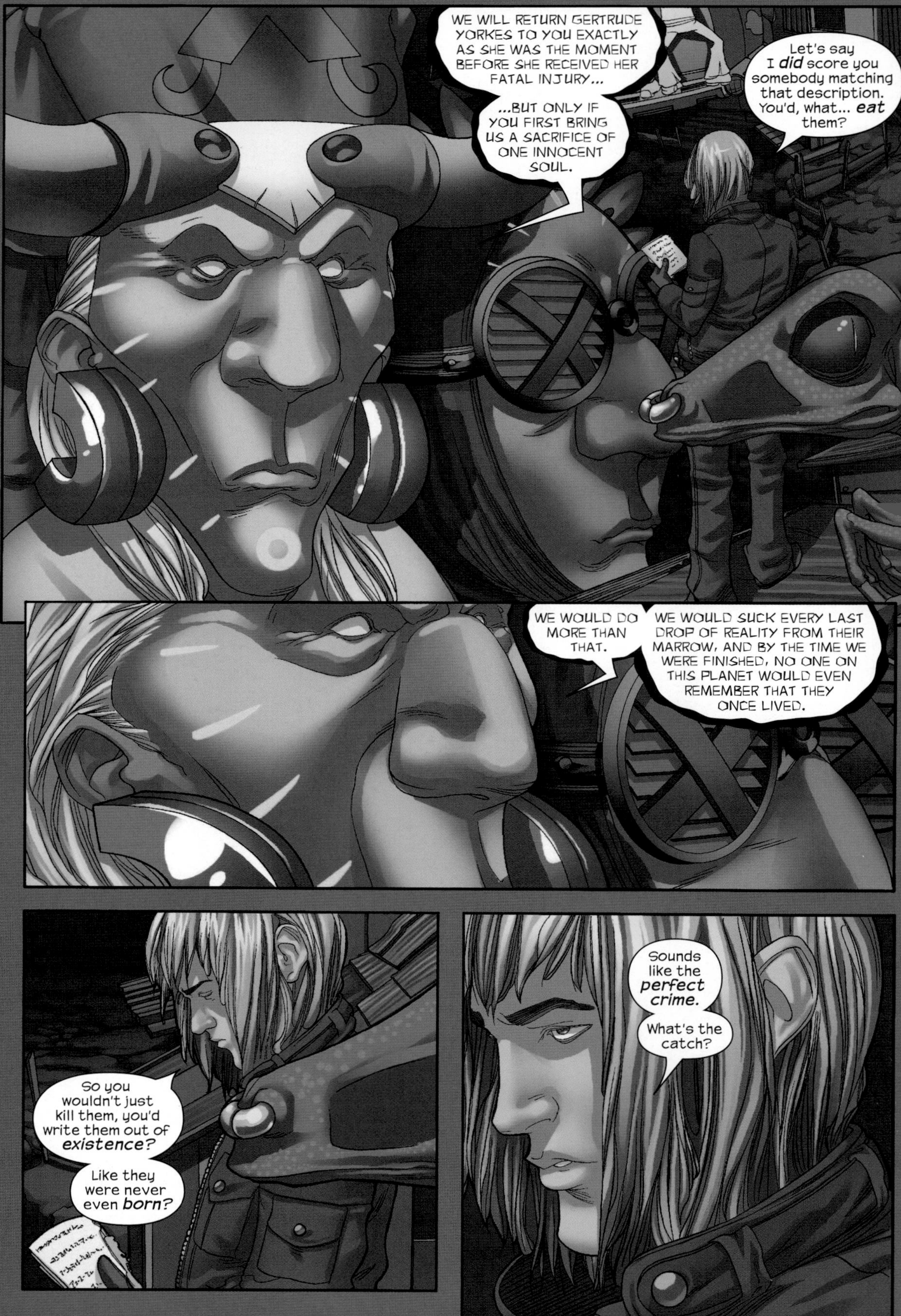
WE WILL RETURN GERTRUDE YORKES TO YOU EXACTLY AS SHE WAS THE MOMENT BEFORE SHE RECEIVED HER FATAL INJURY...
...BUT ONLY IF YOU FIRST BRING US A SACRIFICE OF ONE INNOCENT SOUL.
Let's say I *did* score you somebody matching that description. You'd, what... *eat* them?
WE WOULD DO MORE THAN THAT.
WE WOULD SUCK EVERY LAST DROP OF REALITY FROM THEIR MARROW, AND BY THE TIME WE WERE FINISHED, NO ONE ON THIS PLANET WOULD EVEN REMEMBER THAT THEY ONCE LIVED.
So you wouldn't just kill them, you'd write them out of *existence*?
Like they were never even *born*?
Sounds like the *perfect crime.*
What's the catch?

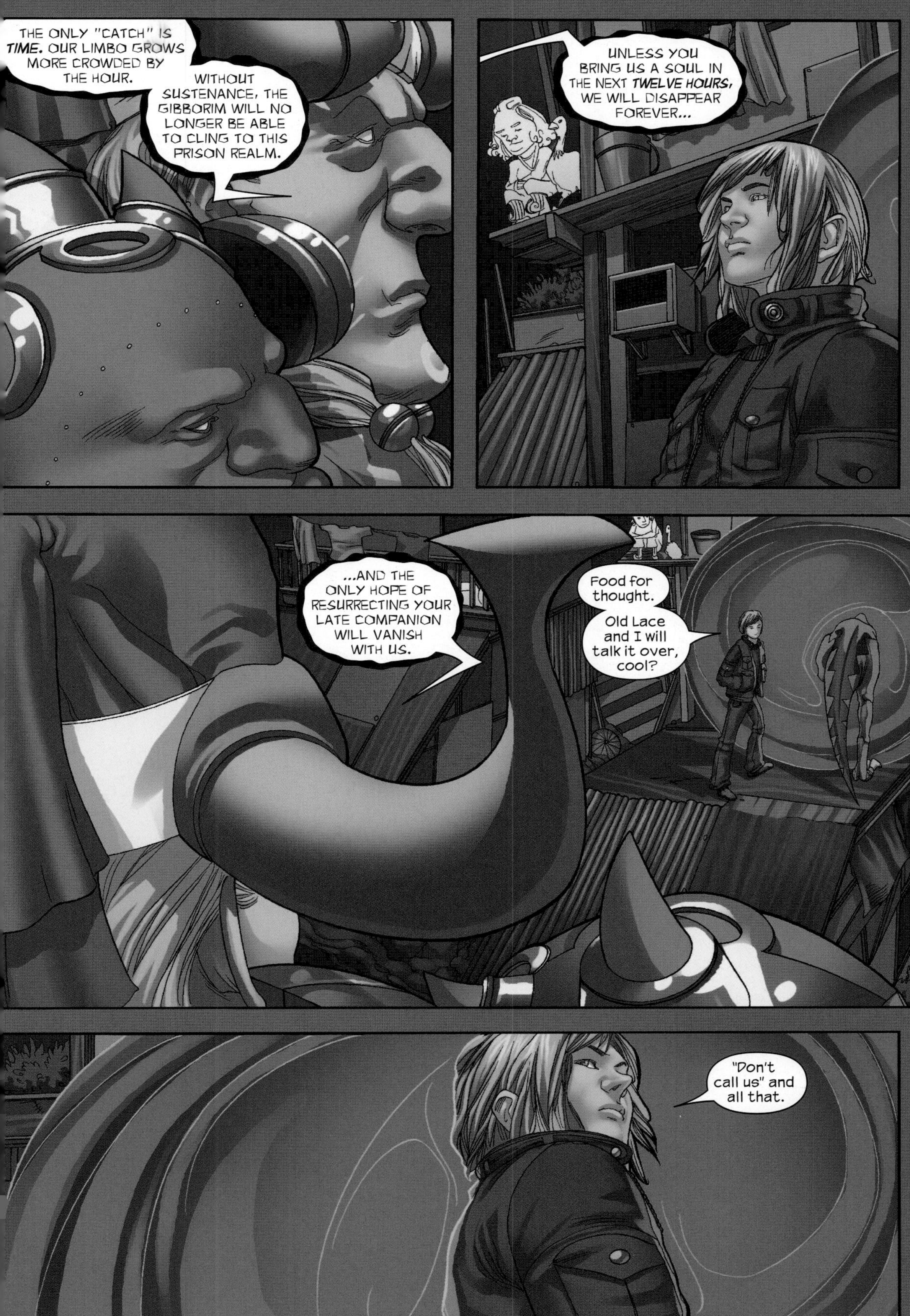
THE ONLY "CATCH" IS TIME. OUR LIMBO GROWS MORE CROWDED BY THE HOUR.
WITHOUT SUSTENANCE, THE GIBBORIM WILL NO LONGER BE ABLE TO CLING TO THIS PRISON REALM.
UNLESS YOU BRING US A SOUL IN THE NEXT TWELVE HOURS, WE WILL DISAPPEAR FOREVER...
...AND THE ONLY HOPE OF RESURRECTING YOUR LATE COMPANION WILL VANISH WITH US.
Food for thought.
Old Lace and I will talk it over, cool?
"Don't call us" and all that.

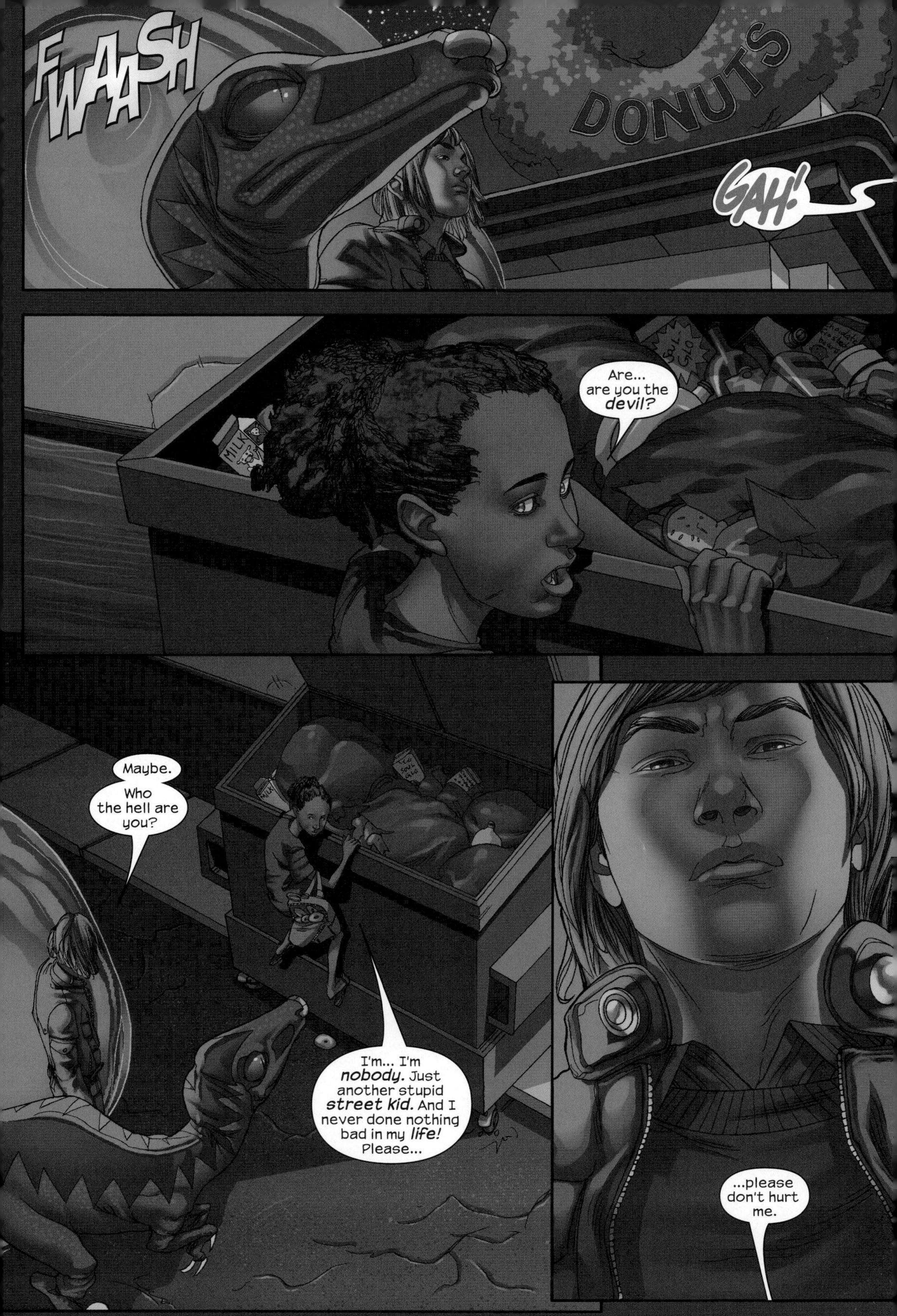
FWAASH
DONUTS
GAH!
Are... are you the *devil?*
Maybe.
Who the hell are you?
I'm... I'm *nobody.* Just another stupid *street kid.* And I never done nothing bad in my *life!* Please...
...please don't hurt me.

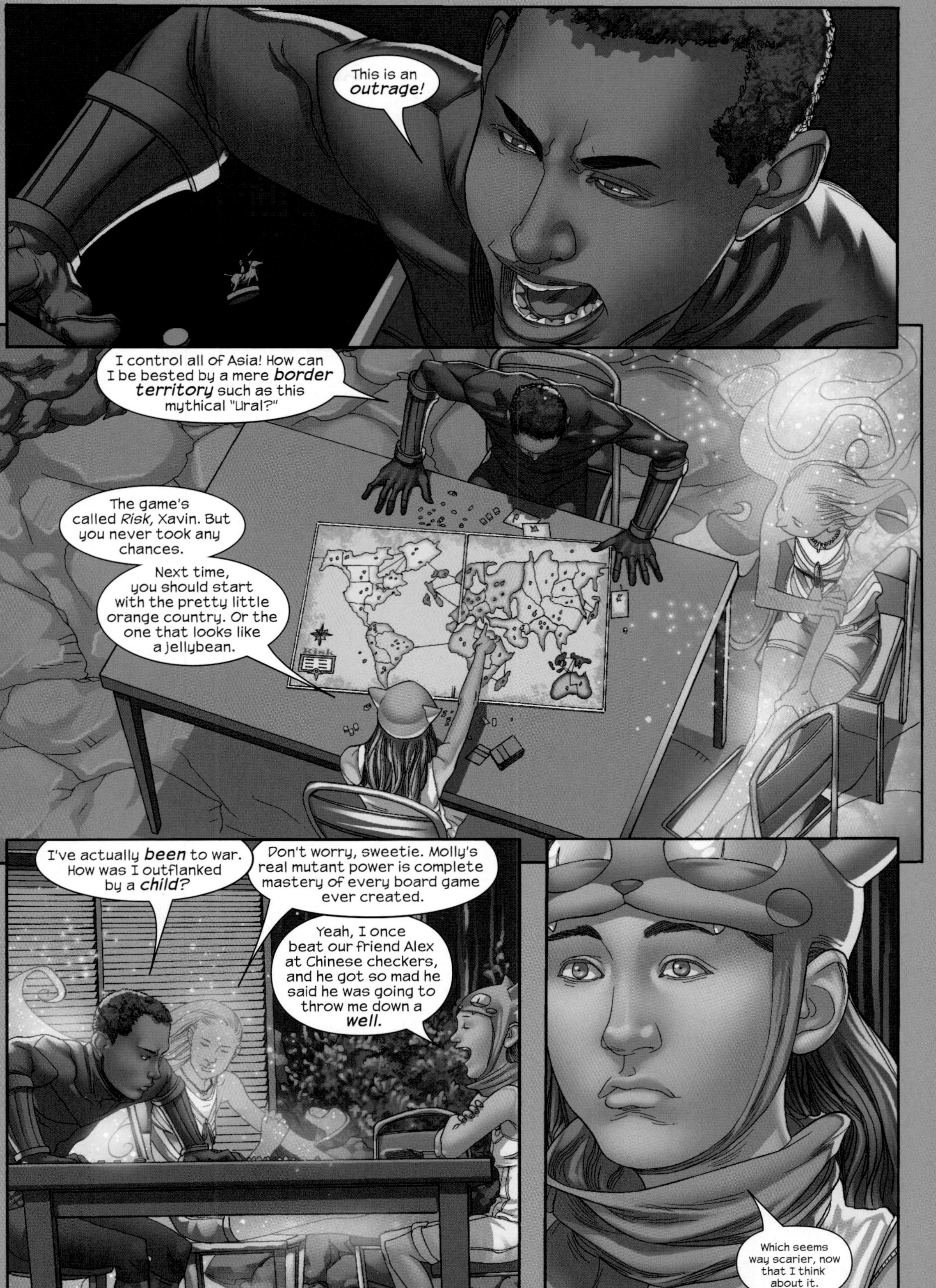
This is an *outrage!*
I control all of Asia! How can I be bested by a mere **border territory** such as this mythical "Ural?"
The game's called *Risk,* Xavin. But you never took any chances.
Next time, you should start with the pretty little orange country. Or the one that looks like a jellybean.
Risk
I've actually **been** to war. How was I outflanked by a **child?**
Don't worry, sweetie. Molly's real mutant power is complete mastery of every board game ever created.
Yeah, I once beat our friend Alex at Chinese checkers, and he got so mad he said he was going to throw me down a **well.**
Which seems way scarier, now that I think about it.

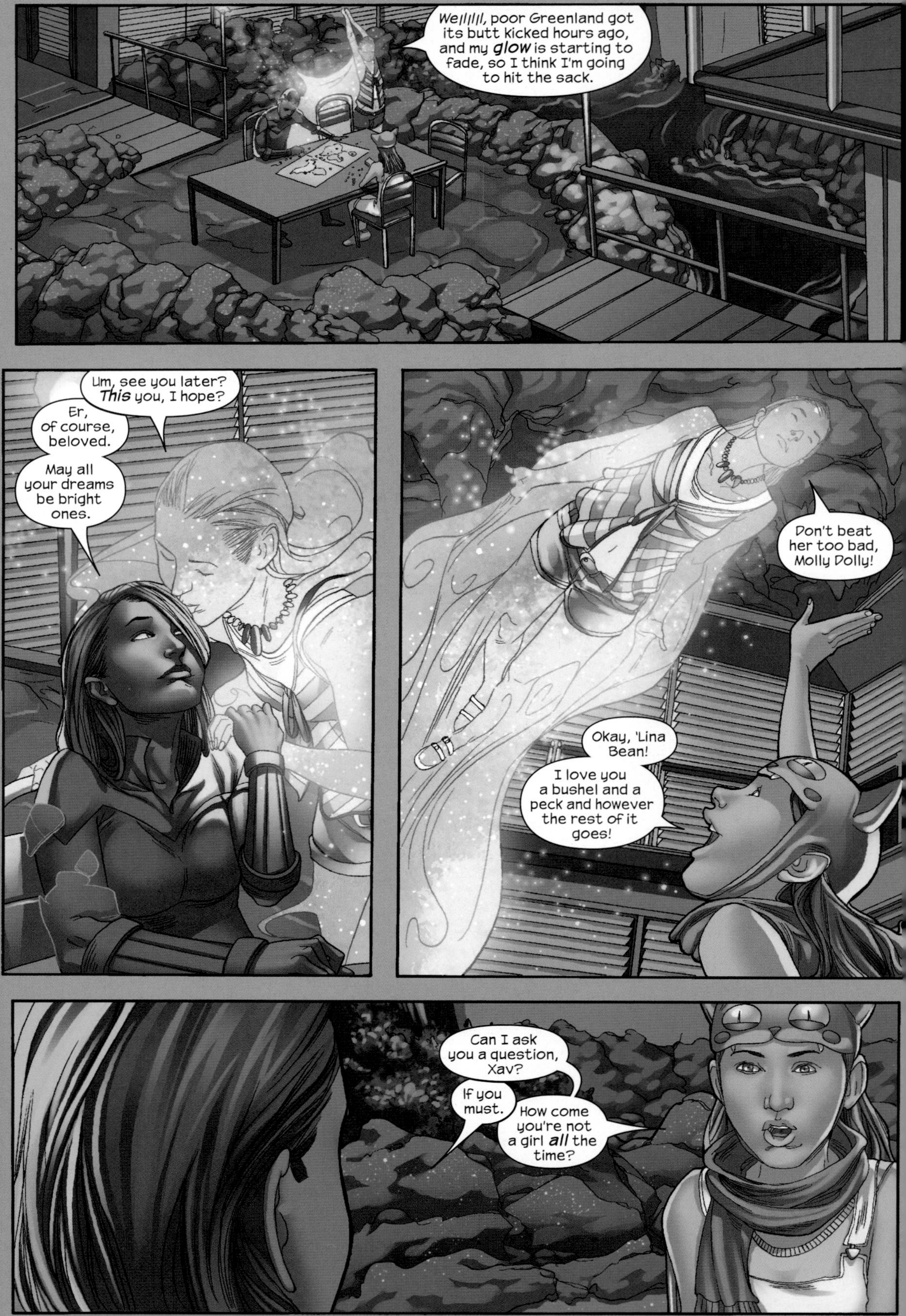
Wellllll, poor Greenland got its butt kicked hours ago, and my *glow* is starting to fade, so I think I'm going to hit the sack.
Um, see you later? *This* you, I hope?
Er, of course, beloved.
May all your dreams be bright ones.
Don't beat her too bad, Molly Dolly!
Okay, 'Lina Bean!
I love you a bushel and a peck and however the rest of it goes!
Can I ask you a question, Xav?
If you must.
How come you're not a girl *all* the time?

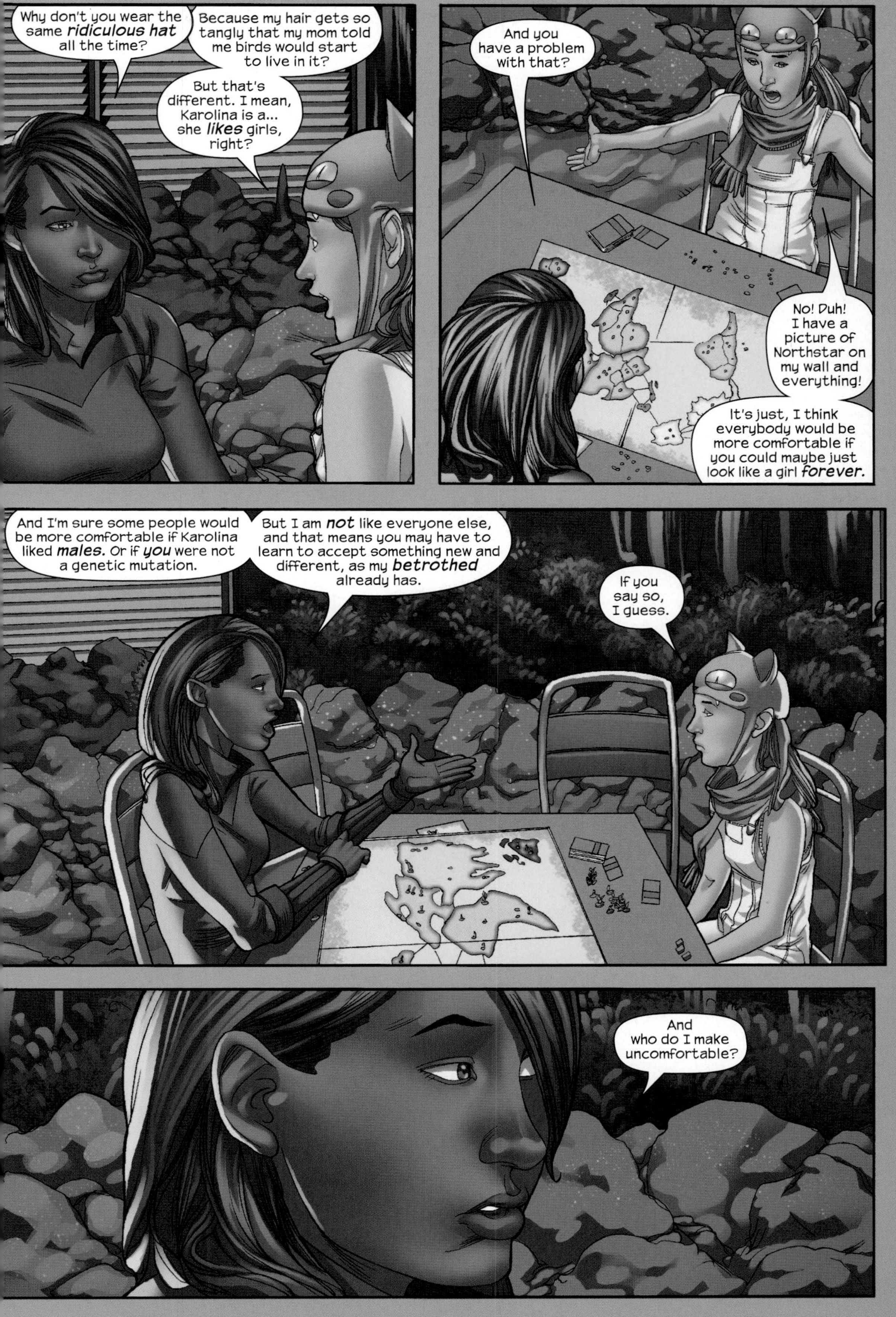

Why don't you wear the same ridiculous hat all the time?
Because my hair gets so tangly that my mom told me birds would start to live in it?
But that's different. I mean, Karolina is a... she likes girls, right?
And you have a problem with that?
No! Duh! I have a picture of Northstar on my wall and everything!
It's just, I think everybody would be more comfortable if you could maybe just look like a girl forever.
And I'm sure some people would be more comfortable if Karolina liked males. Or if you were not a genetic mutation.
But I am not like everyone else, and that means you may have to learn to accept something new and different, as my betrothed already has.
If you say so, I guess.
And who do I make uncomfortable?

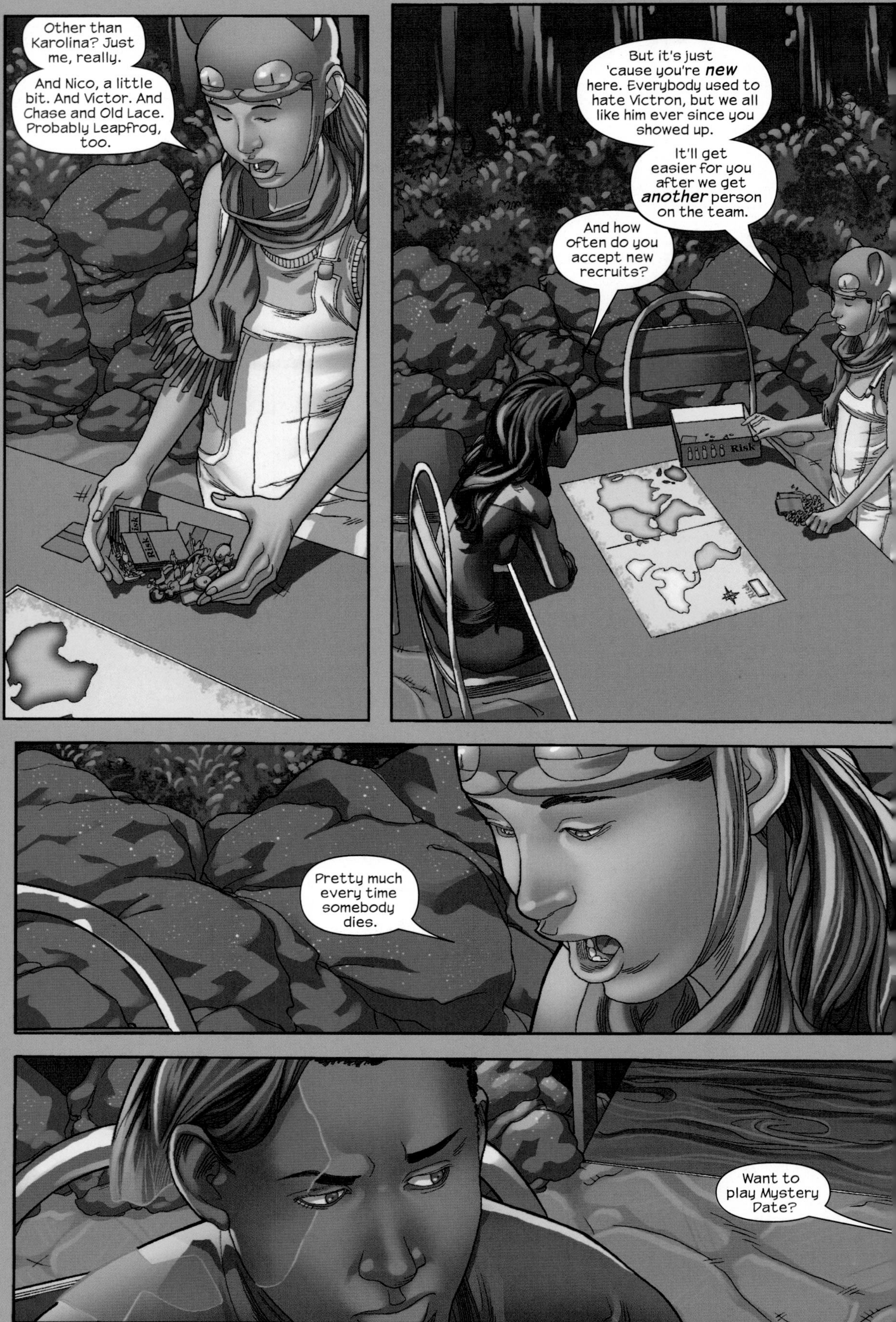

Other than Karolina? Just me, really.
And Nico, a little bit. And Victor. And Chase and Old Lace. Probably Leapfrog, too.
But it's just 'cause you're **new** here. Everybody used to hate Victron, but we all like him ever since you showed up.
It'll get easier for you after we get **another** person on the team.
And how often do you accept new recruits?
Risk
Pretty much every time somebody dies.
Want to play Mystery Date?

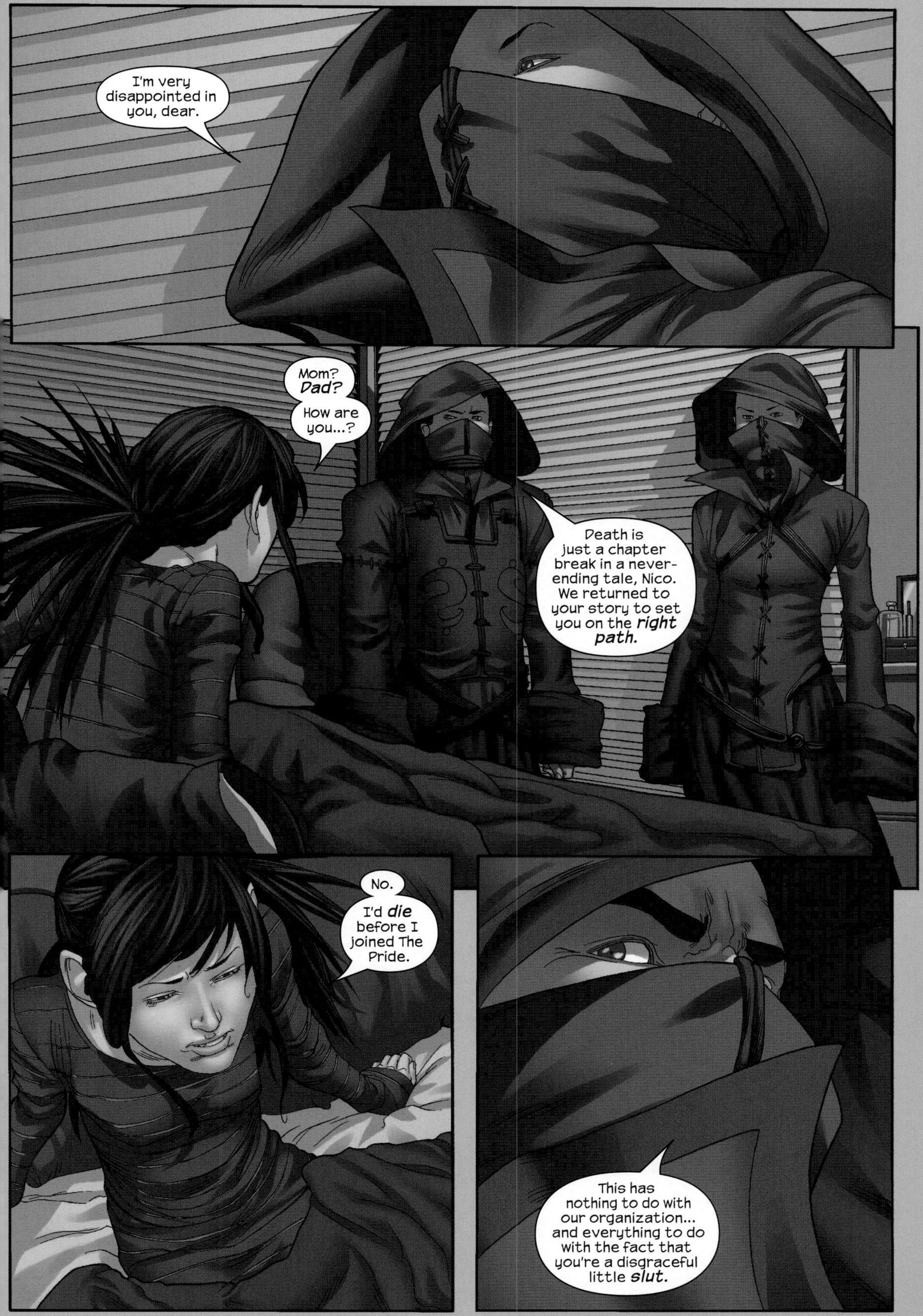

I'm very disappointed in you, dear.
Mom? Dad?
How are you...?
Death is just a chapter break in a never-ending tale, Nico. We returned to your story to set you on the right path.
No.
I'd die before I joined The Pride.
This has nothing to do with our organization... and everything to do with the fact that you're a disgraceful little slut.

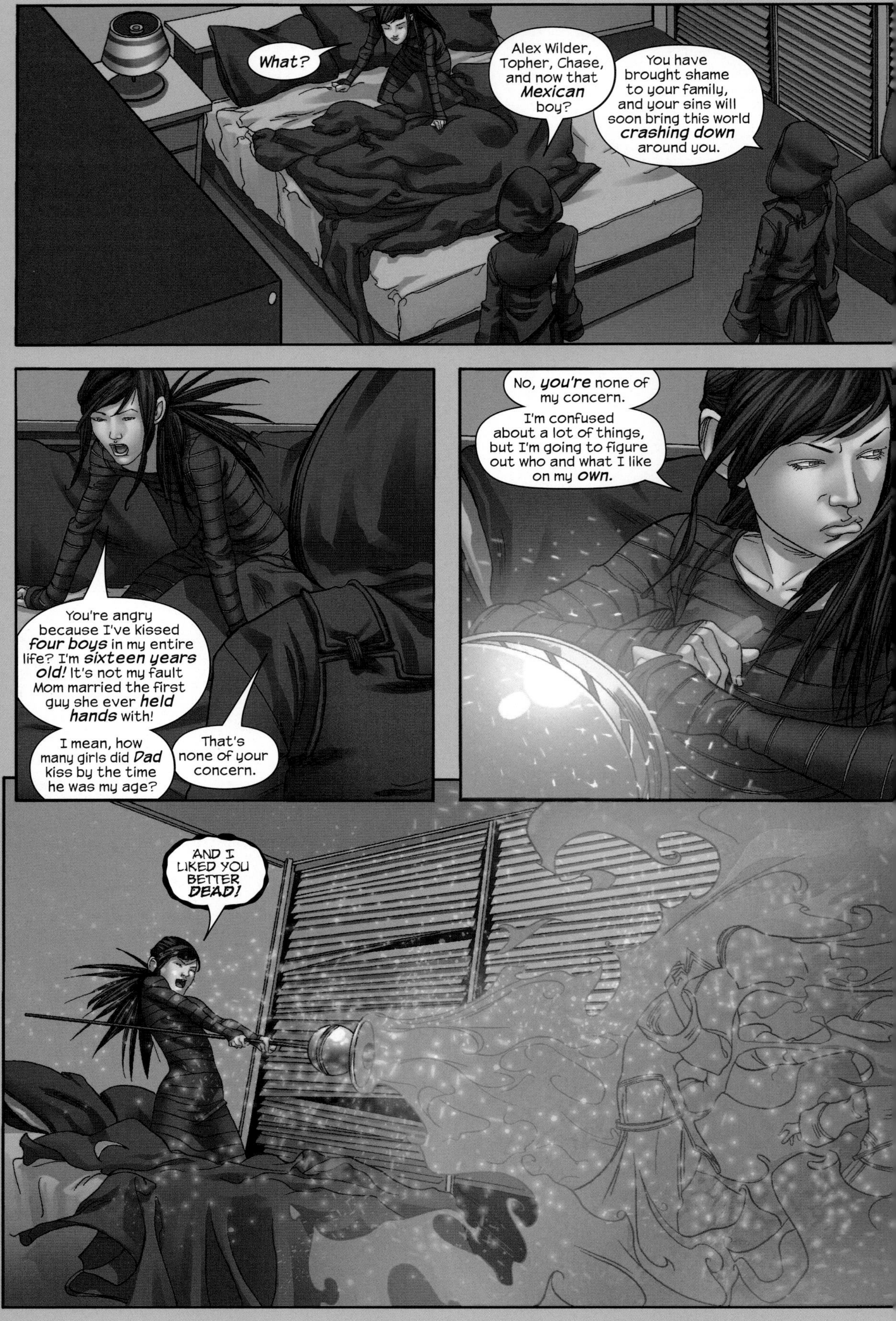
What?
Alex Wilder, Topher, Chase, and now that Mexican boy?
You have brought shame to your family, and your sins will soon bring this world crashing down around you.
You're angry because I've kissed four boys in my entire life? I'm sixteen years old! It's not my fault Mom married the first guy she ever held hands with!
I mean, how many girls did Dad kiss by the time he was my age?
That's none of your concern.
No, you're none of my concern.
I'm confused about a lot of things, but I'm going to figure out who and what I like on my own.
AND I LIKED YOU BETTER DEAD!

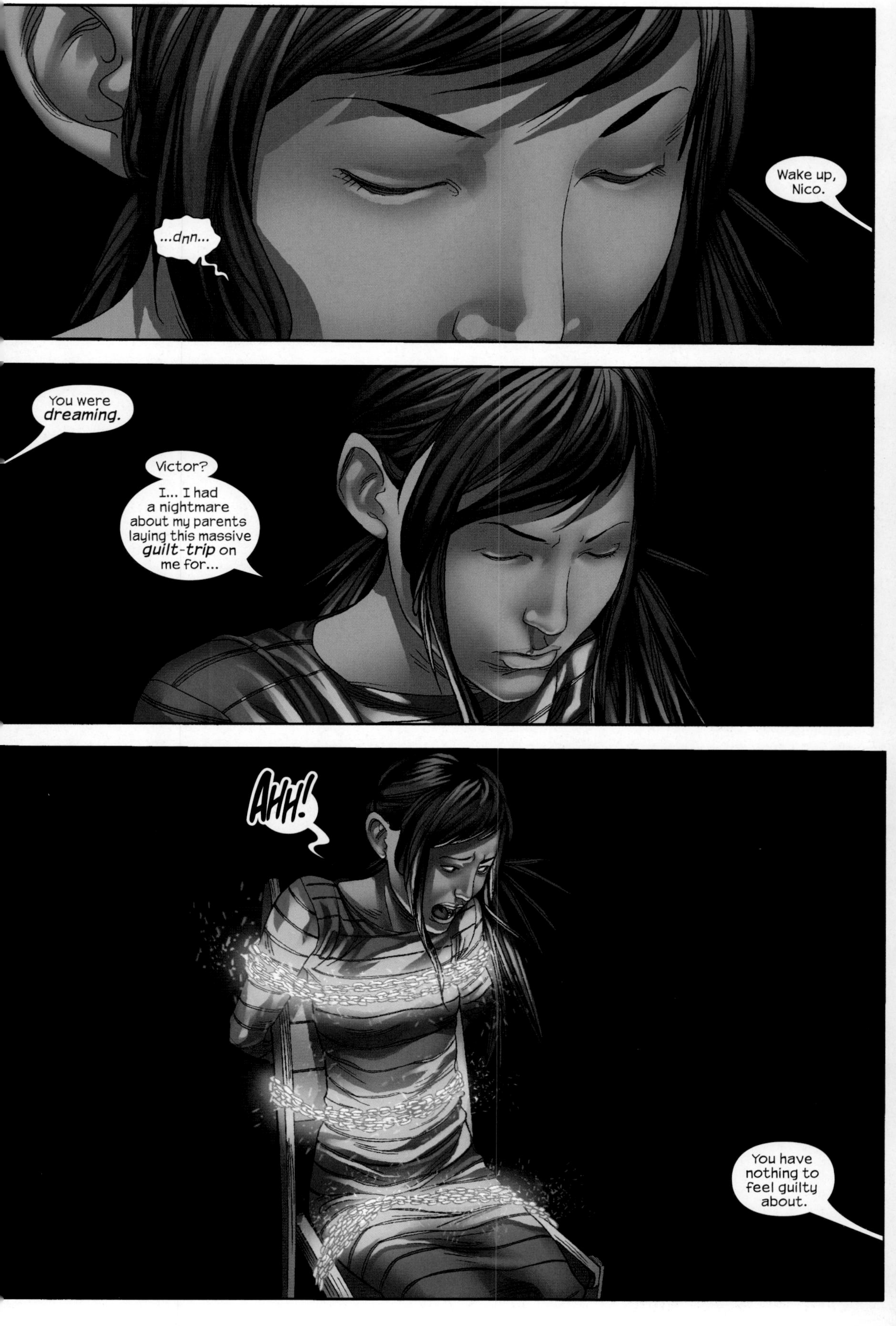
Wake up, Nico.
...dnn...
You were dreaming.
Victor?
I... I had a nightmare about my parents laying this massive guilt-trip on me for...
AHH!
You have nothing to feel guilty about.

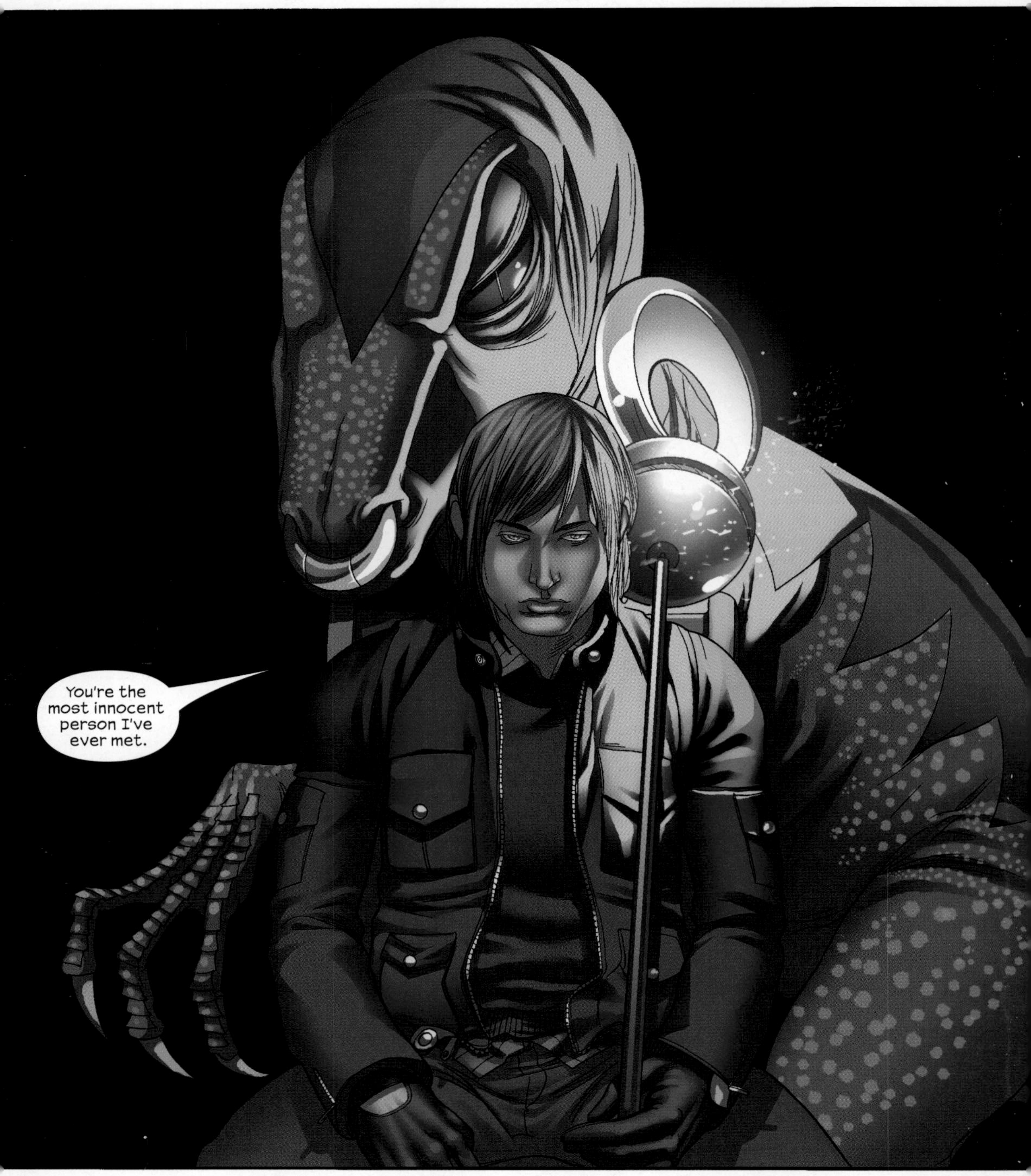
You're the most innocent person I've ever met.

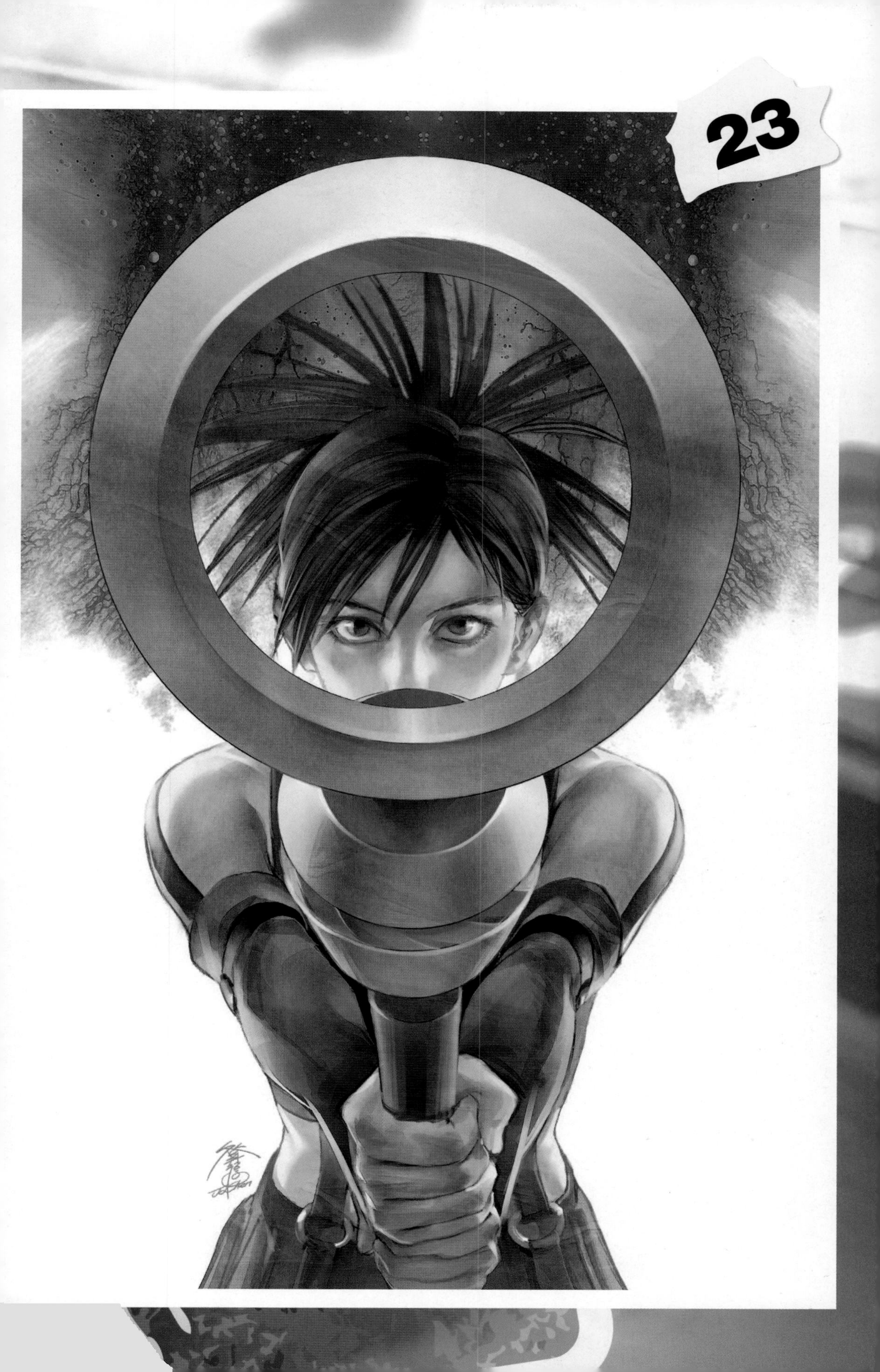
23

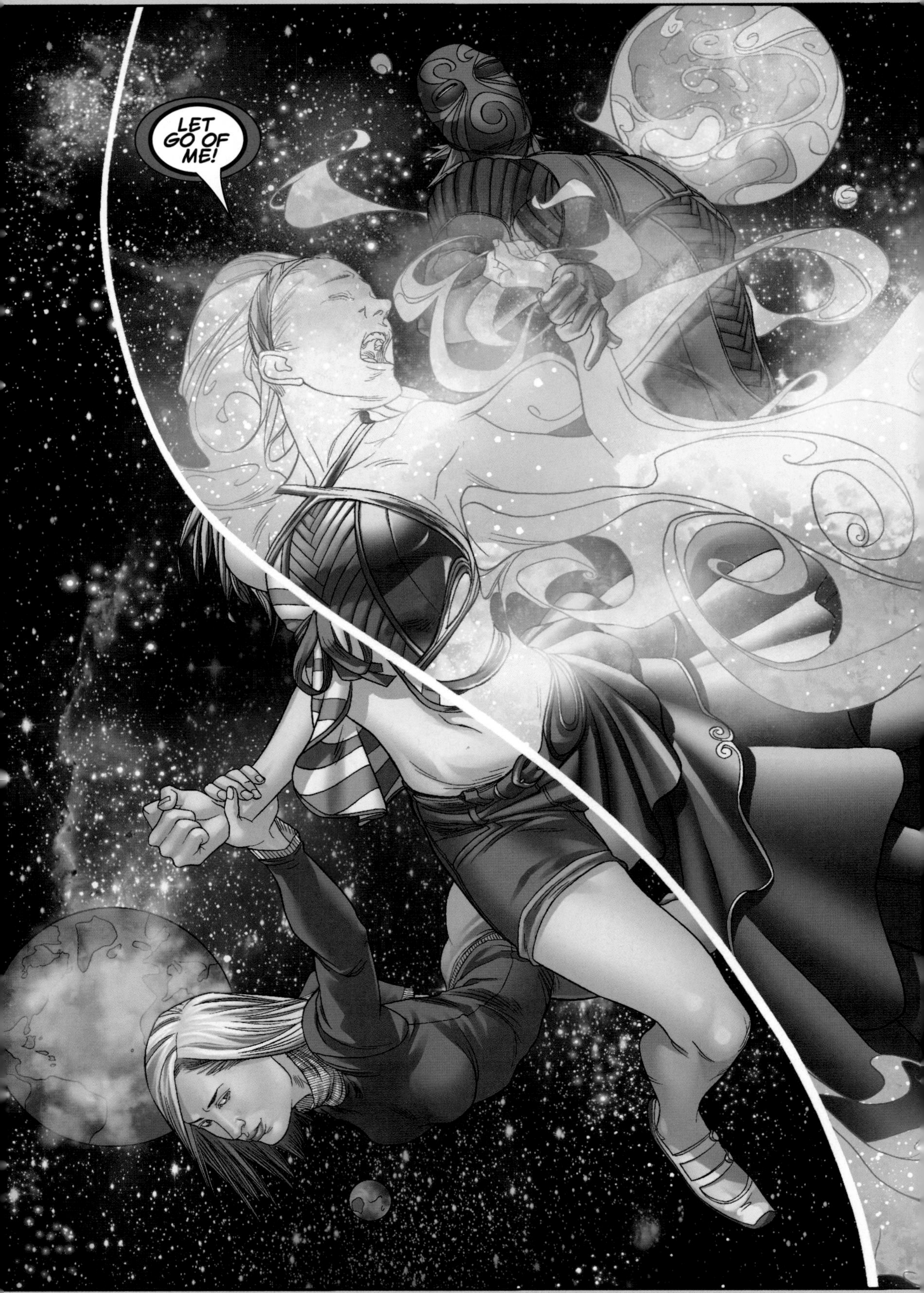
LET GO OF ME!

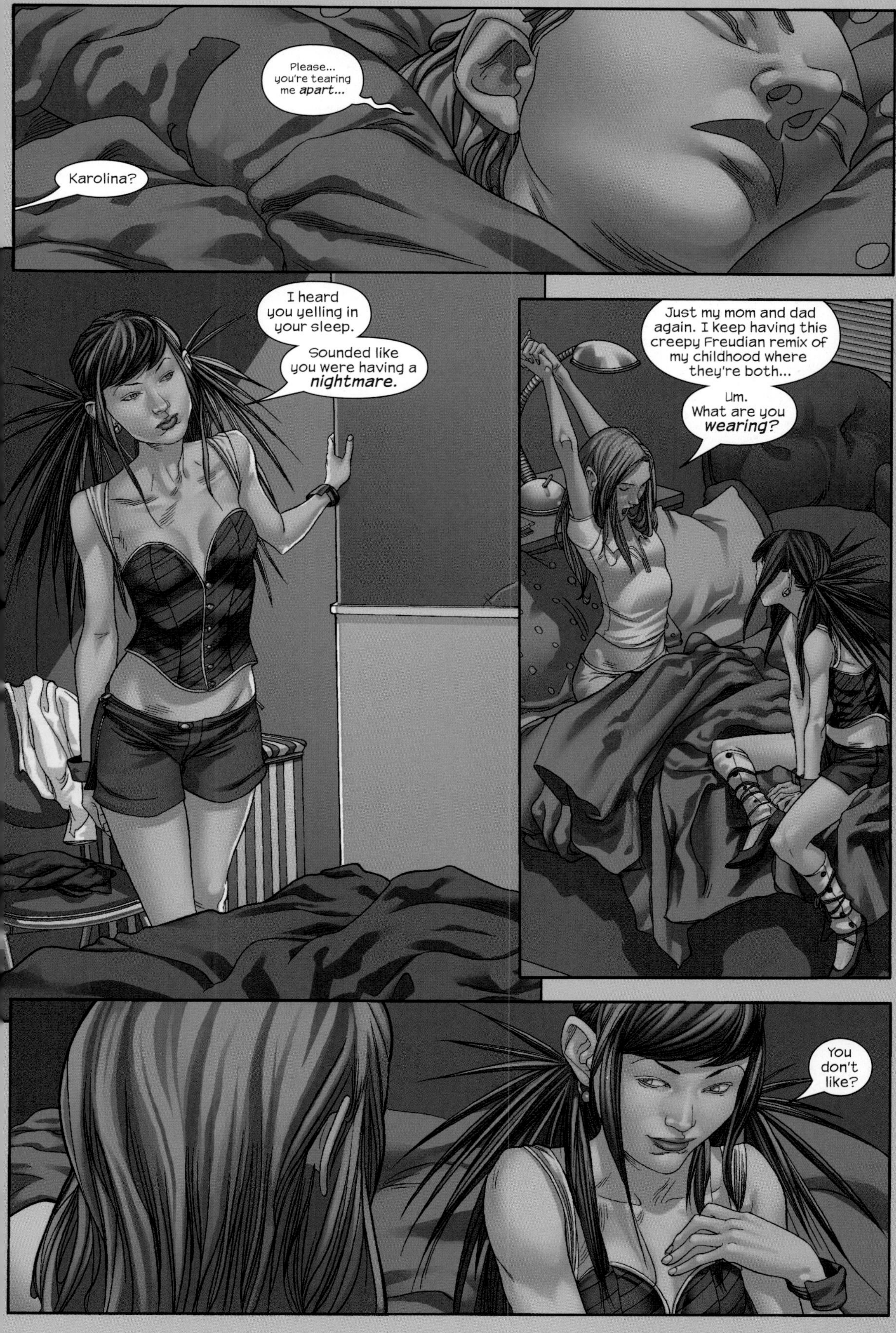

Please... you're tearing me *apart...*
Karolina?
I heard you yelling in your sleep.
Sounded like you were having a *nightmare.*
Just my mom and dad again. I keep having this creepy Freudian remix of my childhood where they're both...
Um. What are you *wearing?*
You don't like?

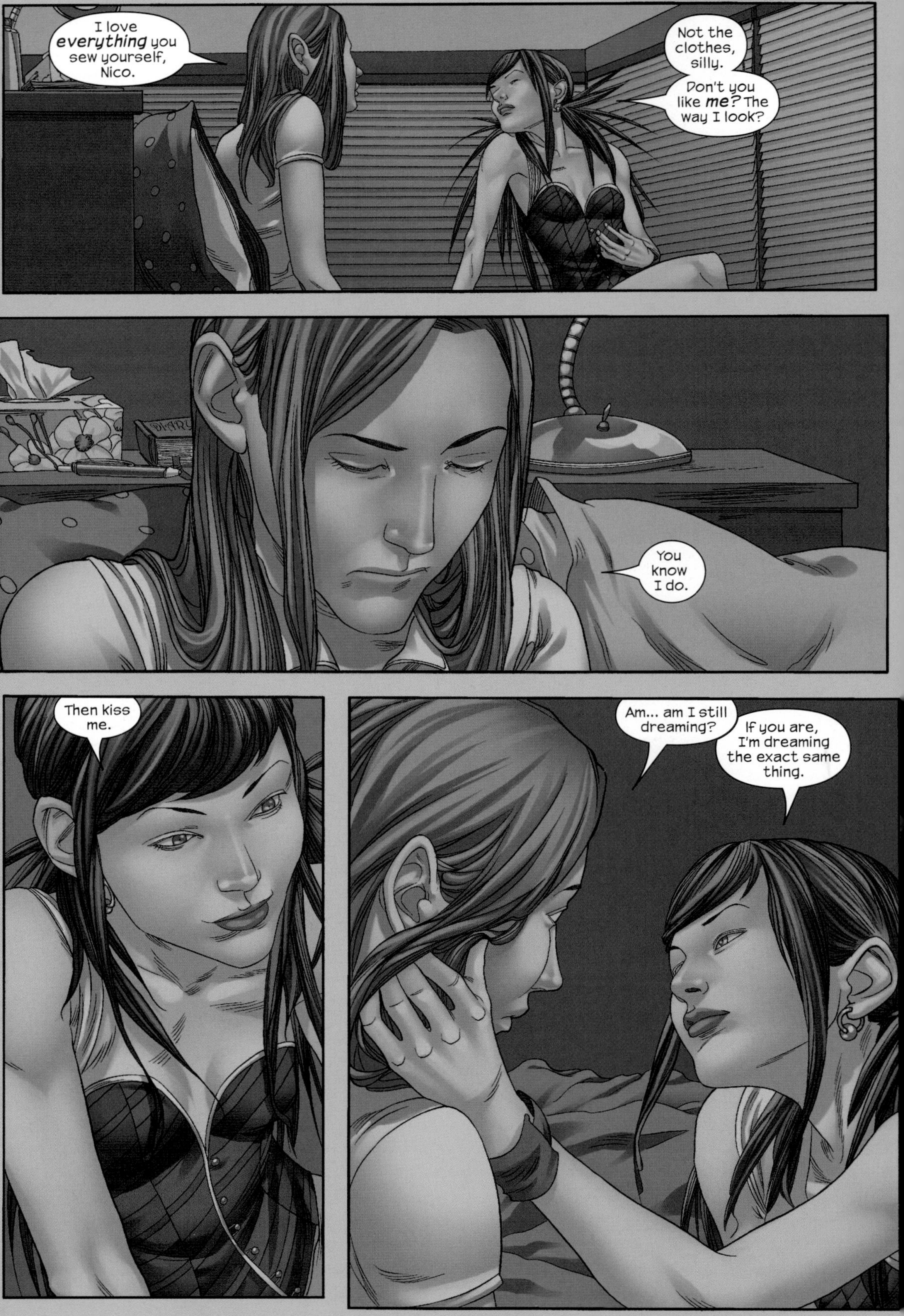
I love everything you sew yourself, Nico.
Not the clothes, silly.
Don't you like me? The way I look?
You know I do.
Then kiss me.
Am... am I still dreaming?
If you are, I'm dreaming the exact same thing.

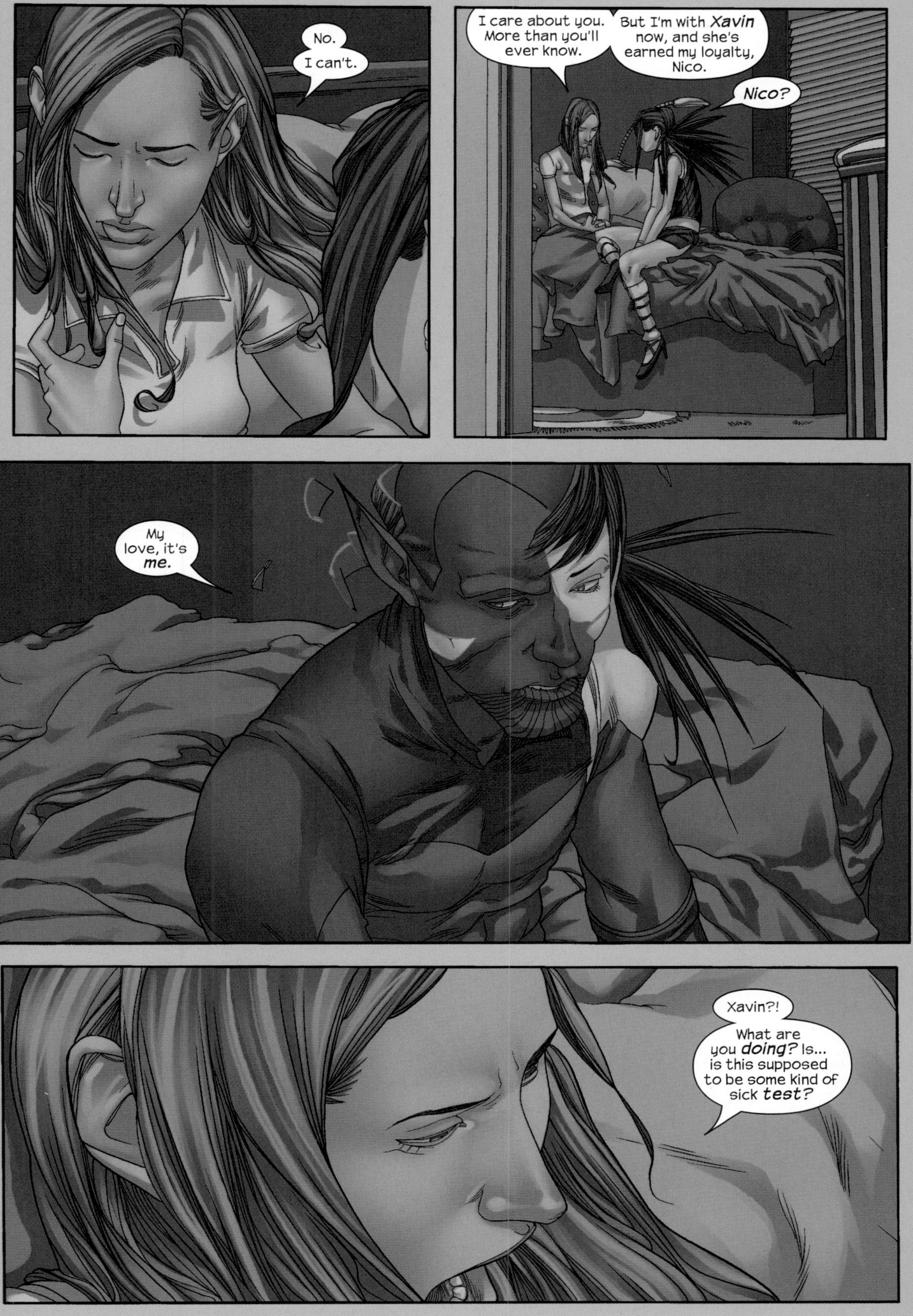
No.
I can't.
I care about you. More than you'll ever know.
But I'm with *Xavin* now, and she's earned my loyalty, Nico.
Nico?
My love, it's *me.*
Xavin?!
What are you *doing?* Is... is this supposed to be some kind of sick *test?*

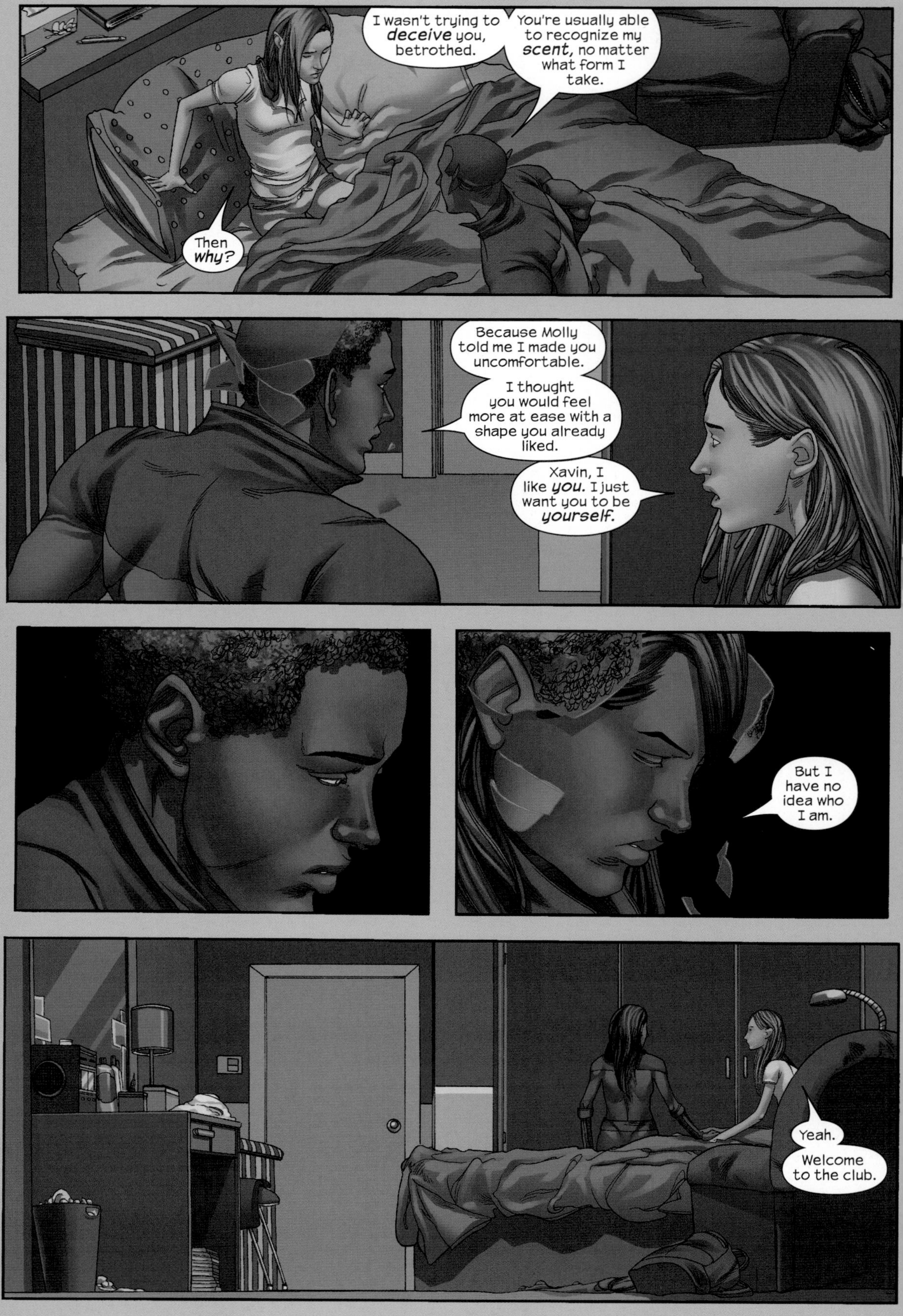
I wasn't trying to deceive you, betrothed.
You're usually able to recognize my scent, no matter what form I take.
Then why?
Because Molly told me I made you uncomfortable.
I thought you would feel more at ease with a shape you already liked.
Xavin, I like you. I just want you to be yourself.
But I have no idea who I am.
Yeah.
Welcome to the club.

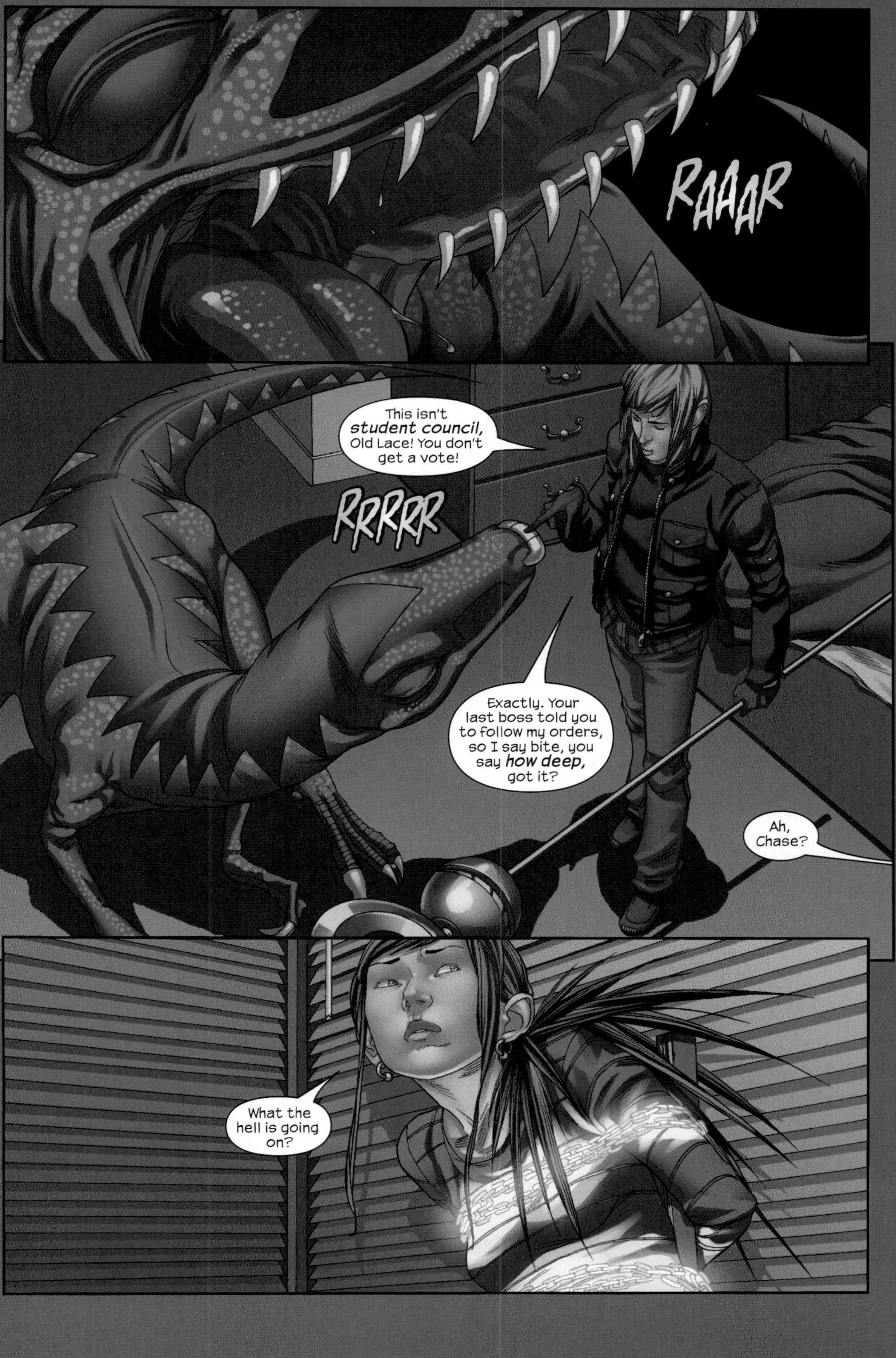
RAAAR
This isn't *student council,* Old Lace! You don't get a vote!
RRRRR
Exactly. Your last boss told you to follow my orders, so I say bite, you say *how deep,* got it?
Ah, Chase?
What the hell is going on?

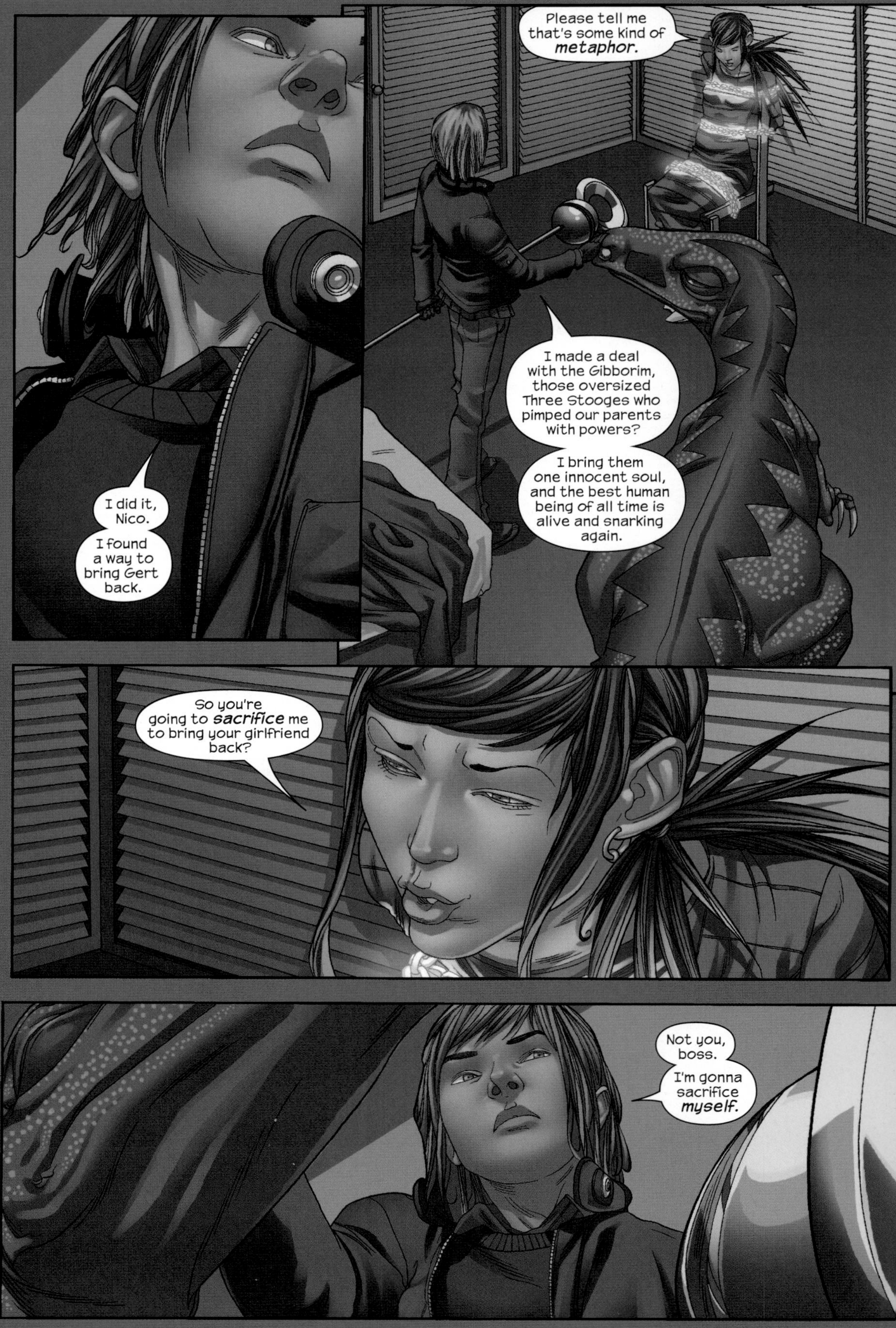
I did it, Nico.
I found a way to bring Gert back.
Please tell me that's some kind of *metaphor.*
I made a deal with the Gibborim, those oversized Three Stooges who pimped our parents with powers?
I bring them one innocent soul, and the best human being of all time is alive and snarking again.
So you're going to *sacrifice* me to bring your girlfriend back?
Not you, boss.
I'm gonna sacrifice *myself.*

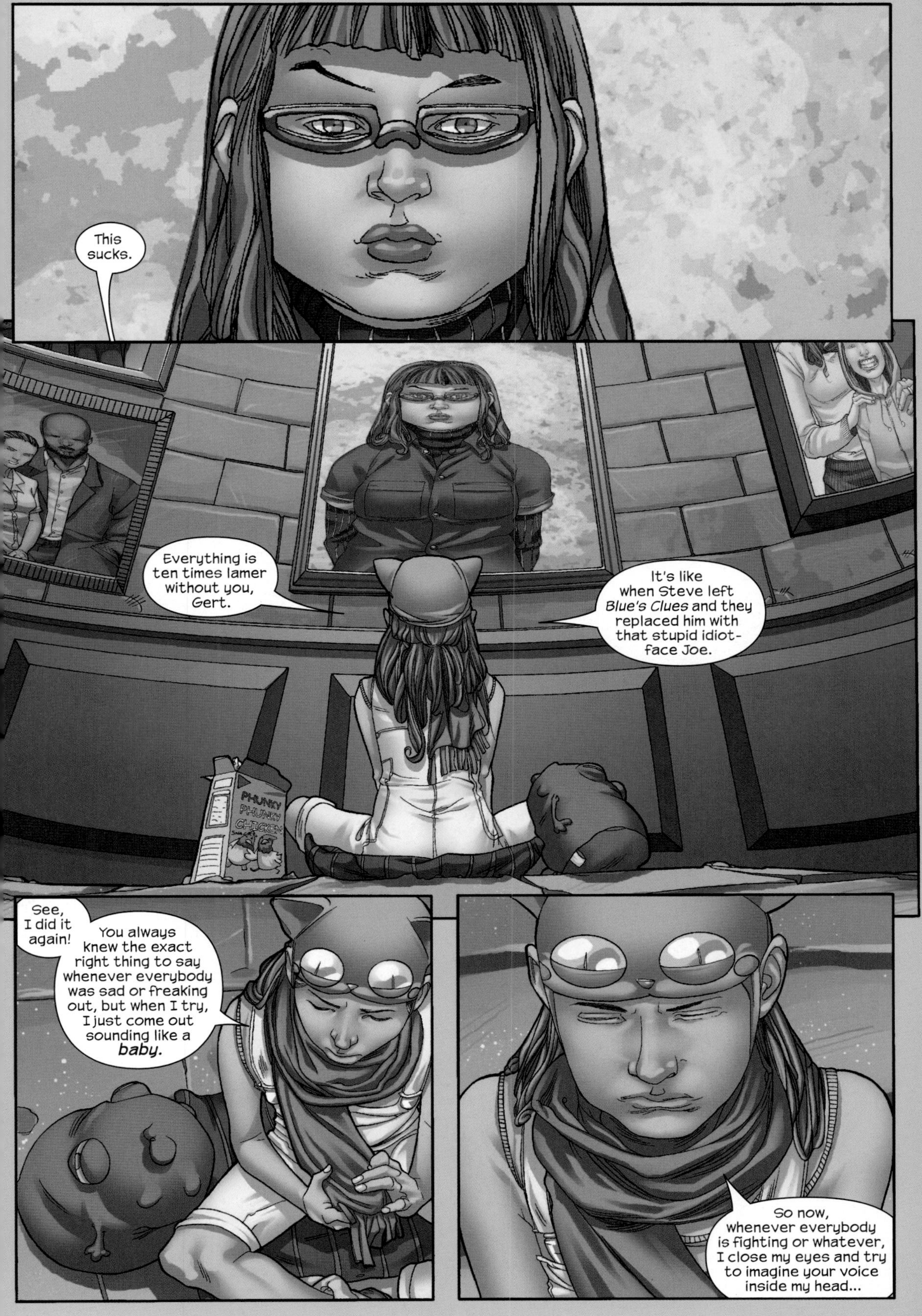
This sucks.
Everything is ten times lamer without you, Gert.
It's like when Steve left *Blue's Clues* and they replaced him with that stupid idiot-face Joe.
PHUNKY PHUNKY CHICKEN
See, I did it again!
You always knew the exact right thing to say whenever everybody was sad or freaking out, but when I try, I just come out sounding like a **baby.**
So now, whenever everybody is fighting or whatever, I close my eyes and try to imagine your voice inside my head...

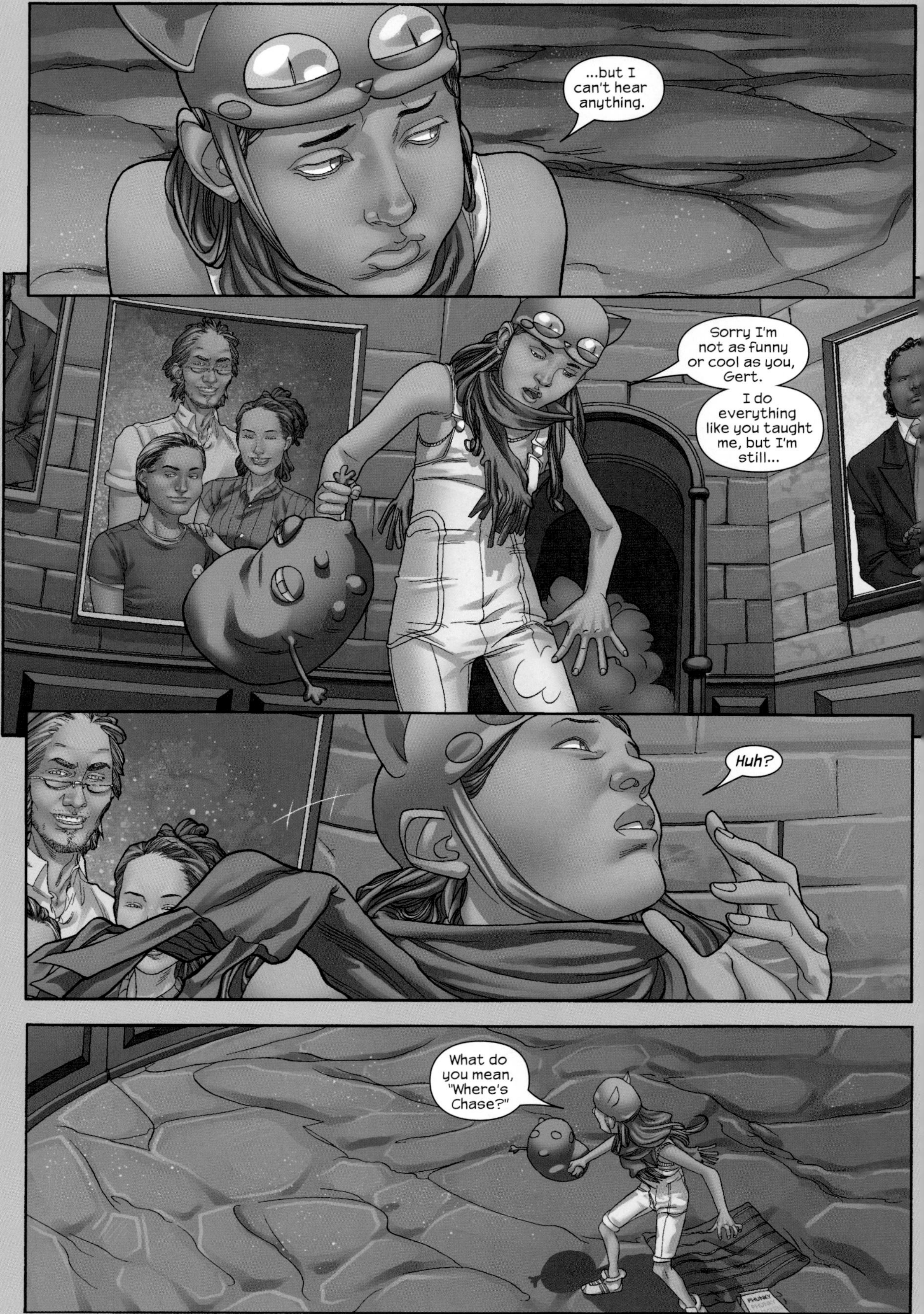
...but I can't hear anything.
Sorry I'm not as funny or cool as you, Gert.
I do everything like you taught me, but I'm still...
Huh?
What do you mean, "Where's Chase?"

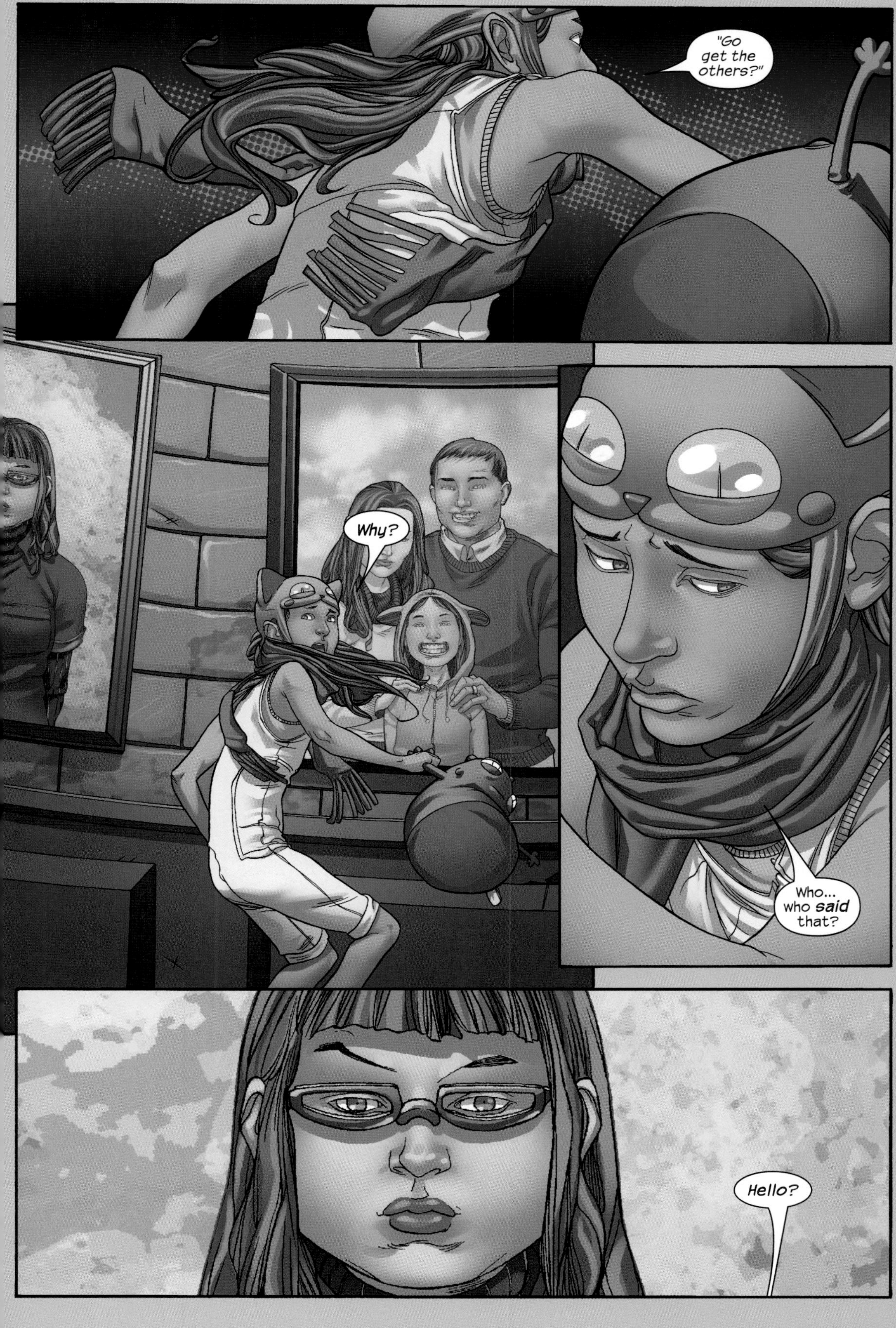
"Go get the others?"
Why?
Who... who said that?
Hello?

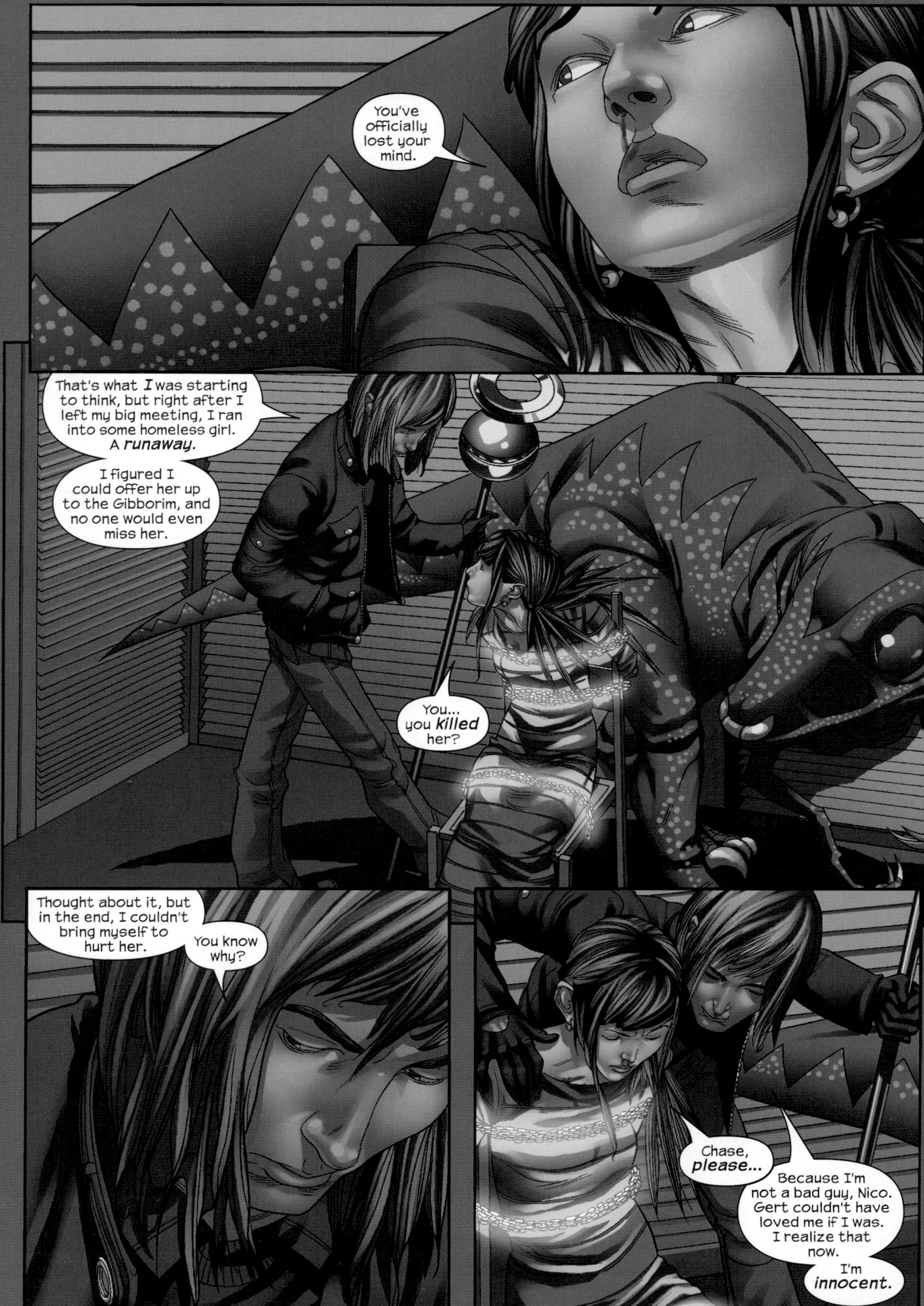
You've officially lost your mind.
That's what *I* was starting to think, but right after I left my big meeting, I ran into some homeless girl. A *runaway.*
I figured I could offer her up to the Gibborim, and no one would even miss her.
You... you *killed* her?
Thought about it, but in the end, I couldn't bring myself to hurt her.
You know why?
Chase, *please...*
Because I'm not a bad guy, Nico. Gert couldn't have loved me if I was. I realize that now.
I'm *innocent.*

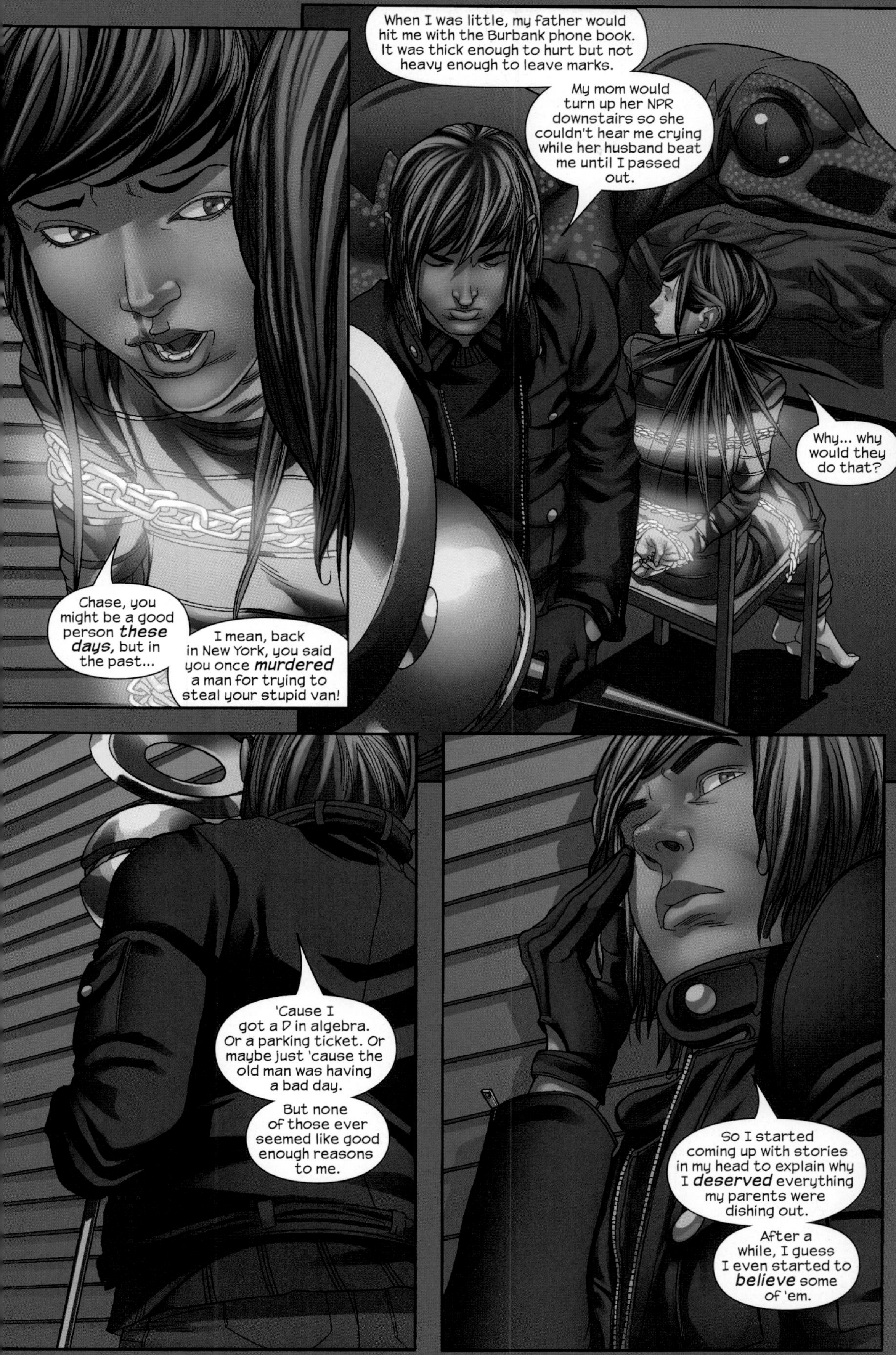
When I was little, my father would hit me with the Burbank phone book. It was thick enough to hurt but not heavy enough to leave marks.
My mom would turn up her NPR downstairs so she couldn't hear me crying while her husband beat me until I passed out.
Why... why would they do that?
Chase, you might be a good person these days, but in the past...
I mean, back in New York, you said you once murdered a man for trying to steal your stupid van!
'Cause I got a D in algebra. Or a parking ticket. Or maybe just 'cause the old man was having a bad day.
But none of those ever seemed like good enough reasons to me.
So I started coming up with stories in my head to explain why I deserved everything my parents were dishing out.
After a while, I guess I even started to believe some of 'em.

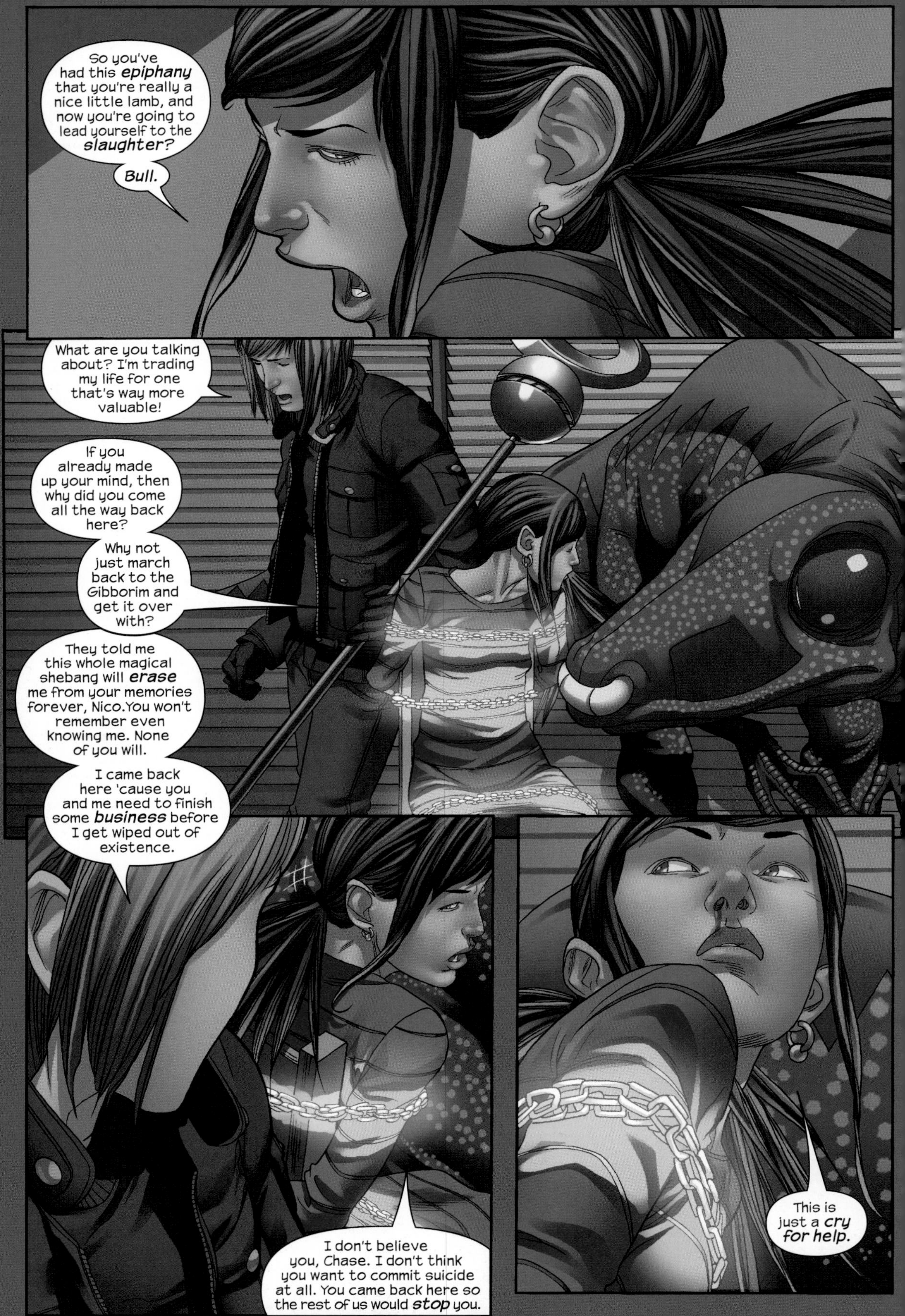
So you've had this *epiphany* that you're really a nice little lamb, and now you're going to lead yourself to the *slaughter*?
Bull.
What are you talking about? I'm trading my life for one that's way more valuable!
If you already made up your mind, then why did you come all the way back here?
Why not just march back to the Gibborim and get it over with?
They told me this whole magical shebang will *erase* me from your memories forever, Nico. You won't remember even knowing me. None of you will.
I came back here 'cause you and me need to finish some *business* before I get wiped out of existence.
I don't believe you, Chase. I don't think you want to commit suicide at all. You came back here so the rest of us would *stop* you.
This is just a *cry for help*.

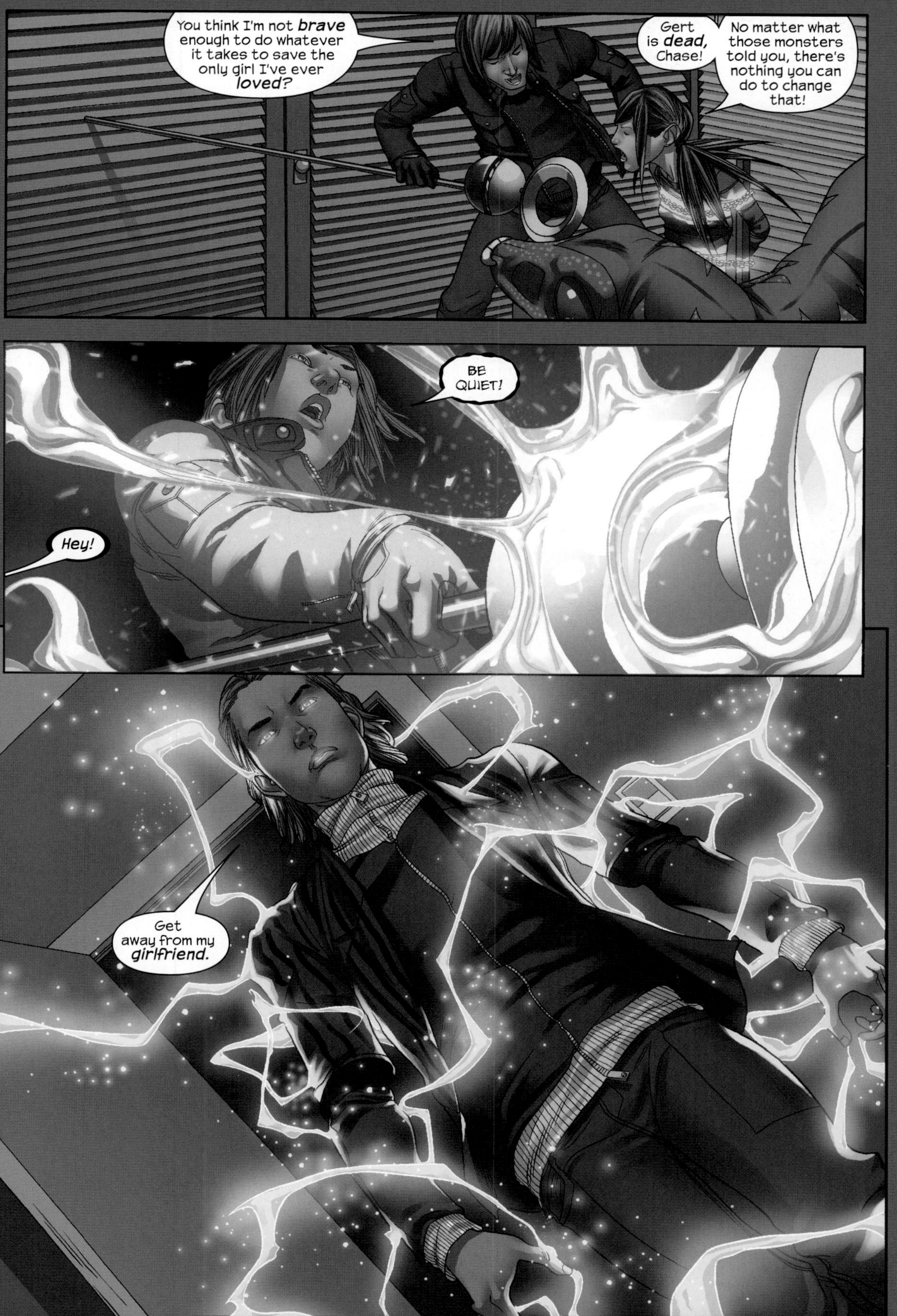
You think I'm not *brave* enough to do whatever it takes to save the only girl I've ever *loved?*
Gert is *dead,* Chase!
No matter what those monsters told you, there's nothing you can do to change that!
BE QUIET!
Hey!
Get away from my *girlfriend.*

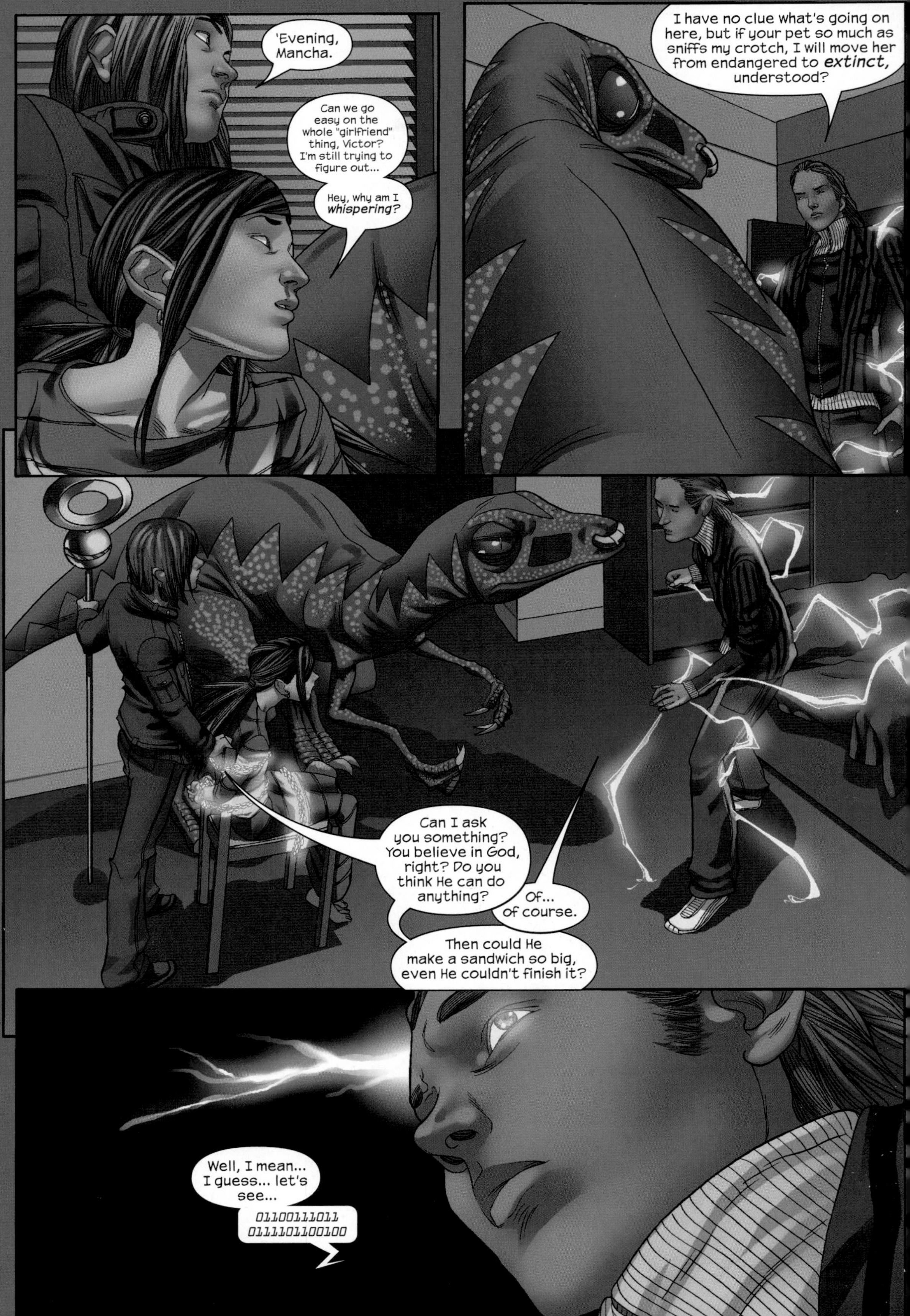
'Evening, Mancha.
Can we go easy on the whole "girlfriend" thing, Victor? I'm still trying to figure out...
Hey, why am I *whispering*?
I have no clue what's going on here, but if your pet so much as sniffs my crotch, I will move her from endangered to *extinct*, understood?
Can I ask you something? You believe in God, right? Do you think He can do anything?
Of... of course.
Then could He make a sandwich so big, even He couldn't finish it?
Well, I mean... I guess... let's see...
01100111011 0111101100100

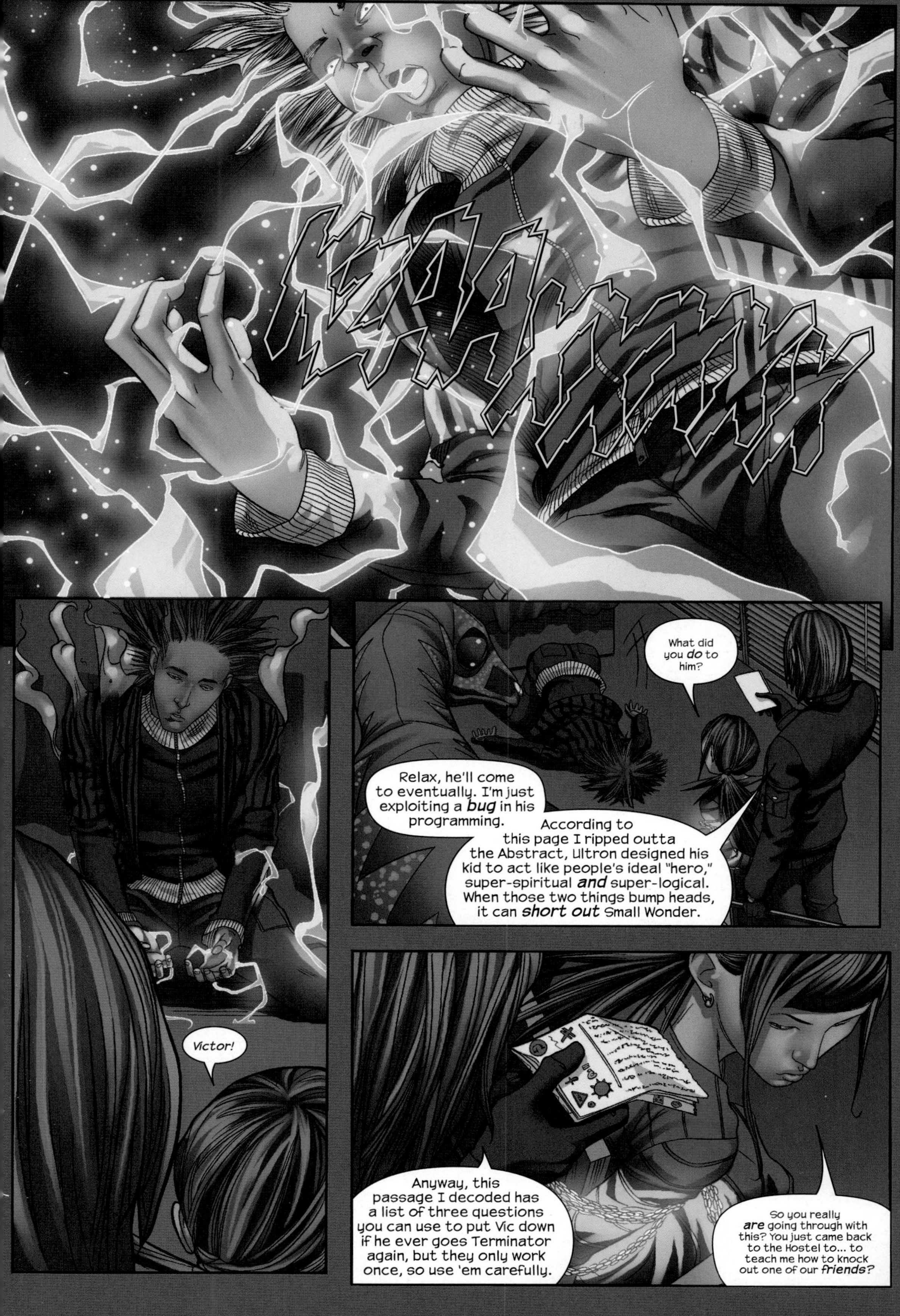

KZZAAAKK
Victor!
What did you *do* to him?
Relax, he'll come to eventually. I'm just exploiting a *bug* in his programming.
According to this page I ripped outta the Abstract, Ultron designed his kid to act like people's ideal "hero," super-spiritual *and* super-logical. When those two things bump heads, it can *short out* Small Wonder.
Anyway, this passage I decoded has a list of three questions you can use to put Vic down if he ever goes Terminator again, but they only work once, so use 'em carefully.
So you really *are* going through with this? You just came back to the Hostel to... to teach me how to knock out one of our *friends*?

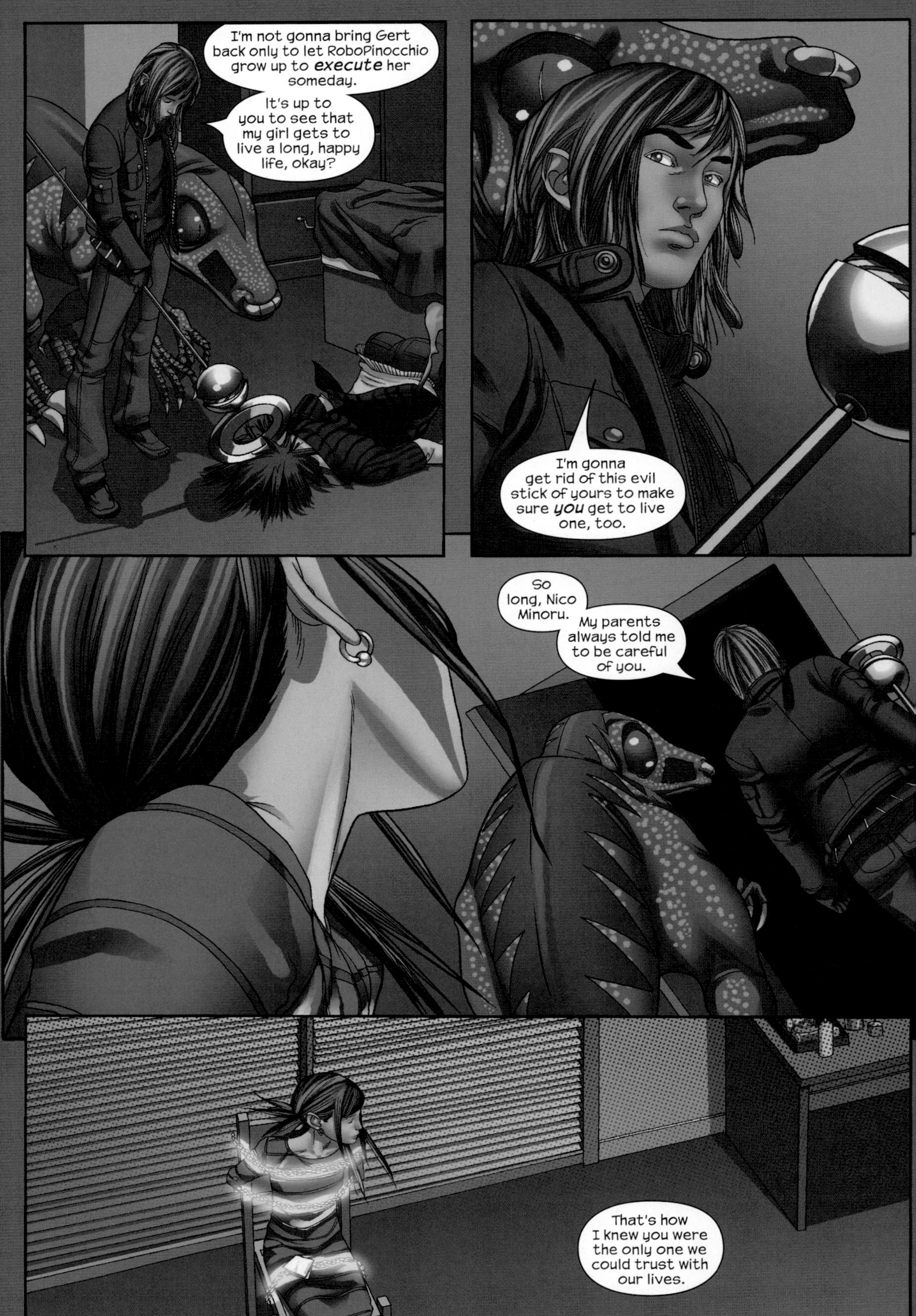
I'm not gonna bring Gert back only to let RoboPinocchio grow up to *execute* her someday.
It's up to you to see that my girl gets to live a long, happy life, okay?
I'm gonna get rid of this evil stick of yours to make sure *you* get to live one, too.
So long, Nico Minoru.
My parents always told me to be careful of you.
That's how I knew you were the only one we could trust with our lives.

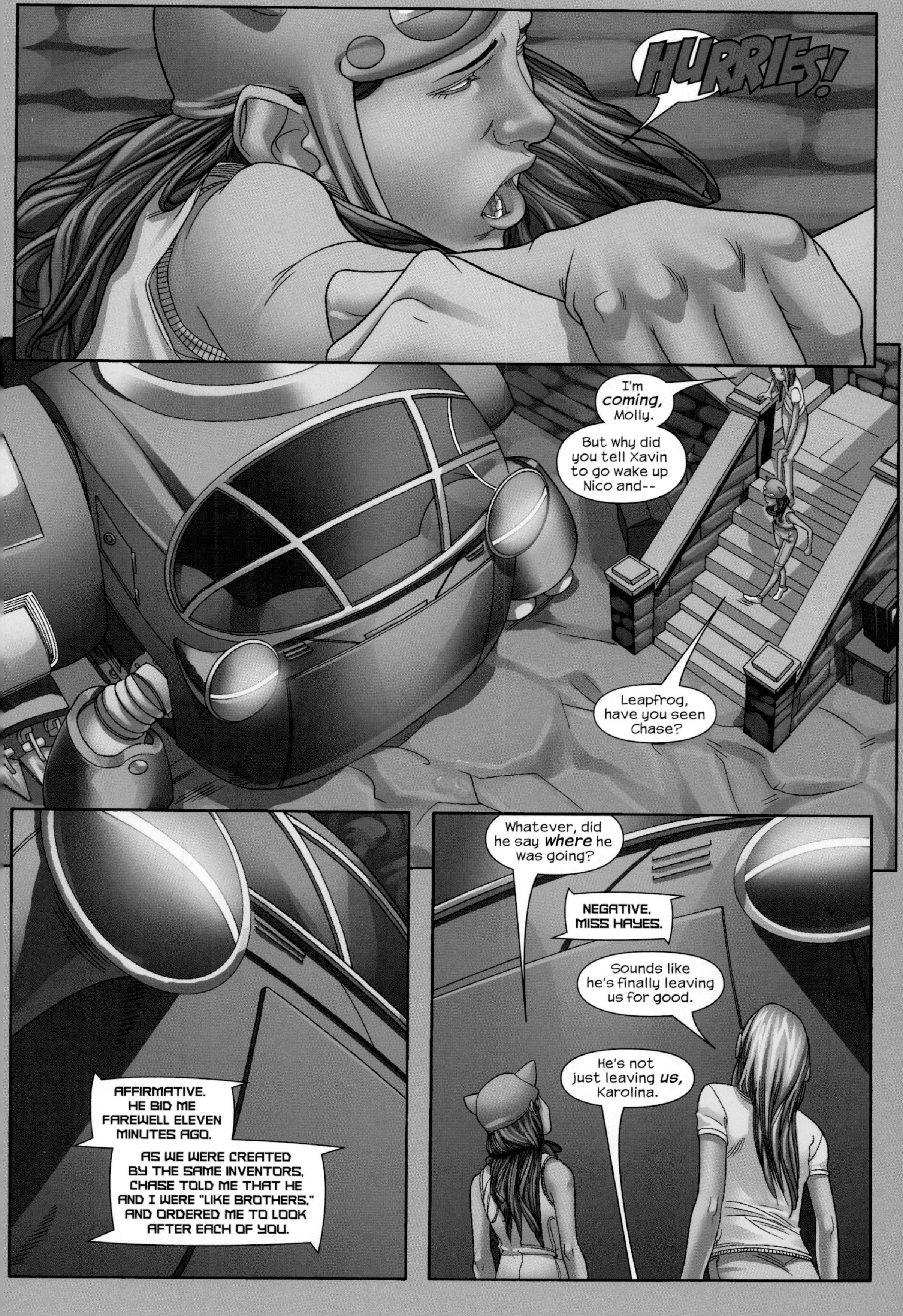
HURRIES!
I'm *coming,* Molly.
But why did you tell Xavin to go wake up Nico and--
Leapfrog, have you seen Chase?
AFFIRMATIVE. HE BID ME FAREWELL ELEVEN MINUTES AGO.
AS WE WERE CREATED BY THE SAME INVENTORS, CHASE TOLD ME THAT HE AND I WERE "LIKE BROTHERS," AND ORDERED ME TO LOOK AFTER EACH OF YOU.
Whatever, did he say *where* he was going?
NEGATIVE, MISS HAYES.
Sounds like he's finally leaving us for good.
He's not just leaving *us,* Karolina.

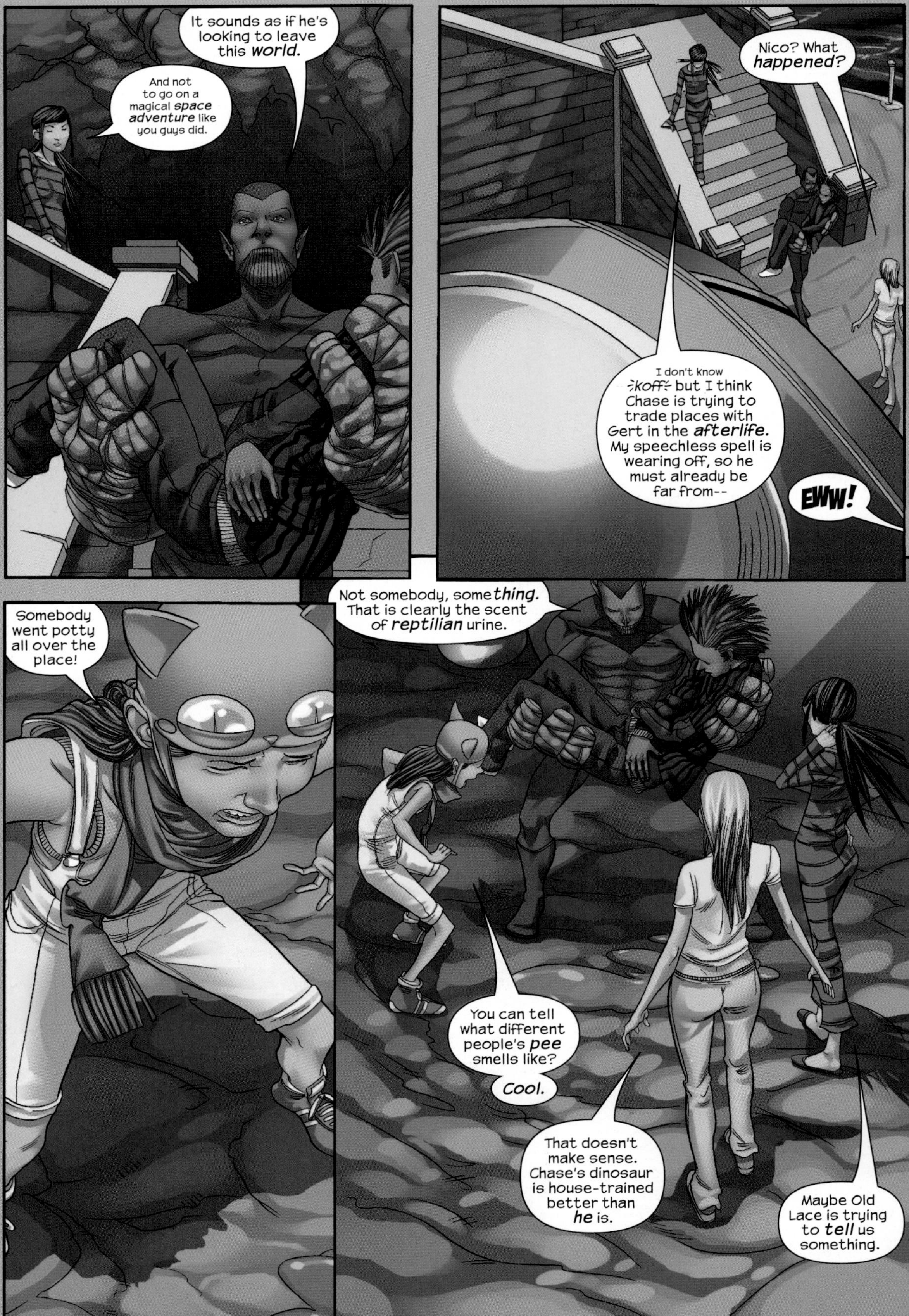

It sounds as if he's looking to leave this *world.*
And not to go on a magical *space adventure* like you guys did.
Nico? What *happened?*
I don't know -koff- but I think Chase is trying to trade places with Gert in the *afterlife.* My speechless spell is wearing off, so he must already be far from--
EWW!
Somebody went potty all over the place!
Not somebody, some*thing.* That is clearly the scent of *reptilian* urine.
You can tell what different people's *pee* smells like?
Cool.
That doesn't make sense. Chase's dinosaur is house-trained better than *he* is.
Maybe Old Lace is trying to *tell* us something.

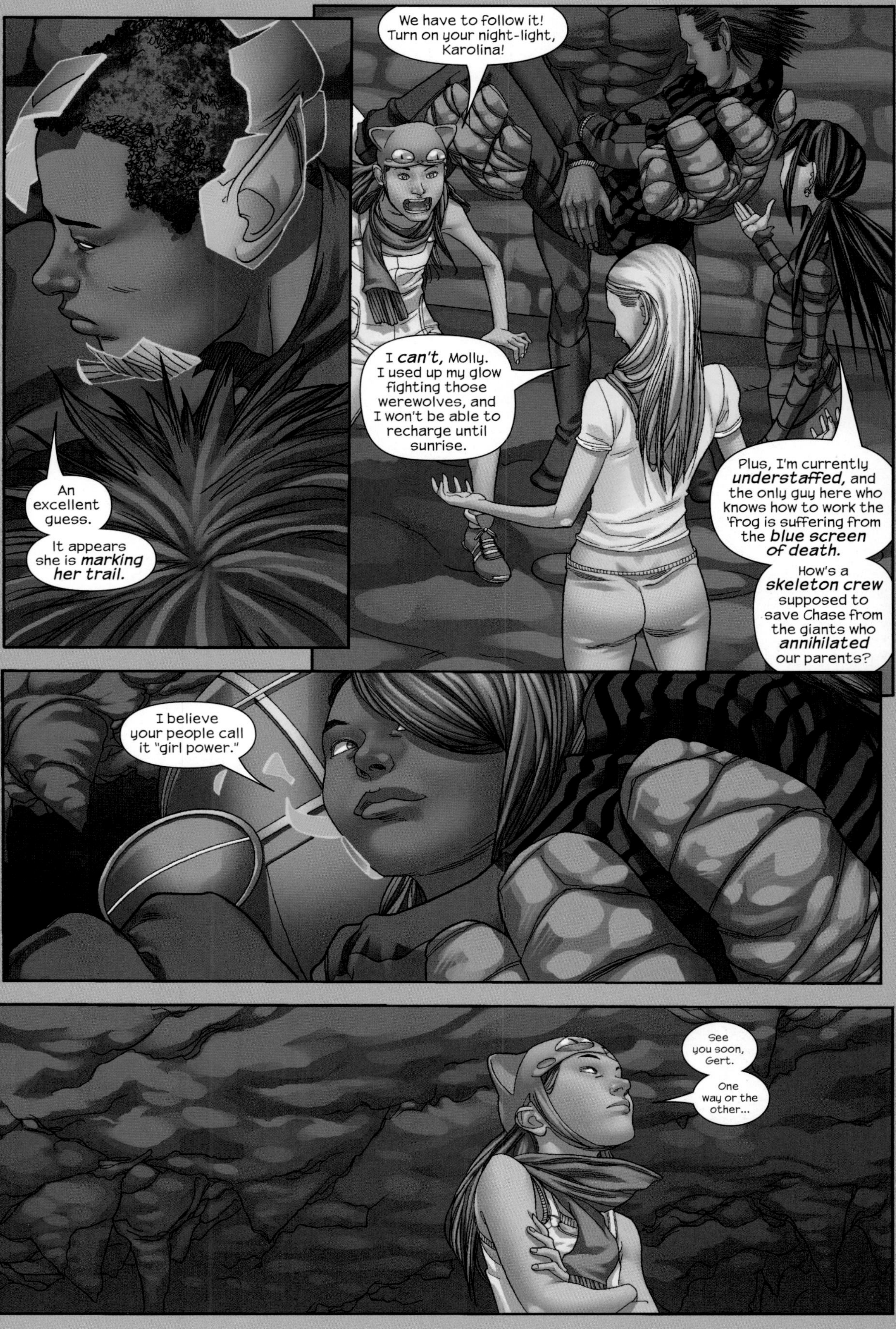

An excellent guess.
It appears she is *marking her trail.*
We have to follow it! Turn on your night-light, Karolina!
I *can't,* Molly. I used up my glow fighting those werewolves, and I won't be able to recharge until sunrise.
Plus, I'm currently *understaffed,* and the only guy here who knows how to work the 'frog is suffering from the *blue screen of death.*
How's a *skeleton crew* supposed to save Chase from the giants who *annihilated* our parents?
I believe your people call it "girl power."
See you soon, Gert.
One way or the other...

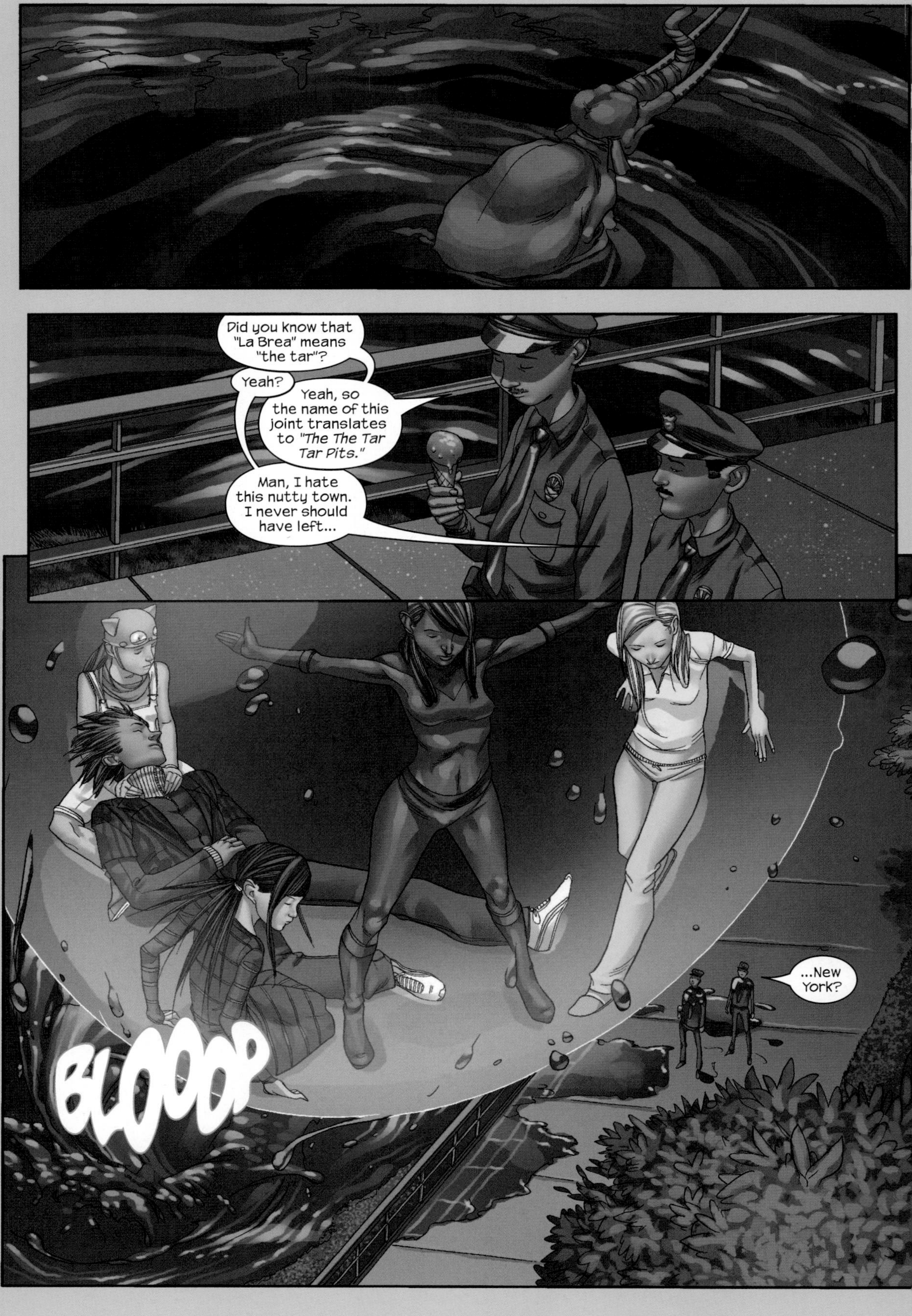
Did you know that "La Brea" means "the tar"?
Yeah?
Yeah, so the name of this joint translates to *"The The Tar Tar Pits."*
Man, I hate this nutty town. I never should have left...
BLOOOP
...New York?

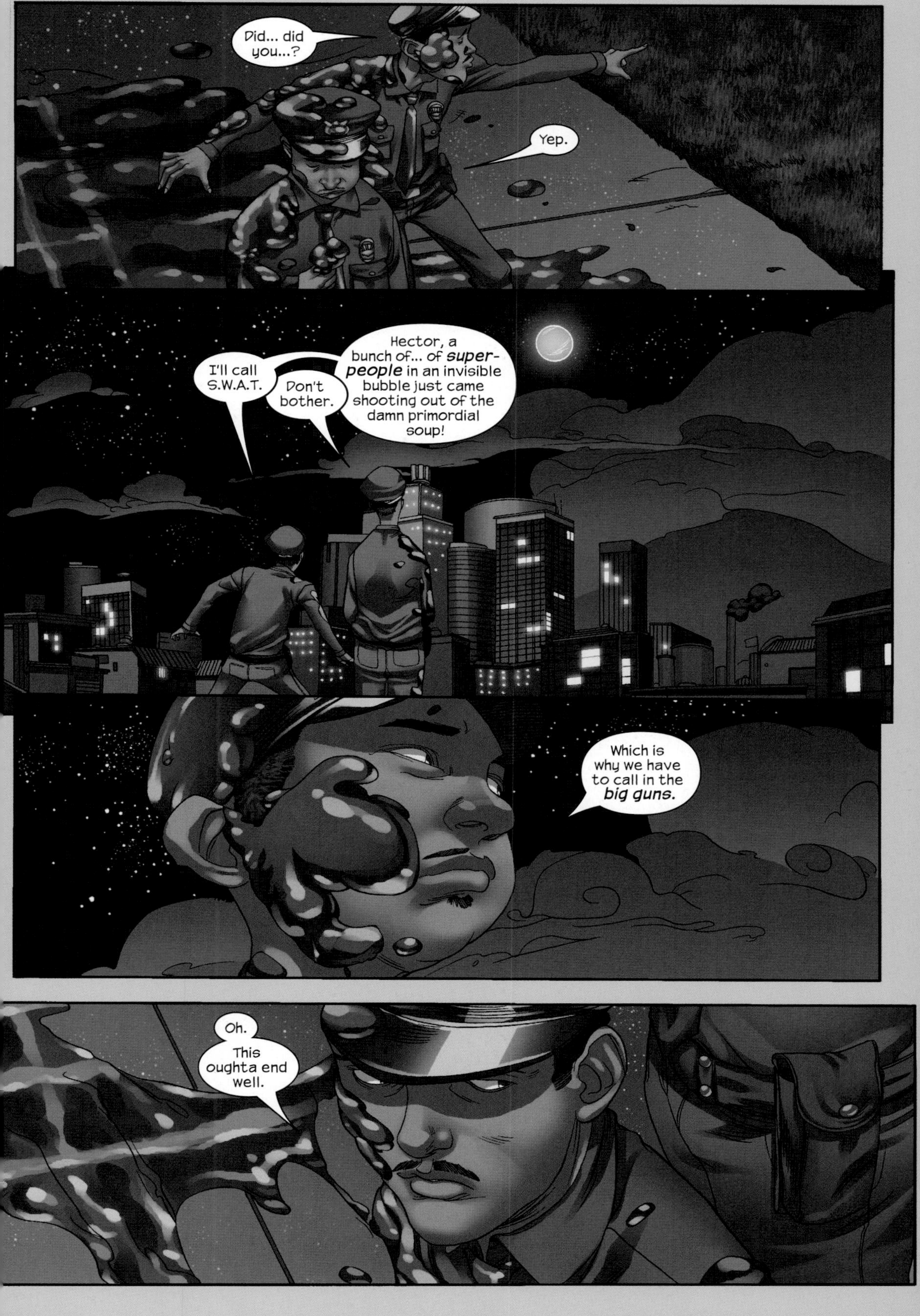
Did... did you...?
Yep.
Hector, a bunch of... of *super-people* in an invisible bubble just came shooting out of the damn primordial soup!
I'll call S.W.A.T.
Don't bother.
Which is why we have to call in the *big guns.*
Oh.
This oughta end well.

24

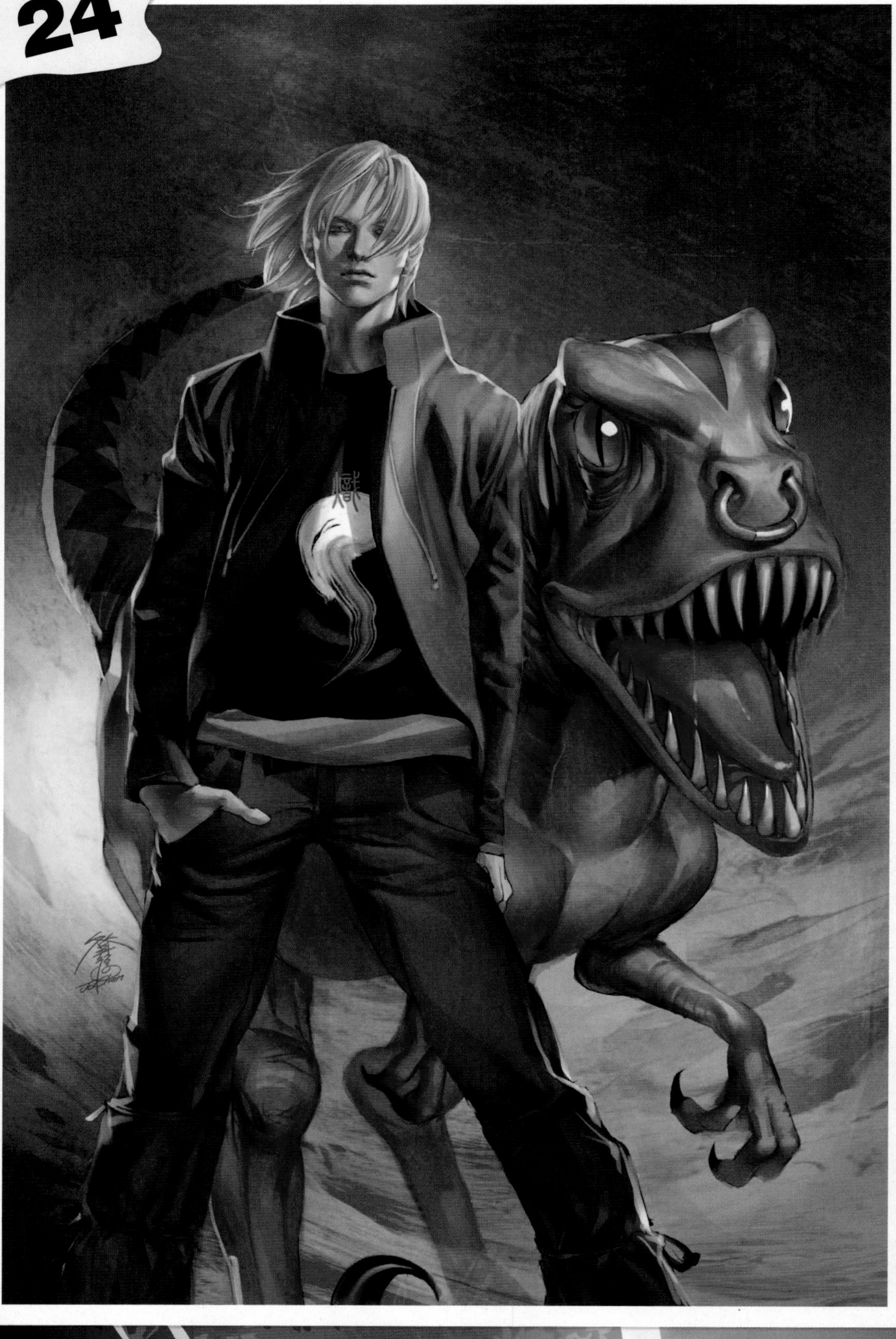

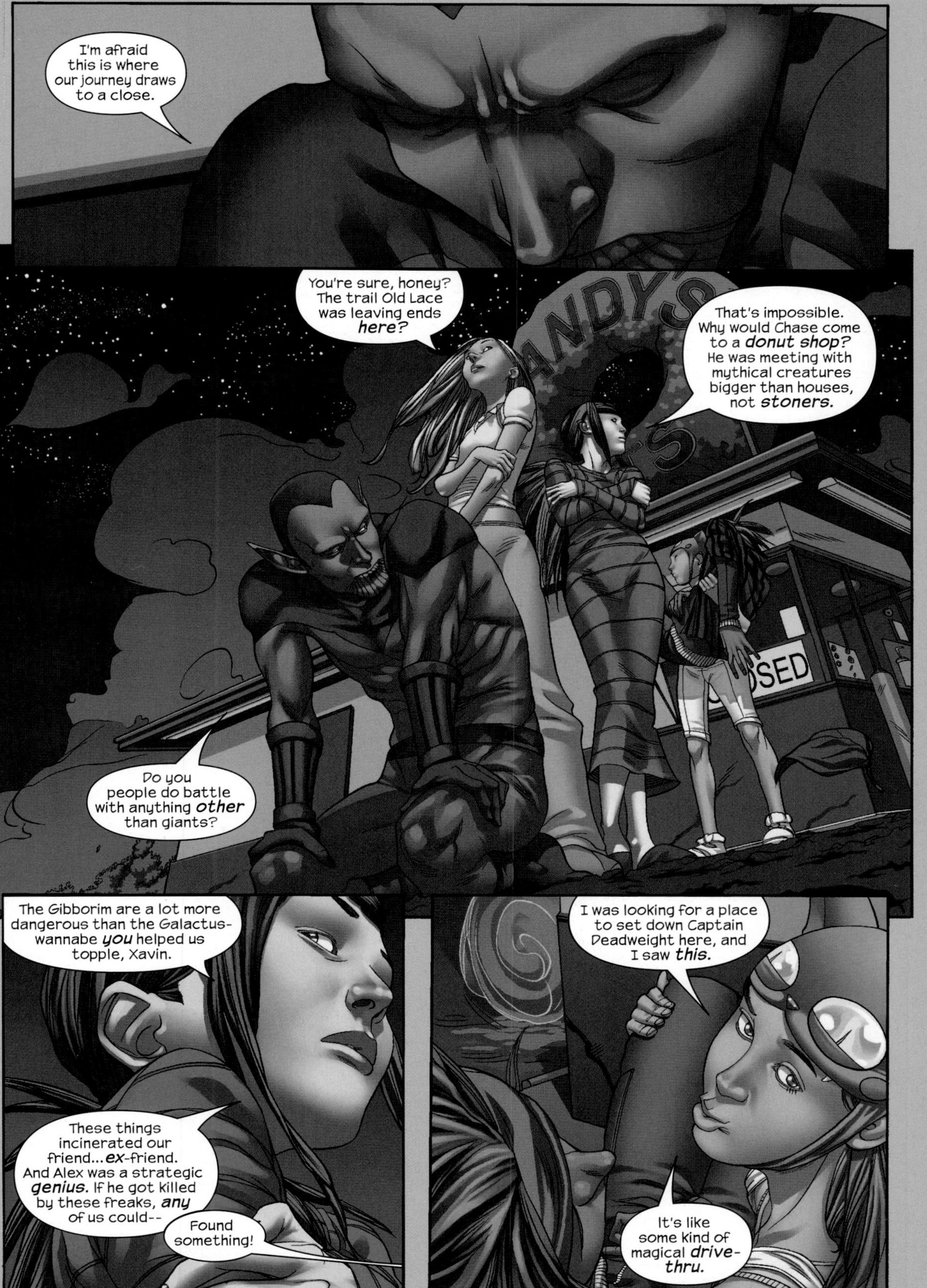
I'm afraid this is where our journey draws to a close.
You're sure, honey? The trail Old Lace was leaving ends *here?*
That's impossible. Why would Chase come to a *donut shop?* He was meeting with mythical creatures bigger than houses, not *stoners.*
Do you people do battle with anything *other* than giants?
The Gibborim are a lot more dangerous than the Galactus-wannabe *you* helped us topple, Xavin.
These things incinerated our friend... *ex*-friend. And Alex was a strategic *genius.* If he got killed by these freaks, *any* of us could--
Found something!
I was looking for a place to set down Captain Deadweight here, and I saw *this.*
It's like some kind of magical *drive-thru.*

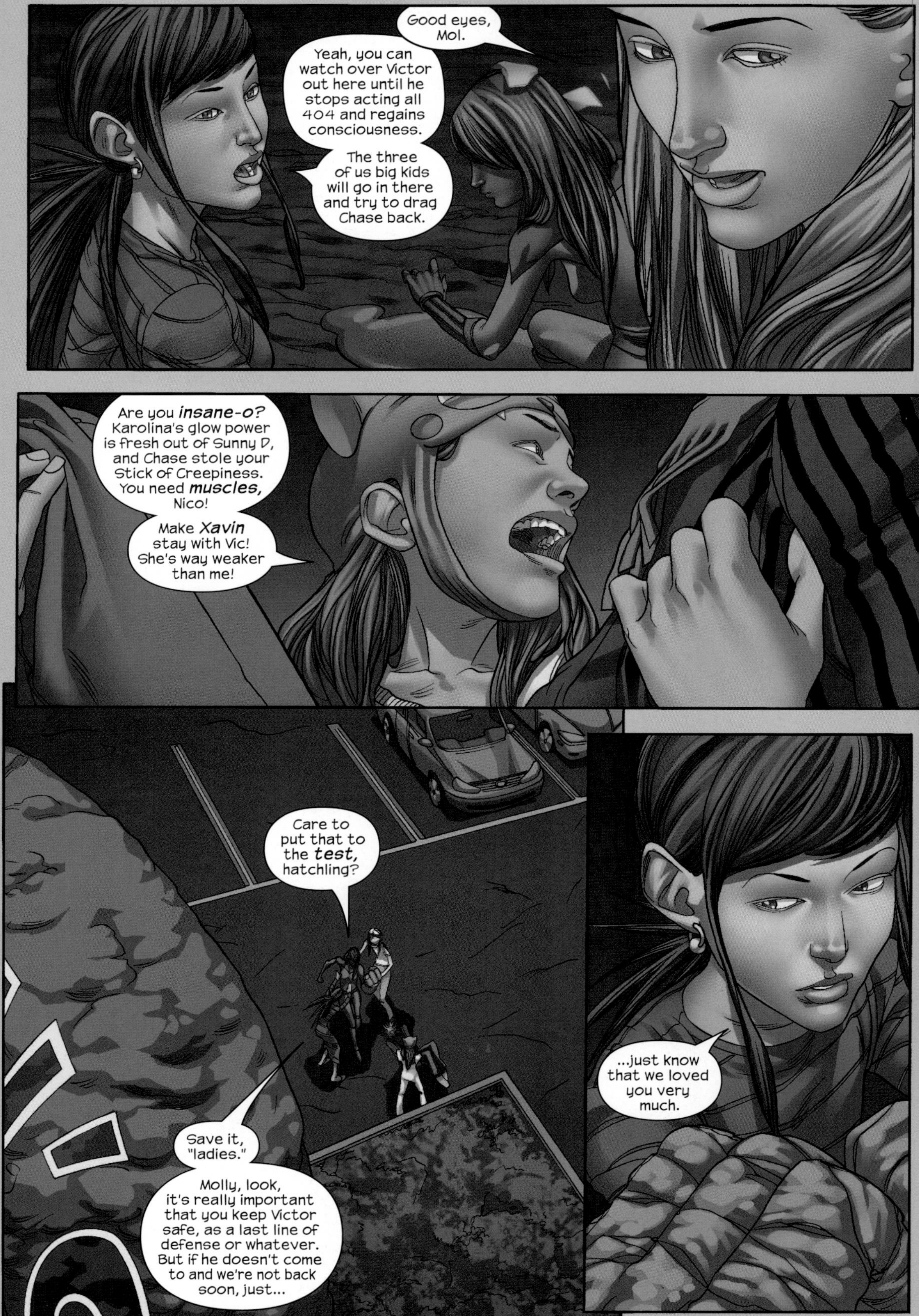
Good eyes, Mol.
Yeah, you can watch over Victor out here until he stops acting all 404 and regains consciousness.
The three of us big kids will go in there and try to drag Chase back.
Are you *insane-o?* Karolina's glow power is fresh out of Sunny D, and Chase stole your Stick of Creepiness. You need *muscles,* Nico!
Make *Xavin* stay with Vic! She's way weaker than me!
Care to put that to the *test,* hatchling?
Save it, "ladies."
Molly, look, it's really important that you keep Victor safe, as a last line of defense or whatever. But if he doesn't come to and we're not back soon, just...
...just know that we loved you very much.

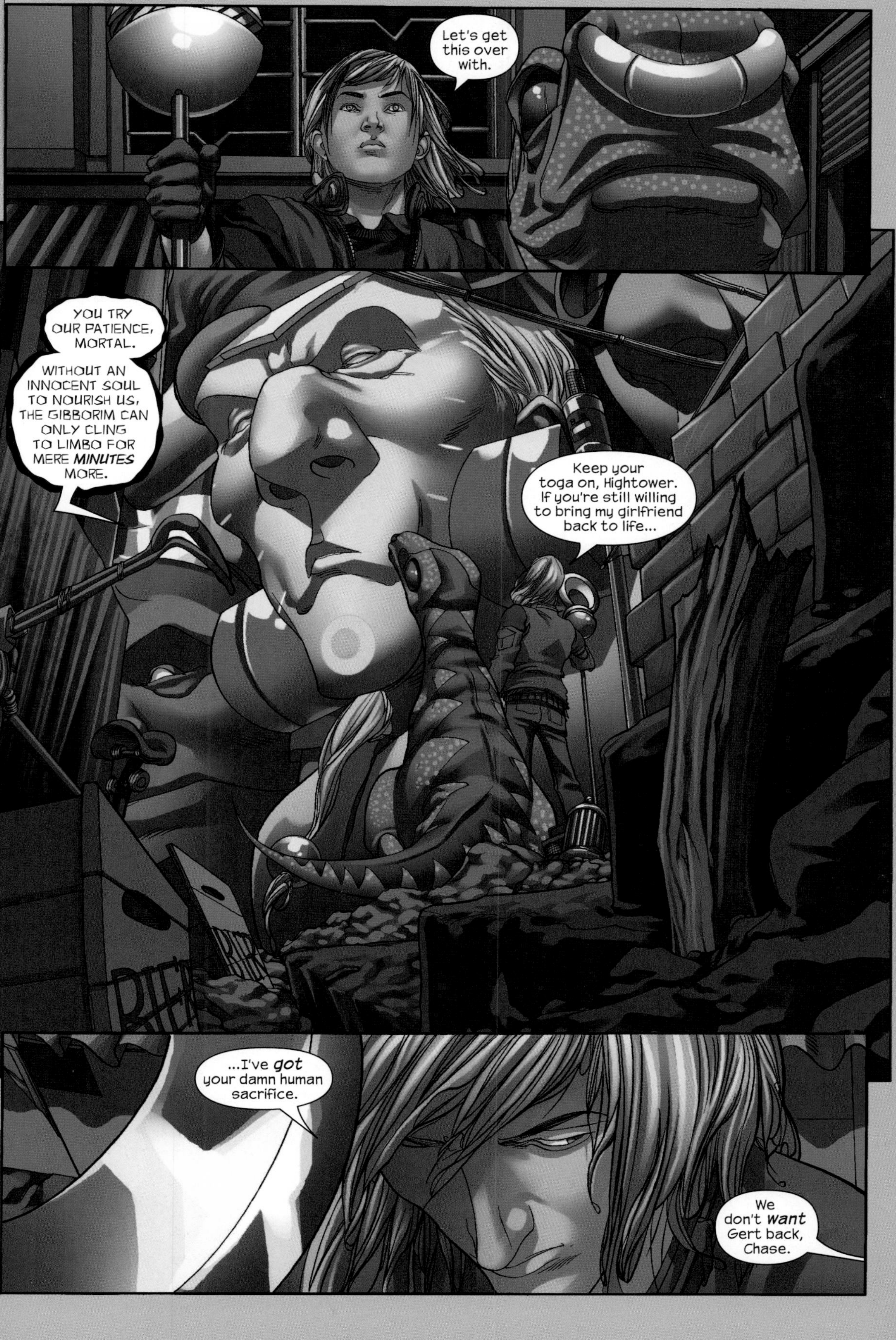
Let's get this over with.
YOU TRY OUR PATIENCE, MORTAL.
WITHOUT AN INNOCENT SOUL TO NOURISH US, THE GIBBORIM CAN ONLY CLING TO LIMBO FOR MERE *MINUTES* MORE.
Keep your toga on, Hightower. If you're still willing to bring my girlfriend back to life...
...I've *got* your damn human sacrifice.
We don't *want* Gert back, Chase.

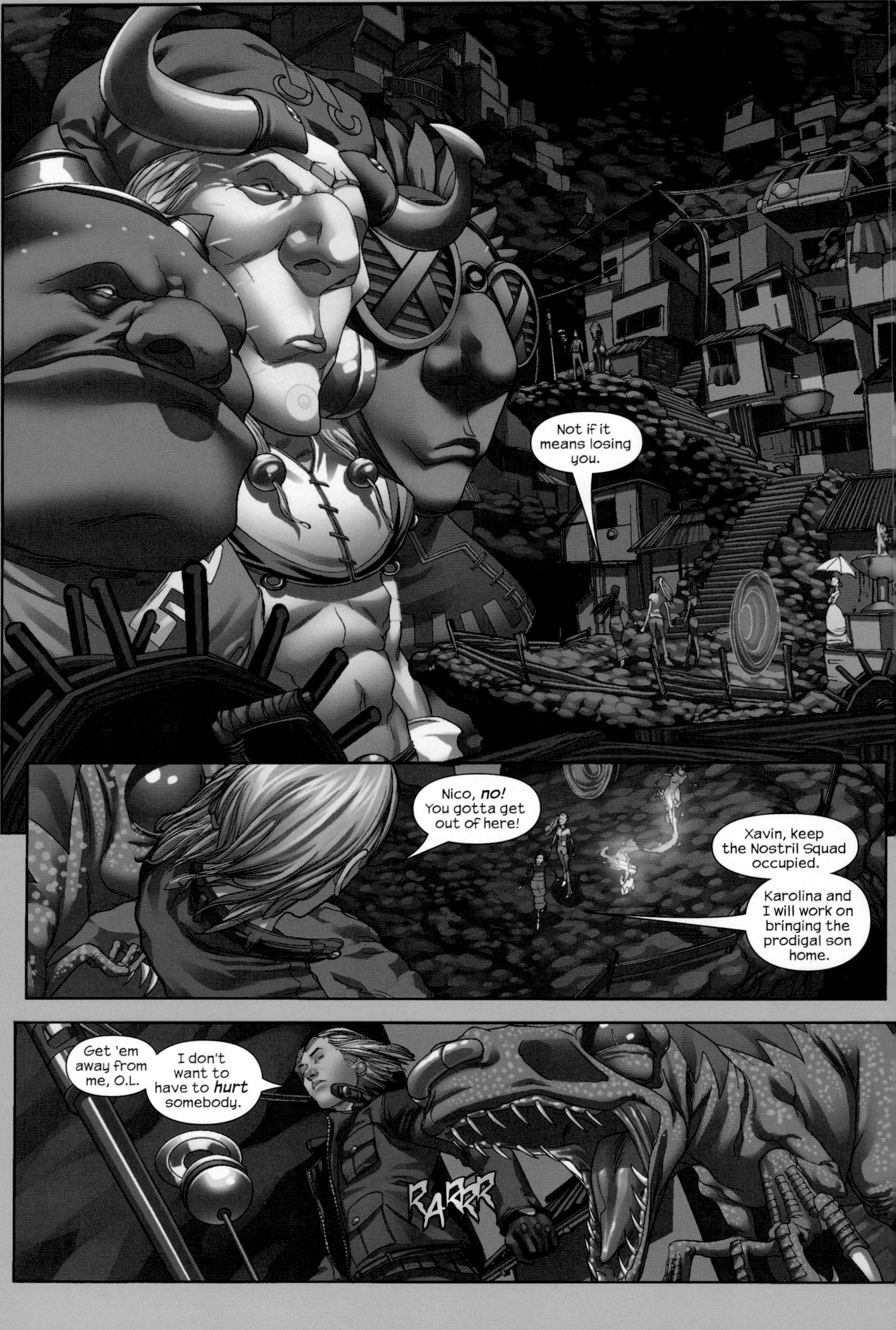

Not if it means losing you.
Nico, **no!** You gotta get out of here!
Xavin, keep the Nostril Squad occupied.
Karolina and I will work on bringing the prodigal son home.
Get 'em away from me, O.L.
I don't want to have to **hurt** somebody.
RARRR

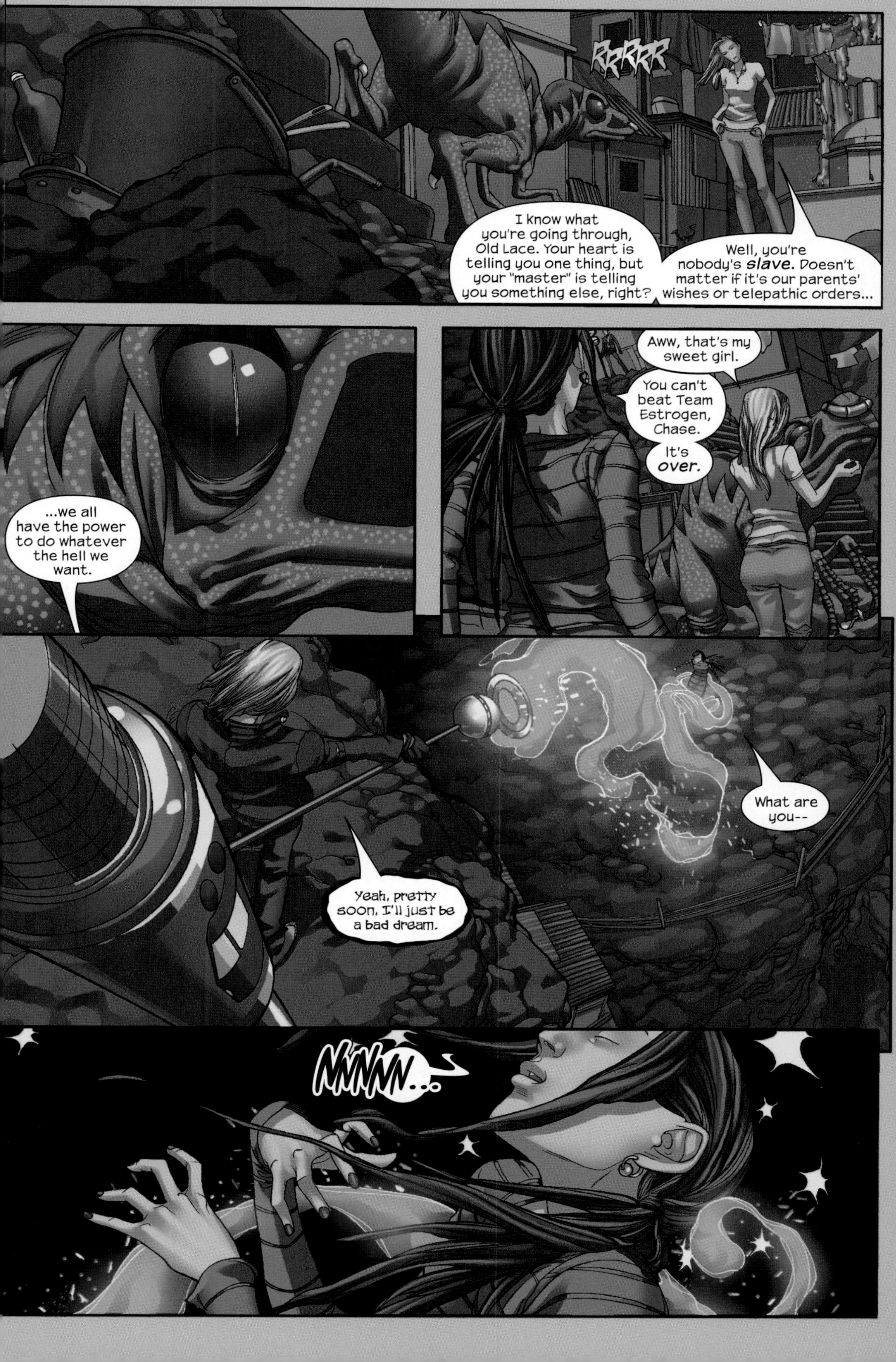
RRRRR
I know what you're going through, Old Lace. Your heart is telling you one thing, but your "master" is telling you something else, right?
Well, you're nobody's *slave.* Doesn't matter if it's our parents' wishes or telepathic orders...
...we all have the power to do whatever the hell we want.
Aww, that's my sweet girl.
You can't beat Team Estrogen, Chase.
It's *over.*
What are you--
Yeah, pretty soon, I'll just be a bad dream.
NNNNN...

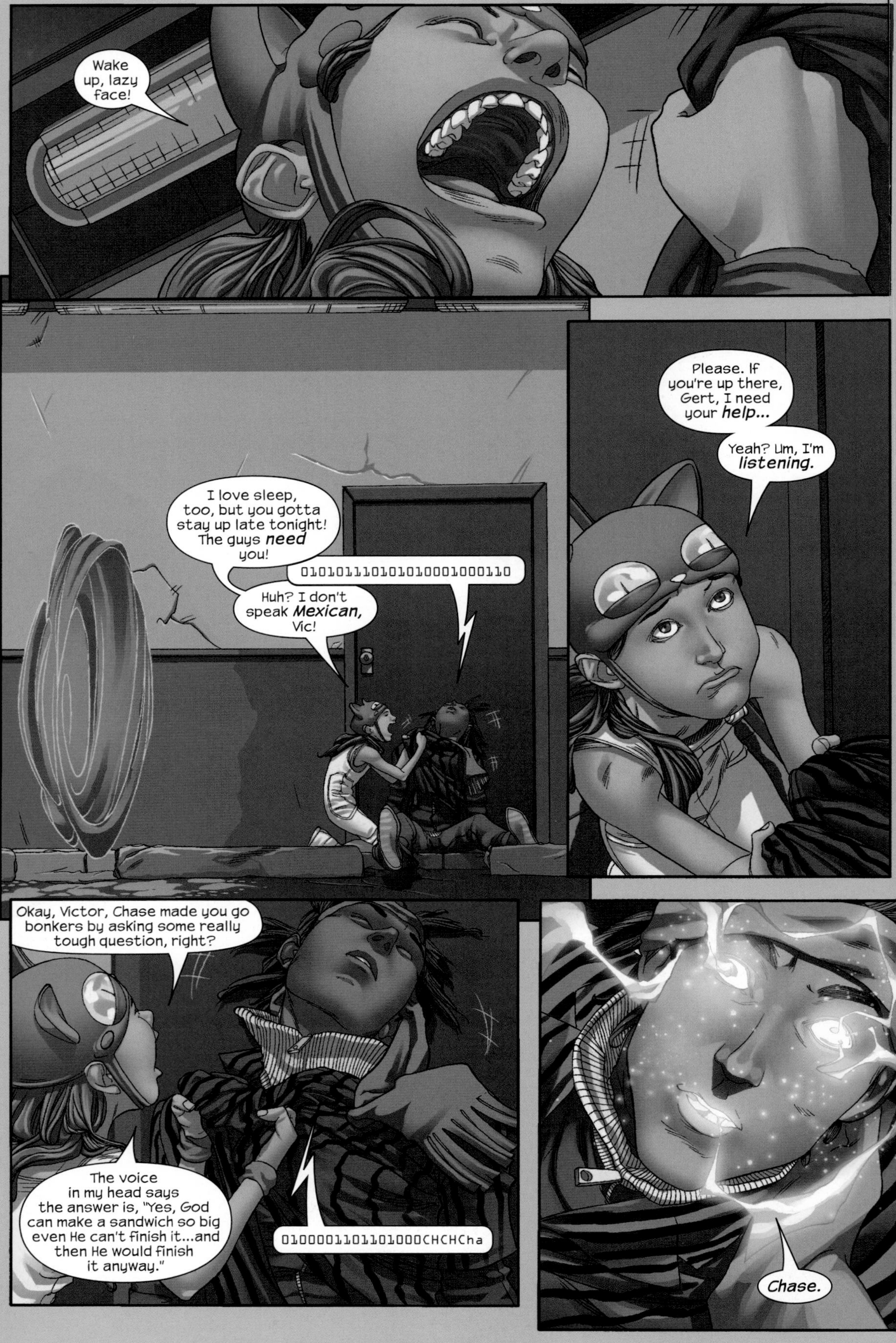

Wake up, lazy face!
I love sleep, too, but you gotta stay up late tonight! The guys need you!
0101011101010100010001 10
Huh? I don't speak Mexican, Vic!
Please. If you're up there, Gert, I need your help...
Yeah? Um, I'm listening.
Okay, Victor, Chase made you go bonkers by asking some really tough question, right?
The voice in my head says the answer is, "Yes, God can make a sandwich so big even He can't finish it...and then He would finish it anyway."
0100001101101000CHCHCha
Chase.

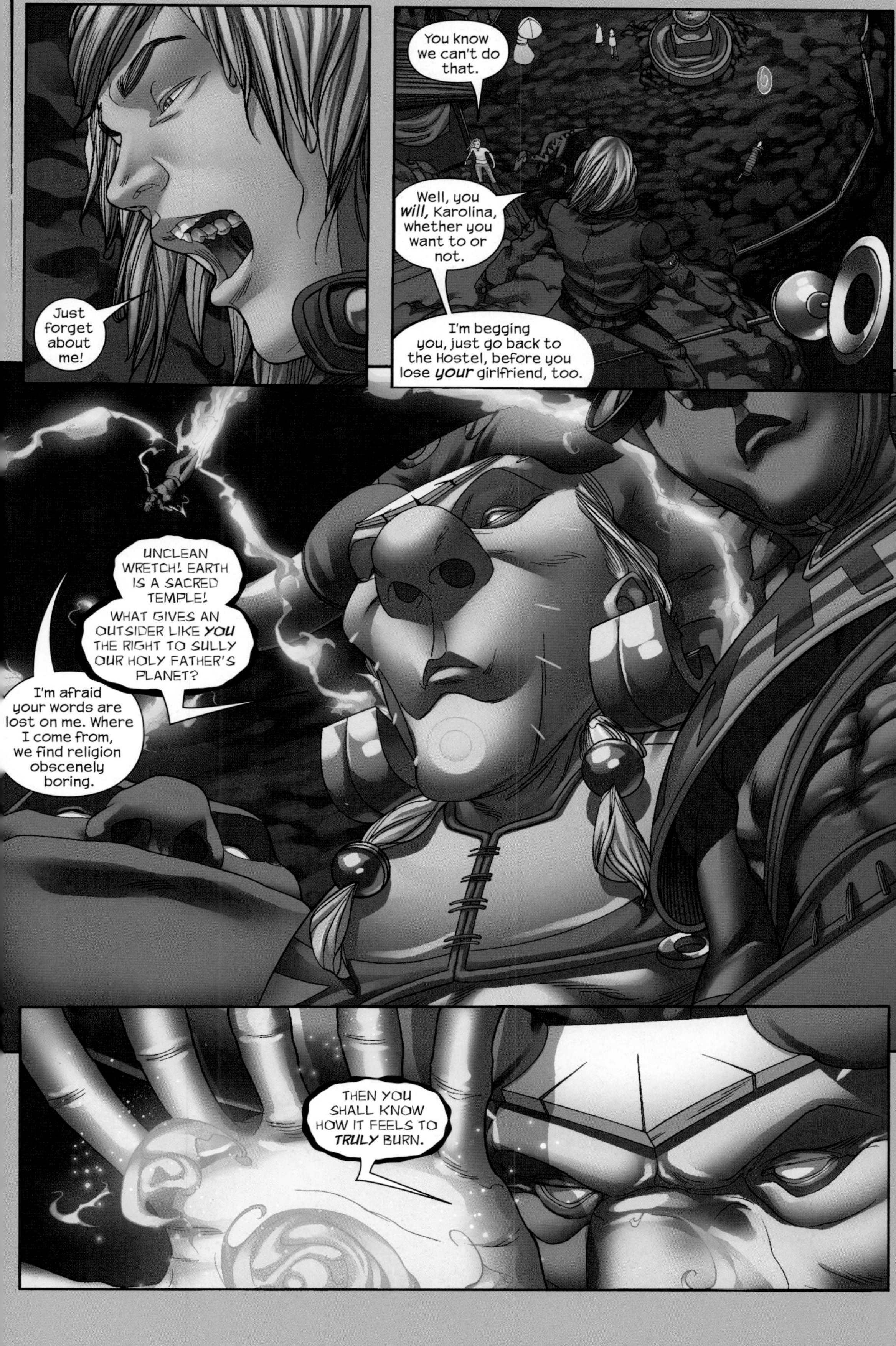

Just forget about me!
You know we can't do that.
Well, you will, Karolina, whether you want to or not.
I'm begging you, just go back to the Hostel, before you lose your girlfriend, too.
UNCLEAN WRETCH! EARTH IS A SACRED TEMPLE!
WHAT GIVES AN OUTSIDER LIKE YOU THE RIGHT TO SULLY OUR HOLY FATHER'S PLANET?
I'm afraid your words are lost on me. Where I come from, we find religion obscenely boring.
THEN YOU SHALL KNOW HOW IT FEELS TO TRULY BURN.

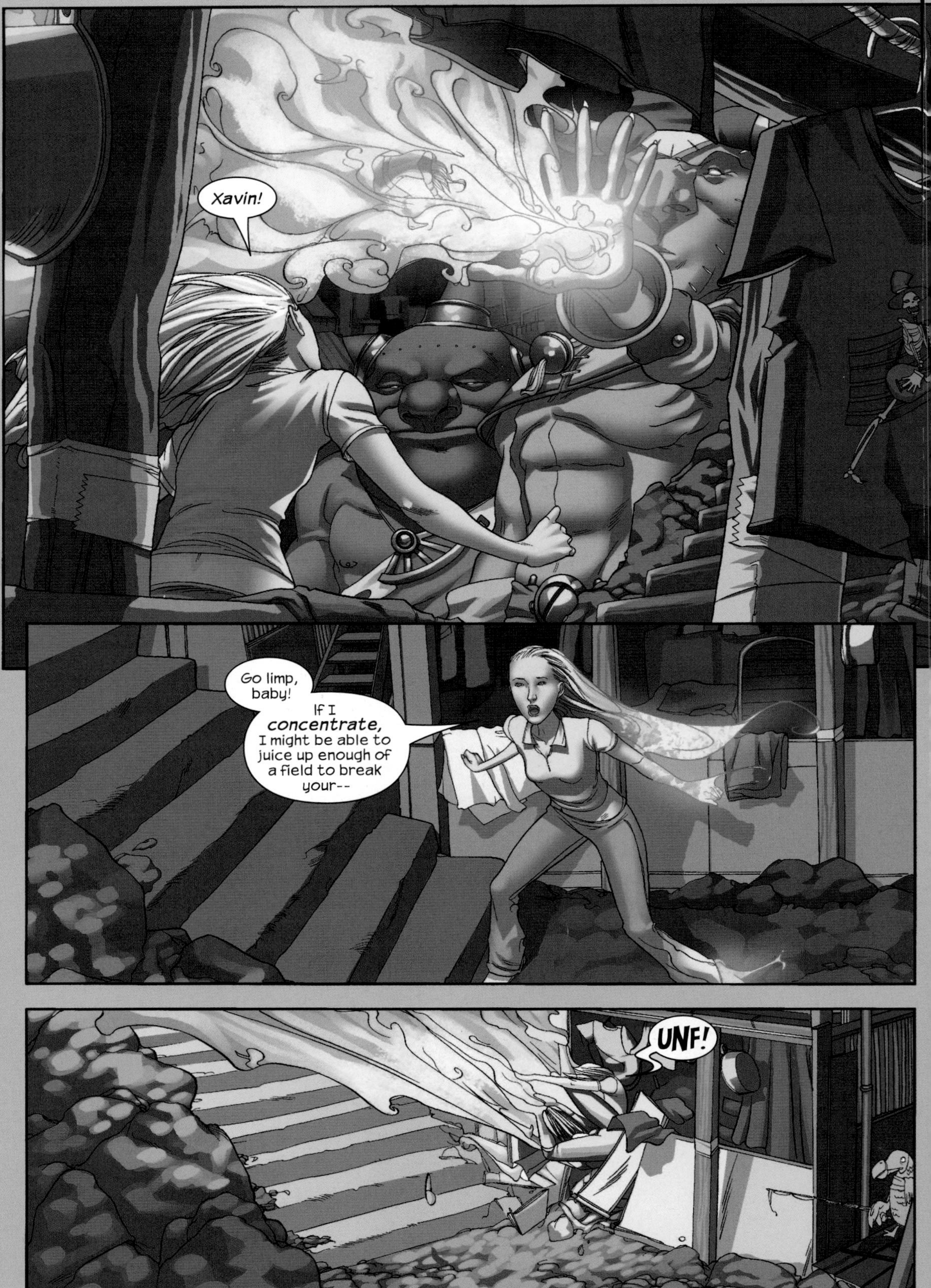
Xavin!
Go limp, baby!
If I *concentrate,* I might be able to juice up enough of a field to break your--
UNF!

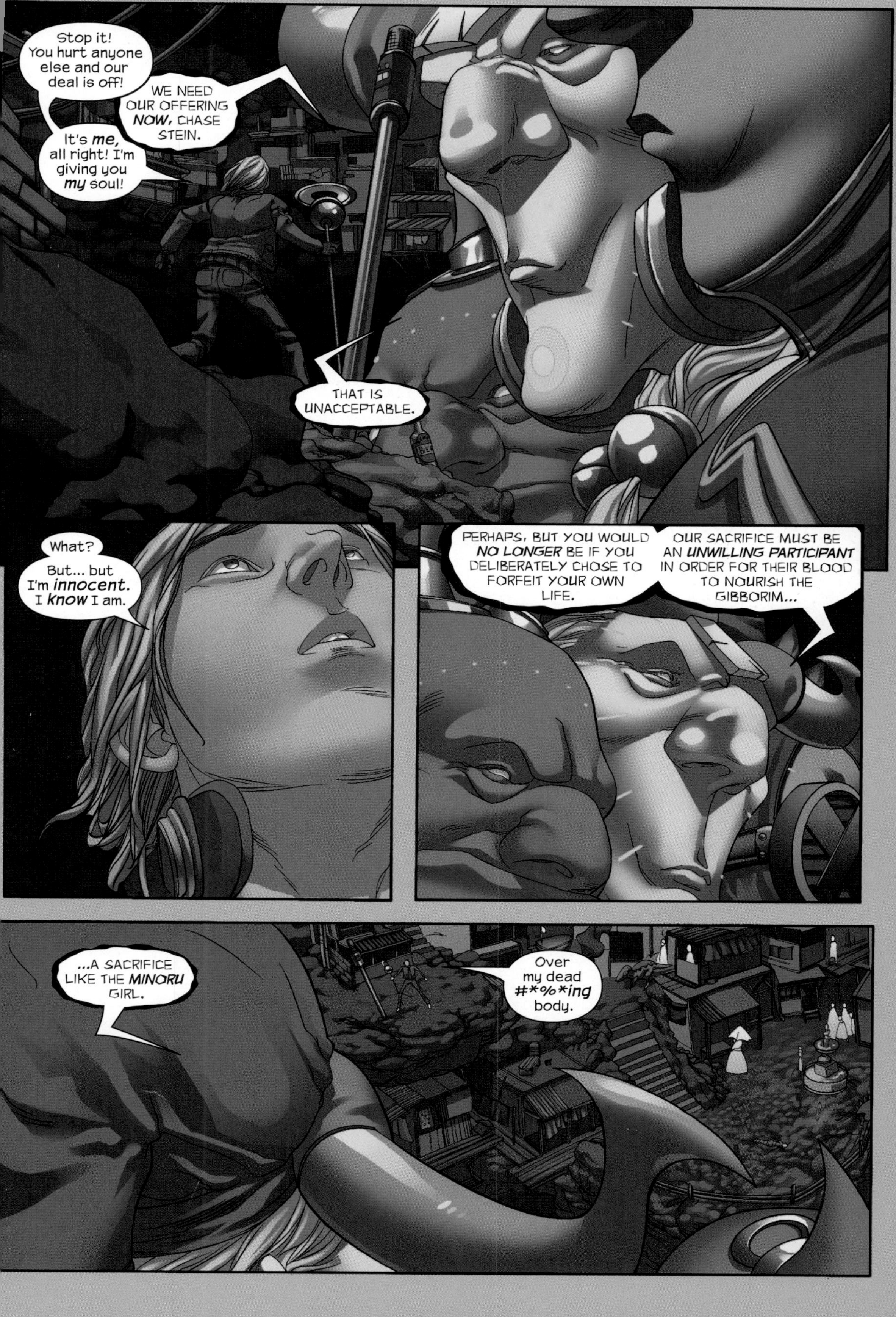
Stop it! You hurt anyone else and our deal is off!
WE NEED OUR OFFERING NOW, CHASE STEIN.
It's me, all right! I'm giving you my soul!
THAT IS UNACCEPTABLE.
What?
But... but I'm innocent. I know I am.
PERHAPS, BUT YOU WOULD NO LONGER BE IF YOU DELIBERATELY CHOSE TO FORFEIT YOUR OWN LIFE.
OUR SACRIFICE MUST BE AN UNWILLING PARTICIPANT IN ORDER FOR THEIR BLOOD TO NOURISH THE GIBBORIM...
...A SACRIFICE LIKE THE MINORU GIRL.
Over my dead #*%*ing body.

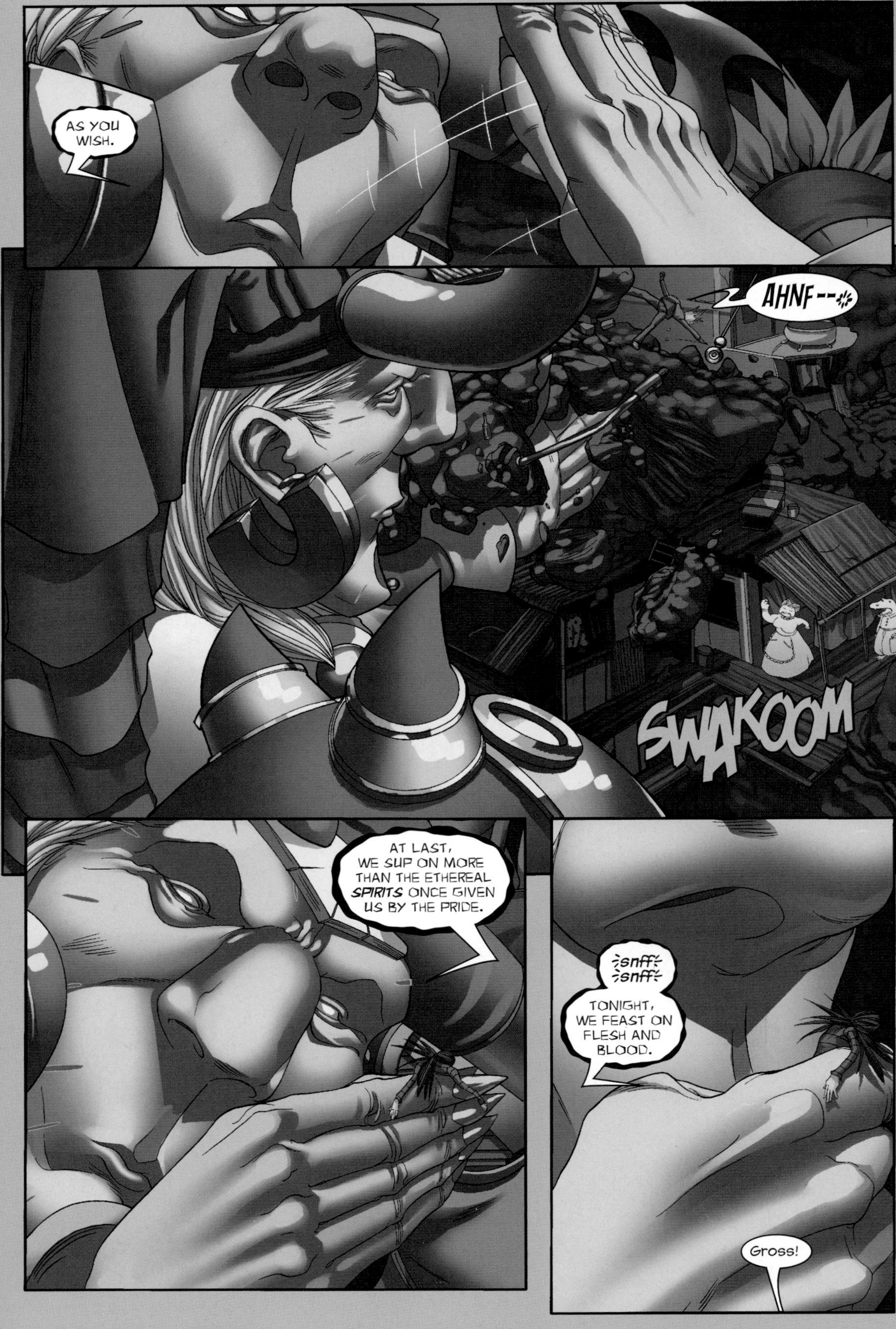

AS YOU WISH.
AHNF--
SWAKOOM
AT LAST, WE SUP ON MORE THAN THE ETHEREAL SPIRITS ONCE GIVEN US BY THE PRIDE.
snff snff
TONIGHT, WE FEAST ON FLESH AND BLOOD.
Gross!

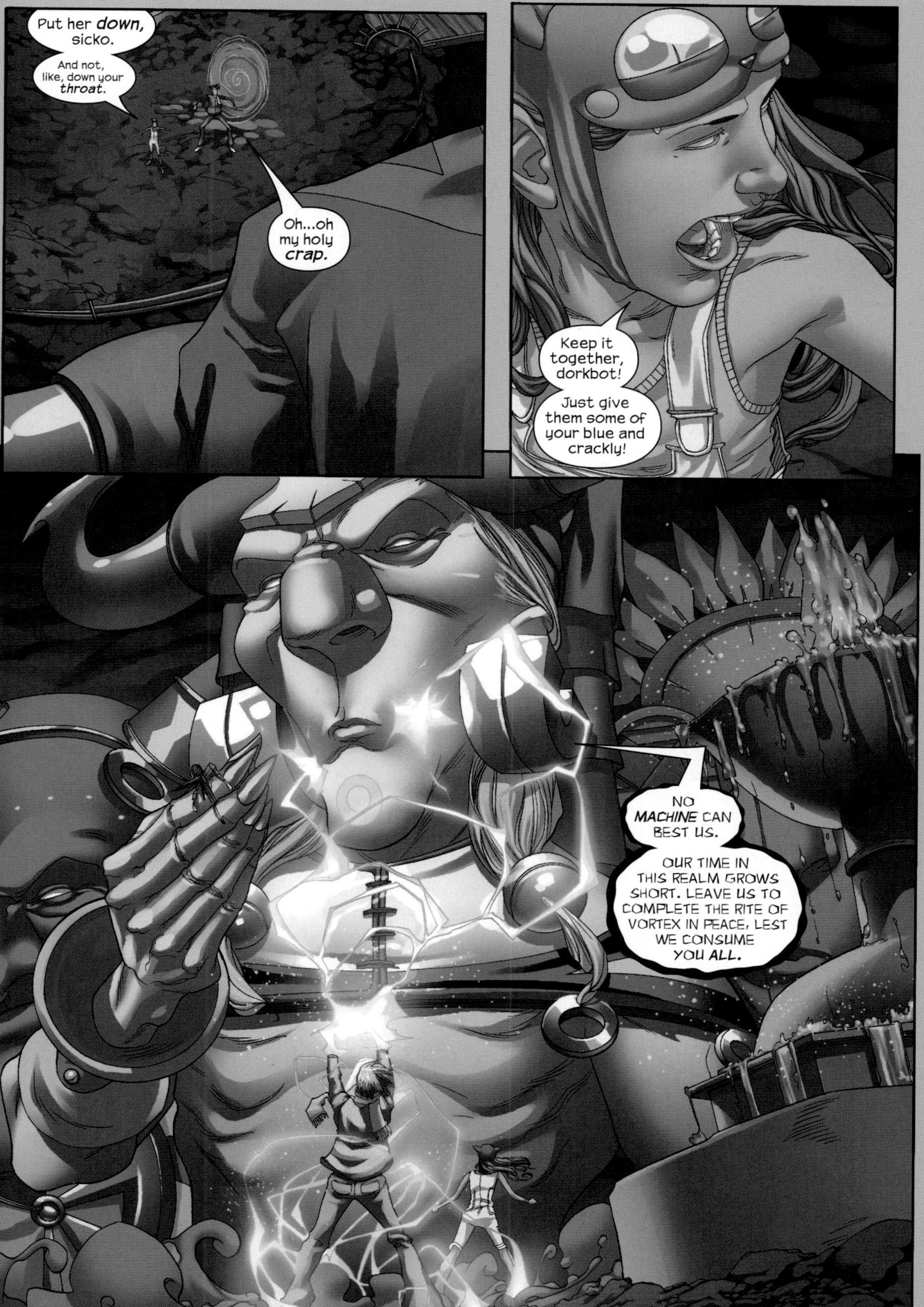

Put her *down,* sicko.
And not, like, down your *throat.*
Oh...oh my holy *crap.*
Keep it together, dorkbot!
Just give them some of your blue and crackly!
NO *MACHINE* CAN BEST US.
OUR TIME IN THIS REALM GROWS SHORT. LEAVE US TO COMPLETE THE RITE OF VORTEX IN PEACE, LEST WE CONSUME YOU *ALL.*

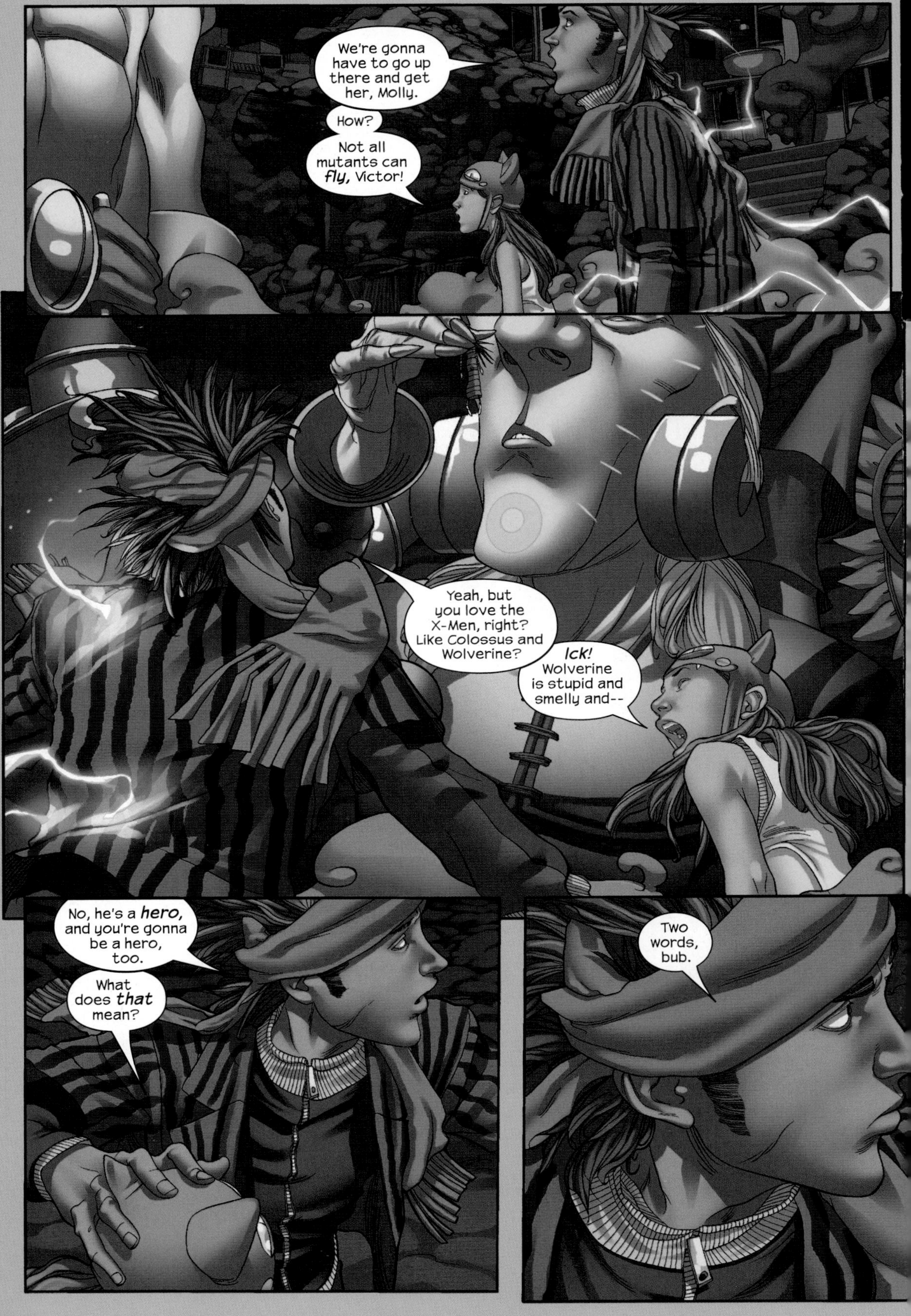

We're gonna have to go up there and get her, Molly.
How?
Not all mutants can *fly,* Victor!
Yeah, but you love the X-Men, right? Like Colossus and Wolverine?
Ick! Wolverine is stupid and smelly and--
No, he's a *hero,* and you're gonna be a hero, too.
What does *that* mean?
Two words, bub.

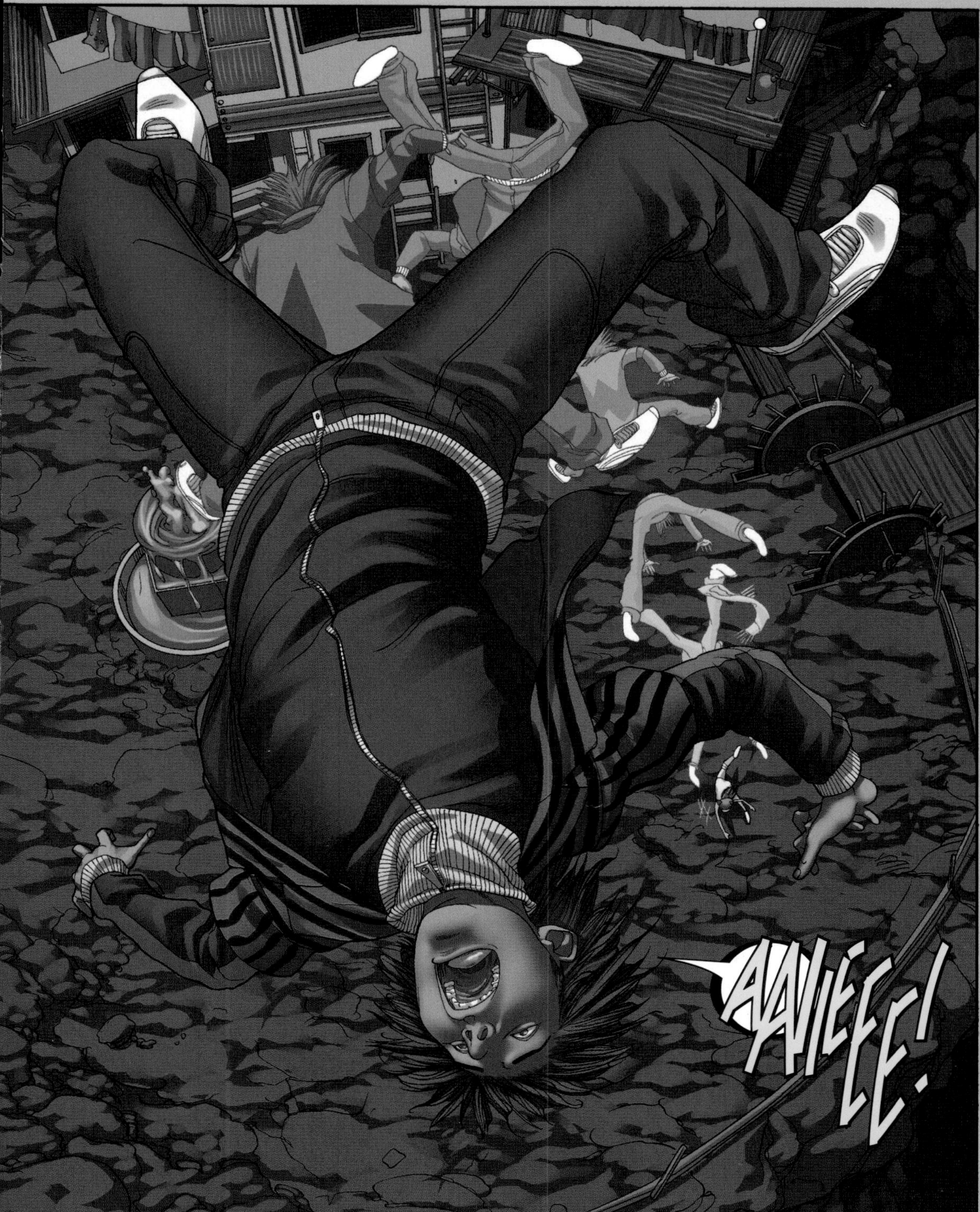
AAIEEEE!

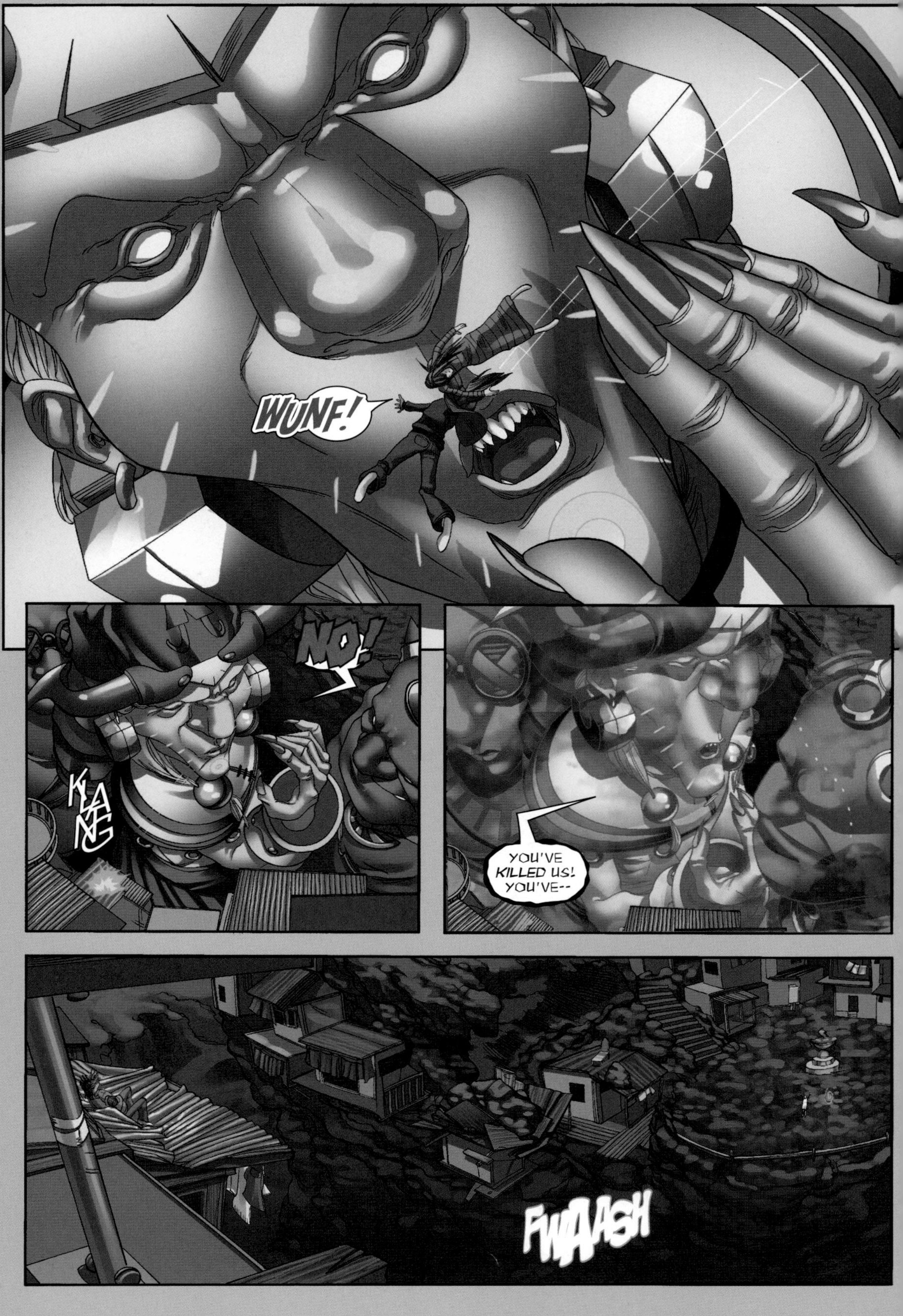
WUNF!
NO!
KLANG
YOU'VE KILLED US! YOU'VE--
FWAASH

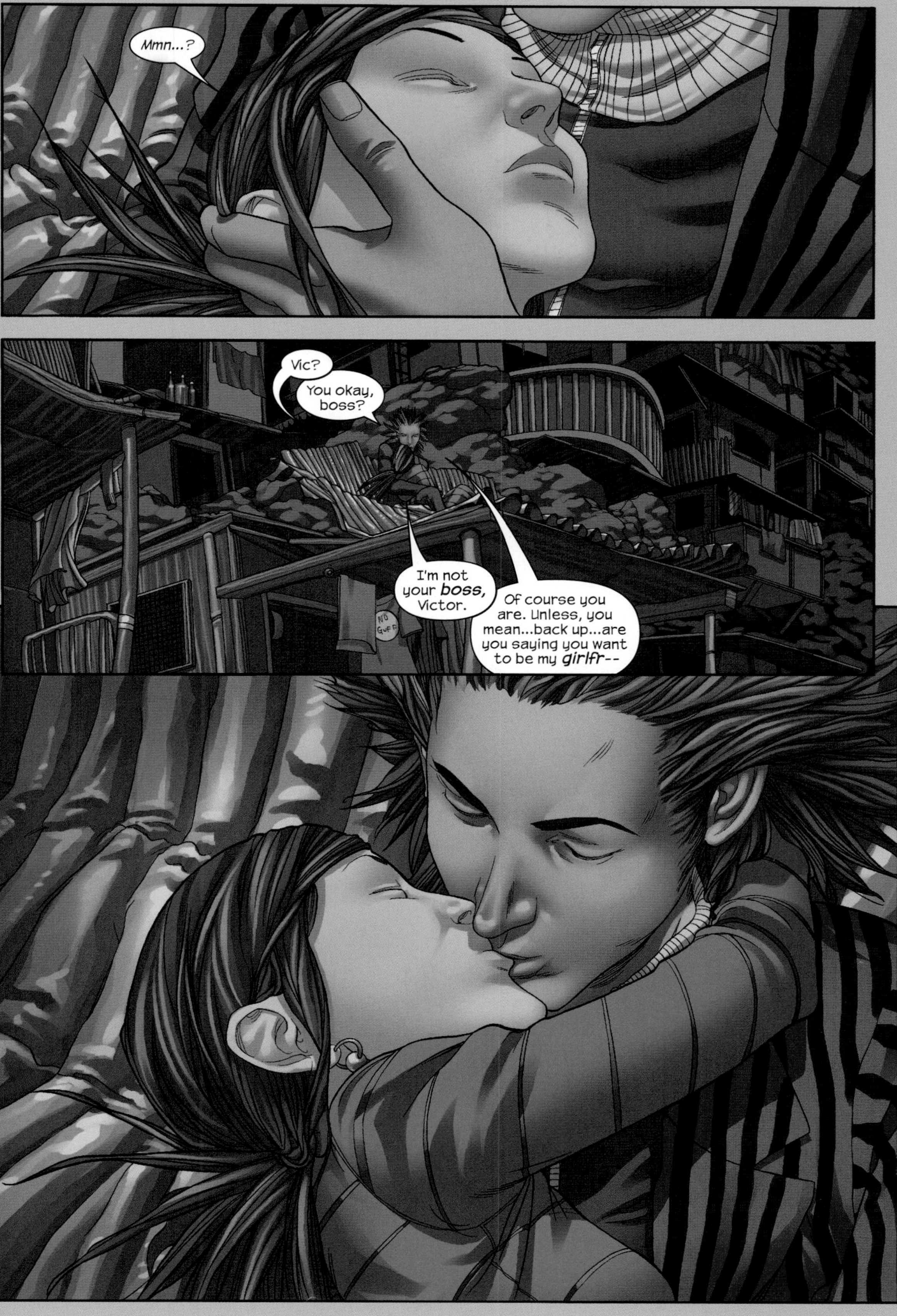
Mmn...?
Vic?
You okay, boss?
I'm not your **boss,** Victor.
Of course you are. Unless, you mean...back up...are you saying you want to be my *girlfr*--

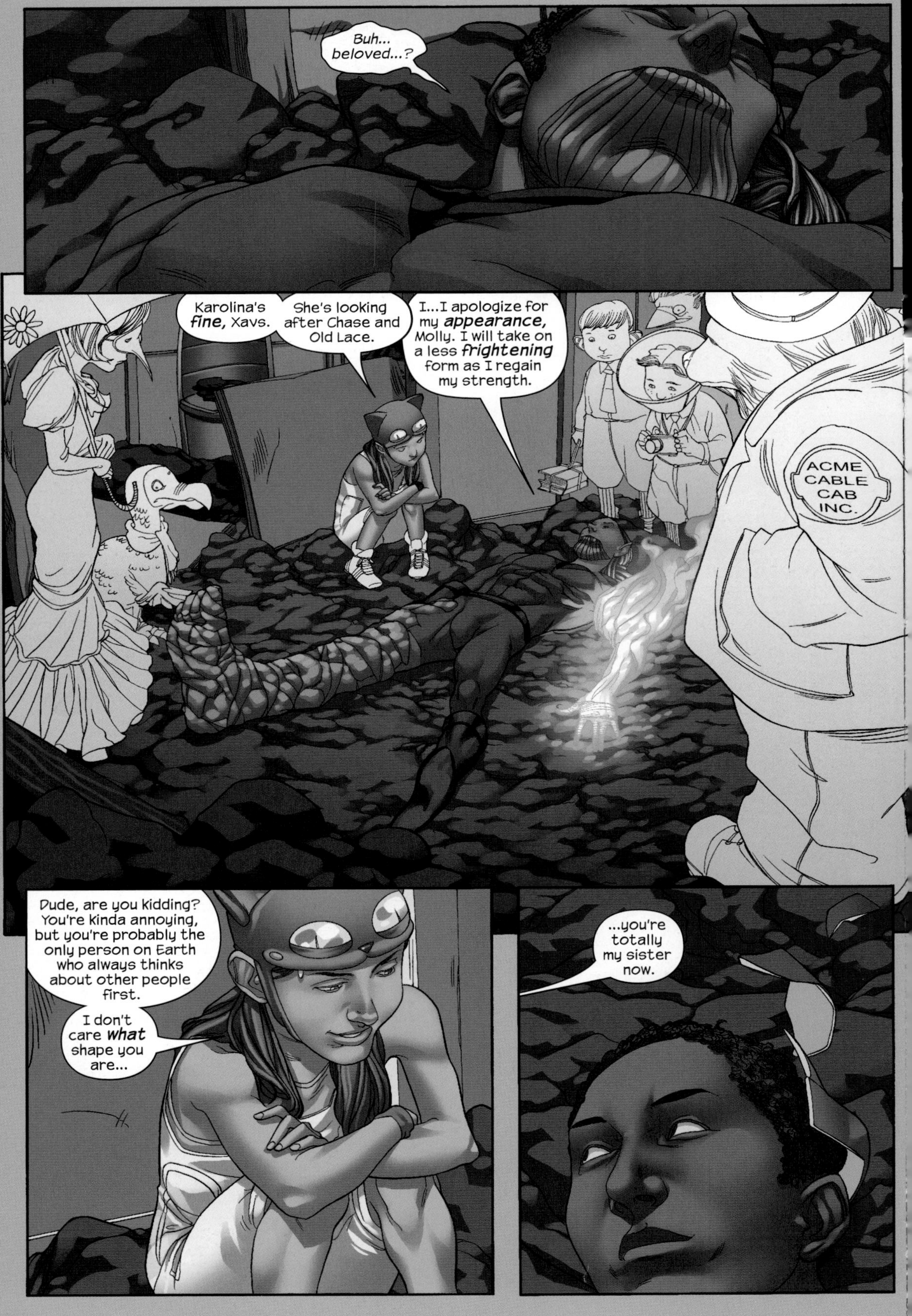
Buh... beloved...?
Karolina's *fine,* Xavs.
She's looking after Chase and Old Lace.
I...I apologize for my *appearance,* Molly. I will take on a less *frightening* form as I regain my strength.
ACME CABLE CAB INC.
Dude, are you kidding? You're kinda annoying, but you're probably the only person on Earth who always thinks about other people first.
I don't care *what* shape you are...
...you're totally my sister now.

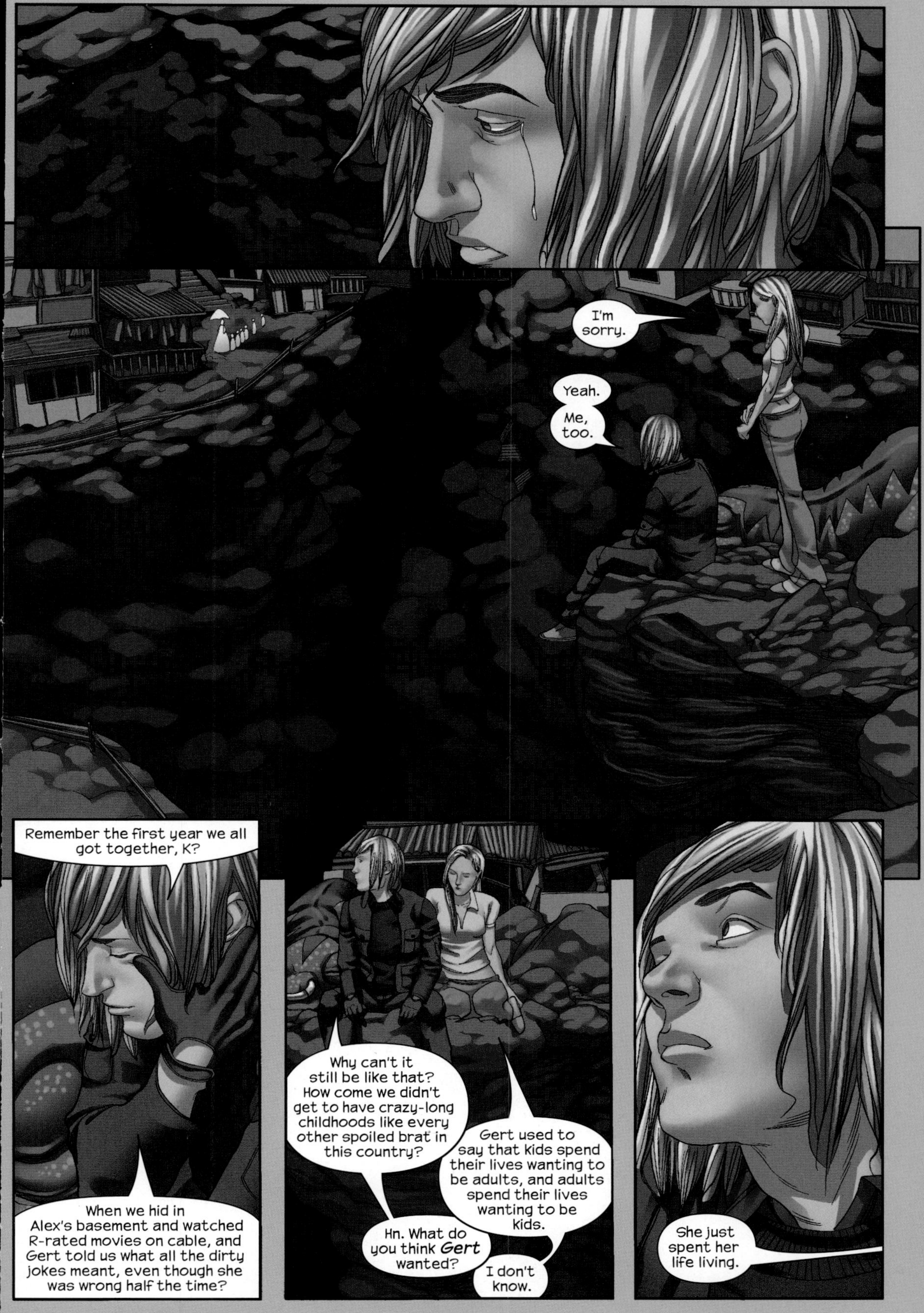
I'm sorry.
Yeah.
Me, too.
Remember the first year we all got together, K?
When we hid in Alex's basement and watched R-rated movies on cable, and Gert told us what all the dirty jokes meant, even though she was wrong half the time?
Why can't it still be like that? How come we didn't get to have crazy-long childhoods like every other spoiled brat in this country?
Gert used to say that kids spend their lives wanting to be adults, and adults spend their lives wanting to be kids.
Hn. What do you think *Gert* wanted?
I don't know.
She just spent her life living.

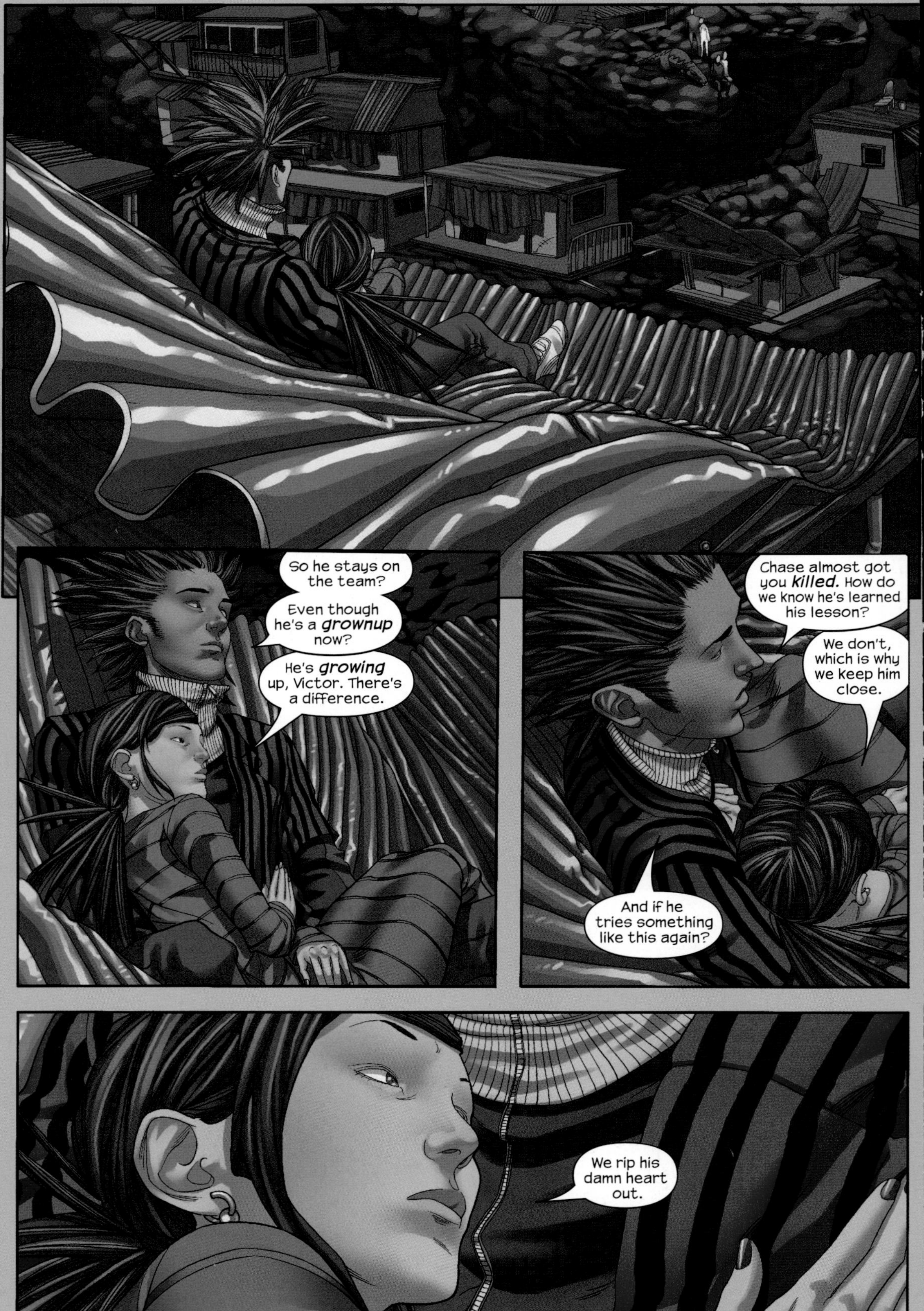
So he stays on the team?
Even though he's a *grownup* now?
He's *growing* up, Victor. There's a difference.
Chase almost got you *killed*. How do we know he's learned his lesson?
We don't, which is why we keep him close.
And if he tries something like this again?
We rip his damn heart out.

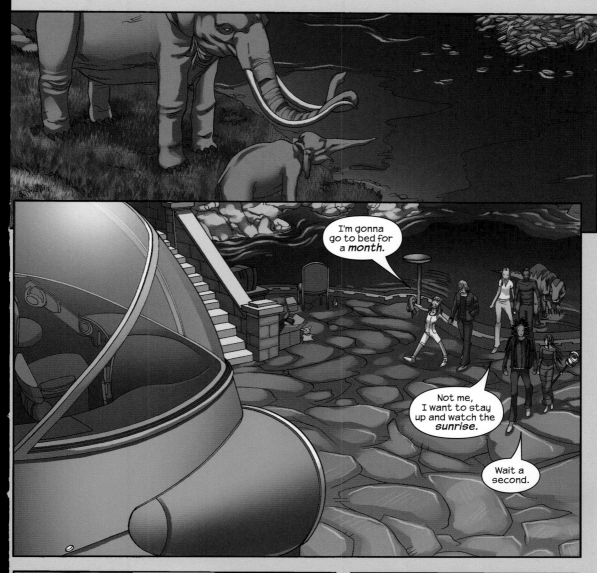

I'm gonna go to bed for a *month*.

Not me, I want to stay up and watch the *sunrise*.

Wait a second.

Isn't this one of our *security daemons*?

Oh, no.

Xavin, when we burned out of the tar pits, did you remember to make *us* invisible, or just the bubble we were zooming around in?

Er...

Hey, kids.

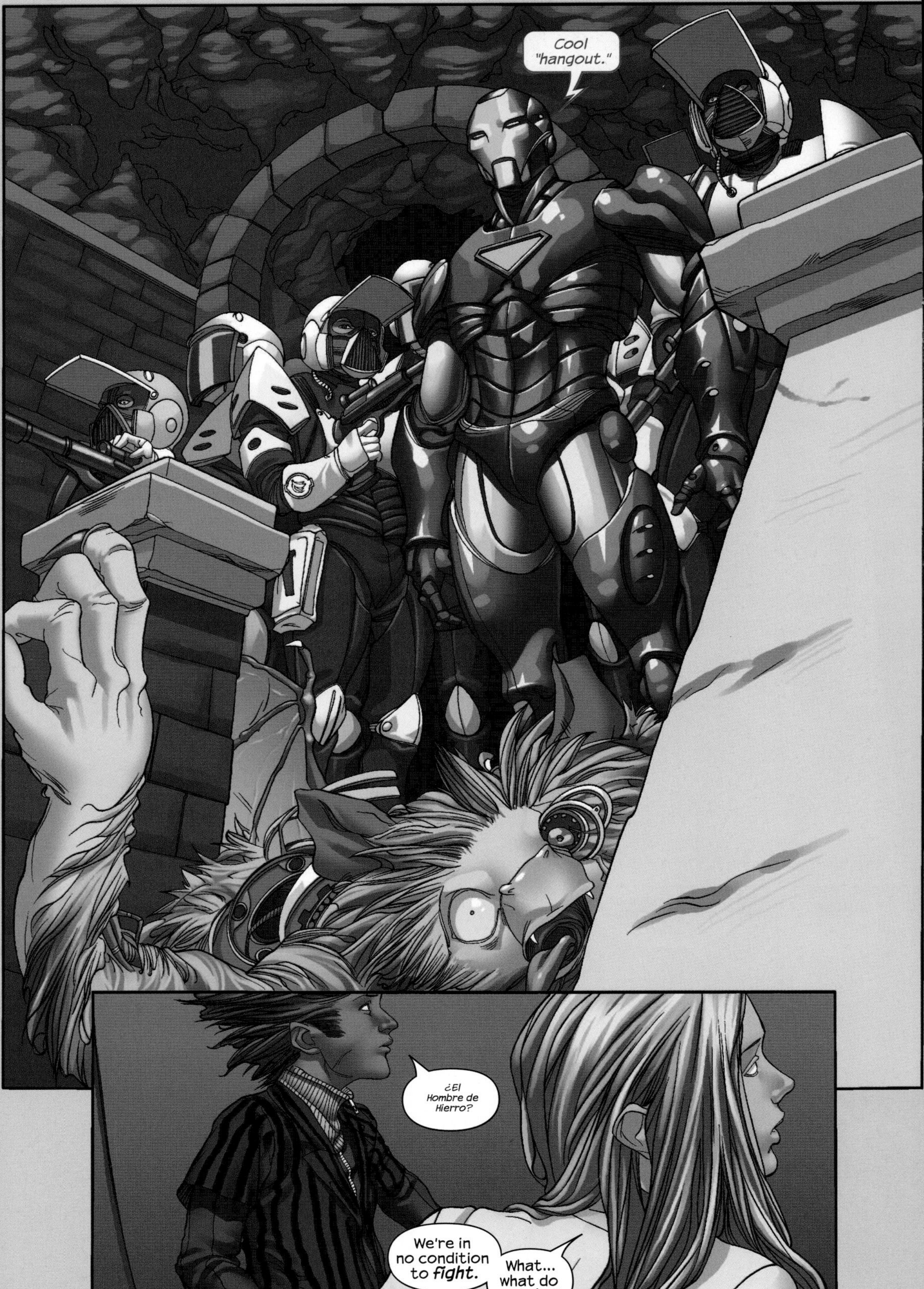
Cool "hangout."
¿El Hombre de Hierro?
We're in no condition to fight.
What... what do we do?

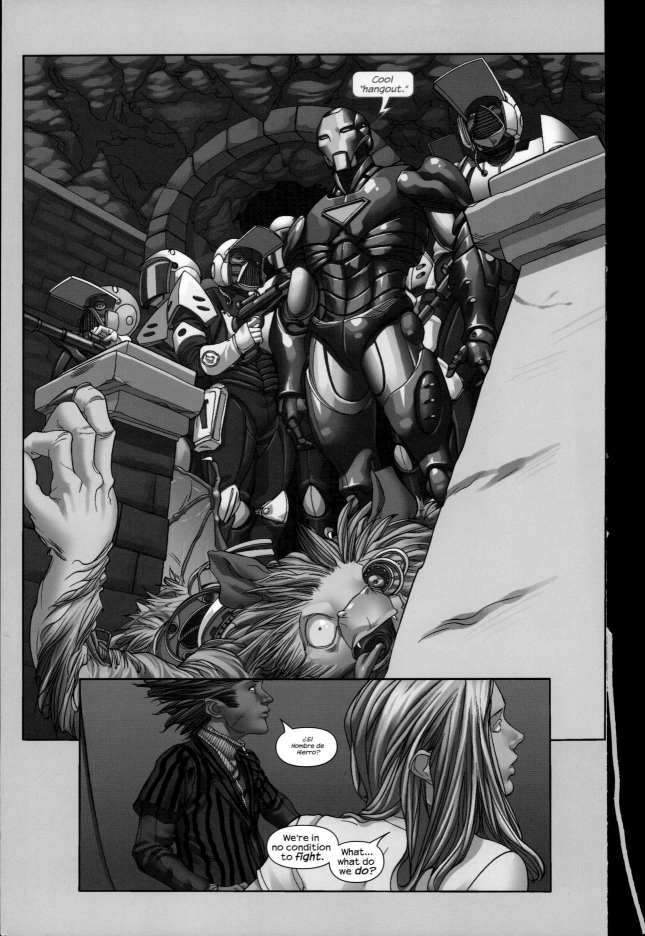

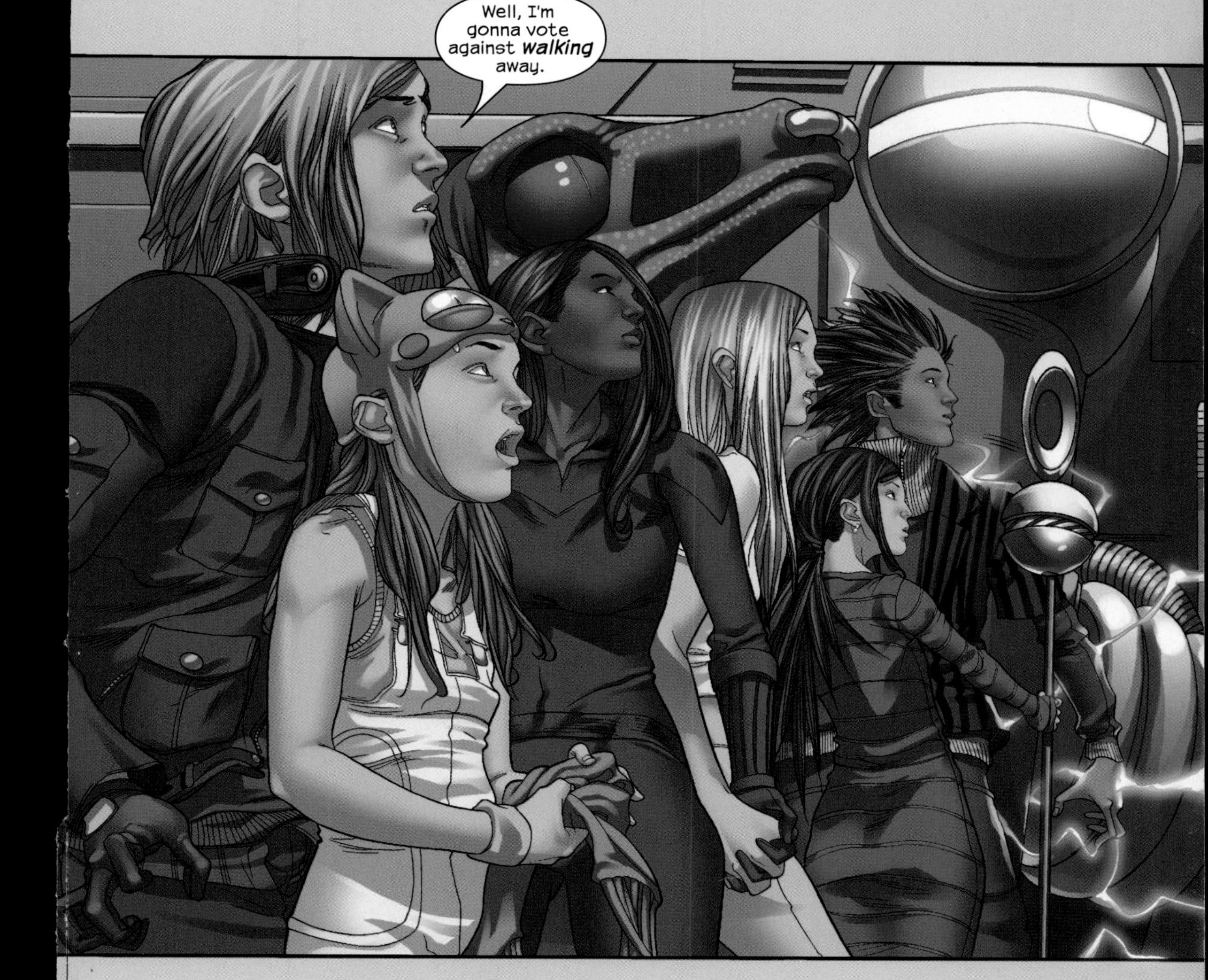
Well, I'm gonna vote against *walking* away.

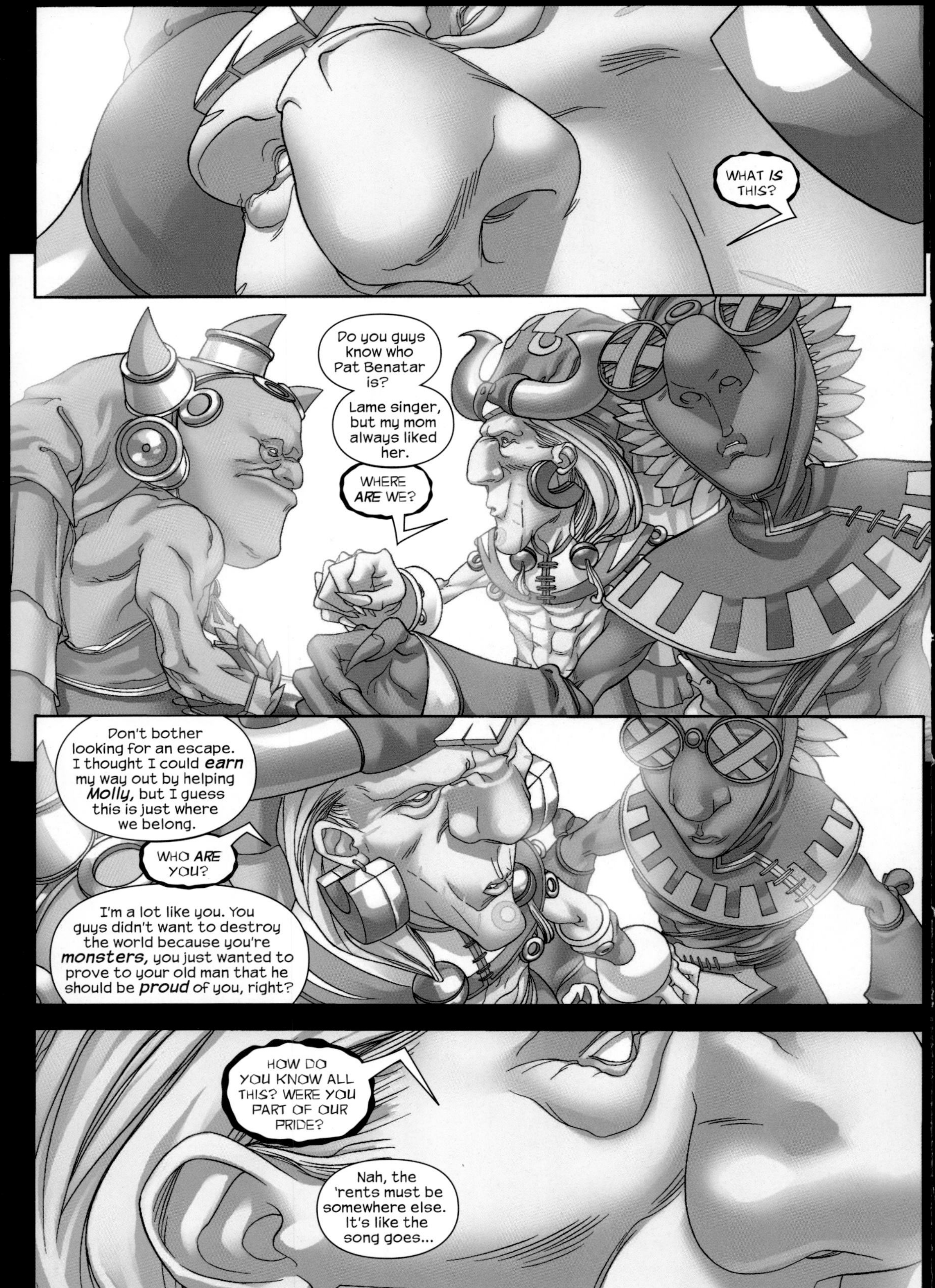
WHAT *IS* THIS?
Do you guys know who Pat Benatar is?
Lame singer, but my mom always liked her.
WHERE *ARE* WE?
Don't bother looking for an escape. I thought I could *earn* my way out by helping *Molly,* but I guess this is just where we belong.
WHO *ARE* YOU?
I'm a lot like you. You guys didn't want to destroy the world because you're *monsters,* you just wanted to prove to your old man that he should be *proud* of you, right?
HOW DO YOU KNOW ALL THIS? WERE *YOU* PART OF OUR PRIDE?
Nah, the 'rents must be somewhere else. It's like the song goes...

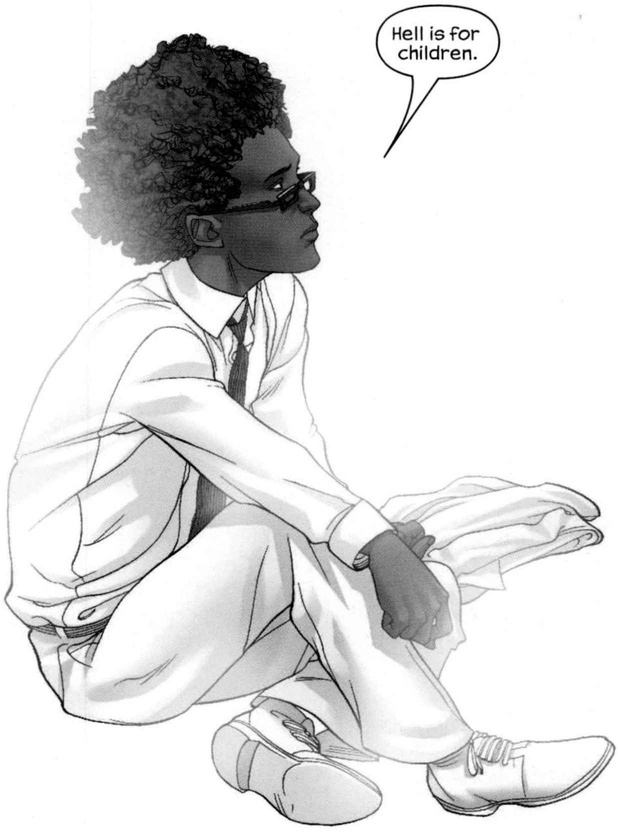
Hell is for children.

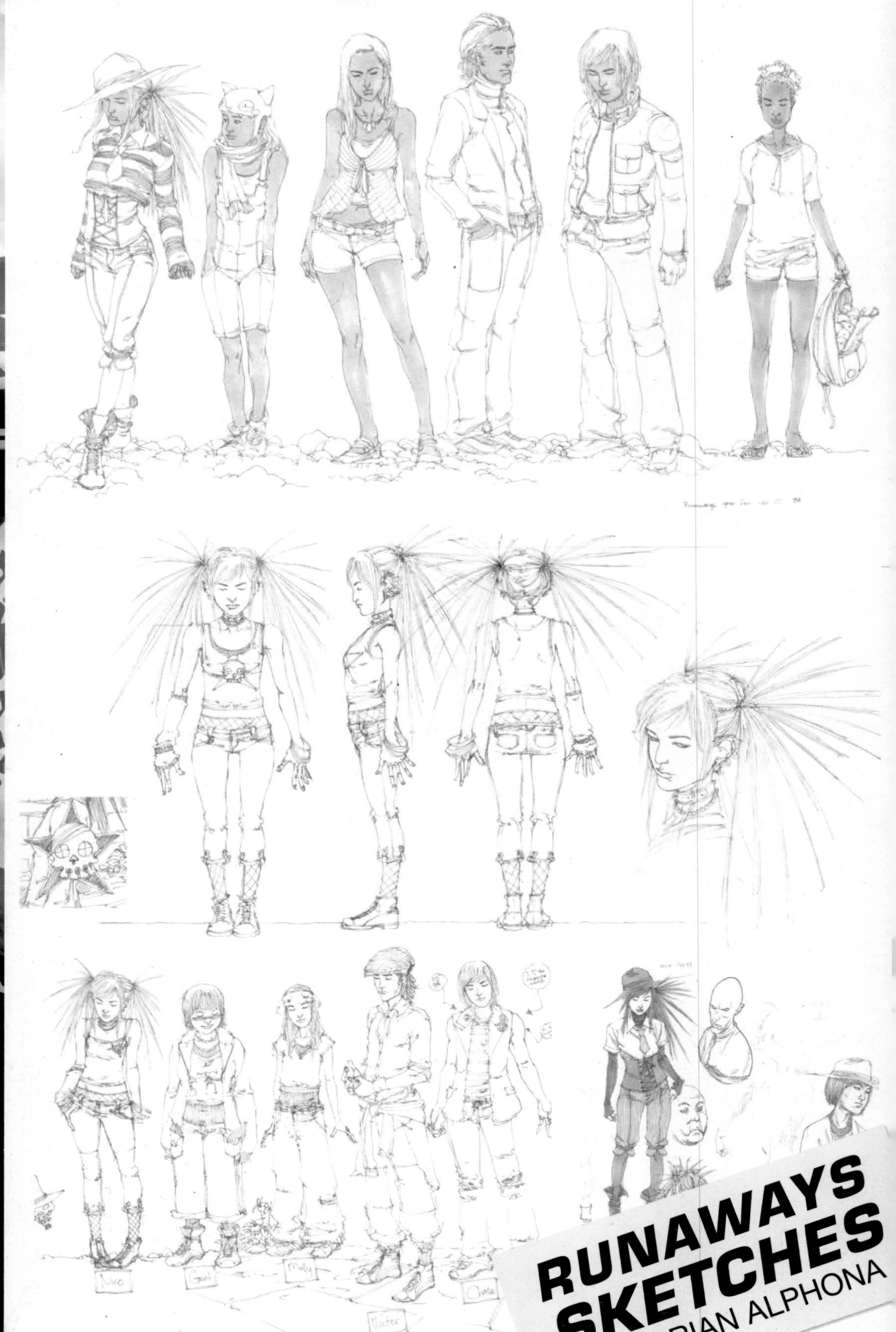
Nico
Gert
Molly
Victor
Chase

RUNAWAYS SKETCHES
BY ADRIAN ALPHONA